EQUAL JUSTICE
in the balance

EQUAL JUSTICE
in the balance

America's Legal Responses to the
Emerging Terrorist Threat

Raneta Lawson Mack
& Michael J. Kelly

With a Foreword by **Michael Ratner**

The University of Michigan Press
Ann Arbor

2007   2006   2005   2004   4   3   2   1

A CIP catalog record for this book is available from the British Library.

Library of Congress Cataloging-in-Publication Data

Mack, Raneta Lawson, 1963–
Equal justice in the balance: America's legal responses to the emerging terrorist threat / Raneta Lawson Mack and Michael J. Kelly ; with a foreword by Michael Ratner.
p.   cm.
Includes bibliographical references and index.
ISBN 0-472-11394-1 (cloth : alk. paper)
1. Dues process of law—United States.   2. Privacy, Right of—United States.   3. Terrorism—United States—Prevention.   4. Law enforcement—United States.   I. Kelly, Michael J., 1968–   II. Title.

KF4765.M23   2004
342.7308'5—dc22   2003027630

Author's note: The bulk of this work was produced during the 2002 calendar year. Consequently, all analyses, case and legislative reviews, references to documents, and supporting material are current as of that period. While the authors have undertaken to selectively update portions of the text during 2003, within the confines of the publishing and production process, any oversight in this regard remains solely their own.

To Helen and Ernest Lawson, with love —R.L.M

To James and Rosemary Kelly, with love —M.J.K

We may assume that the threat to Hawaii was a real one; we may also take it for granted that the general declaration of martial law was justified. But it does not follow from these assumptions that the military was free [to violate the] Constitution . . . especially after the initial shock of the sudden Japanese attack had been dissipated.

From time immemorial despots have used real or imagined threats to the public welfare as an excuse for needlessly abrogating human rights. That excuse is no less unworthy of our traditions when used in this day of atomic warfare or at a future time when some other type of warfare may be devised.

The . . . constitutional rights of an accused individual are too fundamental to be sacrificed merely through a reasonable fear of military assault. There must be some overpowering factor that makes a recognition of those rights incompatible with the public safety before we should consent to their temporary suspension.

—Justice Murphy's concurring opinion in the U.S.
Supreme Court decision against application of
martial law in Hawaii, *Duncan v. Kahanamoku* (1946),
quoted in support of federal district judge Nancy G.
Edmunds's decision to open INS deportation hearings
against the government's request to keep them secret in
Detroit Free Press v. Ashcroft (2002)

Contents

Foreword

Equal Justice in the Balance paints a gloomy picture of the extent to which the executive, Congress, and the judiciary have employed different methods to limit fundamental constitutional rights since September 11, 2001. The authors stress the importance of not giving up these fundamental rights and conclude with a message of optimism, noting an increasing backlash against the administration's more draconian measures. They are right to end on this optimistic note. Although the landscape is still quite bleak, change is in the air.

Growing opposition to the administration's wholesale violations of constitutional rights has sparked a tremendous amount of grassroots organizing. There are now over two hundred city and three state resolutions against the Patriot Act, some of which actually direct city and state employees not to cooperate with the FBI. Libraries all over the country are fighting against the provisions of the Patriot Act that permit the FBI to obtain lists of books checked out by library users; librarians are destroying these lists daily rather than make them available to authorities. A "Freedom to Read Act" that would prohibit such snooping has been introduced in the Senate—by a Republican senator. Many Democratic candidates for president are criticizing passage of the Patriot Act; former vice president Al Gore has made a major speech asking for its repeal; and, as *Equal Justice in the Balance* notes, Attorney General John Ashcroft, in what one newspaper described as "an act of desperation," was forced during the fall of 2003 to go on an eighteen-city road show to defend his policies.

Increasingly, the issues of constitutionality and basic freedoms are moving away from being Left or Right, conservative or liberal, and becoming understood as human rights issues that cross the political spectrum. The conservative columnist William Safire has come out against military tribunals, and the Cato Institute, a libertarian think tank, supported the rights of U.S. citizens to have judicial review of their designations as "enemy combatants." Former generals and POWs have supported hearings for those detained at Guantanamo. This is not to say that this struggle to regain lost liberty will be easy to win; but it is to say that people are beginning to fight back.

Despite popular fears and the overarching claims of a permanent "war on terrorism," there have also been some recent legal developments that are an additional reason for hopefulness. In a December 2003 blow to the Bush administration, the Supreme Court said it would review the incommunicado and indefinite detentions of 660 detainees at Guantanamo Bay, Cuba. Apparently the ruling shocked the administration; the lower courts had refused even to look at the legality of those detentions, and the administration claimed plenary power to do as it wished with the detainees, asserting that no court could even hear a case on behalf of the detainees. This claim of absolute power, a power unrestrained by any court review, seems to have been too much for the Court.

Just a few days after the Supreme Court granted review, the administration said it would release 140 detainees, presumably hoping to demonstrate that it could be trusted to give some kind of process to the prisoners and that a ruling against it would not be necessary. The administration also said that counsel could visit David Hicks, one of the Guantanamo detainees who may be designated for trial before a military commission.

The Supreme Court is also likely to grant review in the case of Yaser Hamdi, the U.S. citizen allegedly picked up in Afghanistan, who has been labeled an enemy combatant and held incommunicado in a military brig in South Carolina. For almost two years Hamdi has been denied access to a lawyer, but on the day prior to filing its opposition to Supreme Court review of his detention, the administration, presumably to avoid review, stated he could see his lawyer.

On December 18, 2003, in another blow to the administration, the Second Circuit Court of Appeals held that Jose Padilla, a U.S. citizen who, like Hamdi, has been labeled an enemy combatant, is entitled to a writ of habeas corpus releasing him from military custody. He had been confined to a brig in South Carolina and held incommunicado over a year without access to a lawyer. The oral argument in the case had gone badly for the administration: Rosemary Pooler, the presiding judge, stated, "As terrible as 9/11 was, it didn't repeal the Constitution." The court, in a 2-1 decision, found that the president did not have the constitutional power to detain as an enemy combatant an American citizen seized within a country outside of a zone of combat.

These developments demonstrate that this administration cannot be trusted to act within the bounds of law unless there is judicial review of its actions. Only after the Supreme Court said it would review the Guantanamo cases did the administration act to ameliorate the unjust conditions under which it is holding prisoners. This is a hopeful sign—a concrete example of the importance of such review and a reaffirmation of the system of checks and balances embodied in the U.S. Constitution.

An issue no court has yet addressed is the administration's use of the classification "enemy combatant." It is a worrisome category without any precise legal meaning that leaves unclear what rights, if any, those designated as "enemy combatants" may have. Those persons captured in the field of battle in Afghanistan and detained at Guantanamo should have been treated as prisoners of war under the Geneva Conventions and given the rights to which the conventions entitle them. Instead, by labeling those persons as "enemy combatants," the administration claims it can treat them as it wishes, with solitary confinement, long periods of interrogation, and trials before military tribunals.

Similarly, those like Padilla who were allegedly attempting to commit acts of terrorism should have been arrested, allowed attorneys, brought before a federal court, and charged with a crime. Instead, by labeling Padilla and others as "enemy combatants," the administration claims it can imprison them indefinitely in military brigs without any rights.

These executive detentions outside the rule of law are one of the most frightening aspects of the "war on terror." For almost eight hundred years, at least since the Magna Carta of 1215, and more recently as embodied in the International Covenant on Civil and Political Rights, it has been widely understood that executive detentions are anathema and one of the primary characteristics of a police state. Recent court activism signals that the courts understand the dangers of such unchecked power.

One of the more draconian administration reactions to 9/11 was the widespread detention of hundreds and possibly thousands of noncitizens living in the United States: America's "disappeared." Most were Muslim and/or of Arabic ethnicity. They had no connection with 9/11, had committed no crime, and were detained mostly because of minor immigration violations. The administration refused to give out their names, delayed allowing them access to attorneys, shackled and chained many of them, and subjected a number of them to beatings. Although litigation was brought under the Freedom of Information Act in an effort to find out the names, the case lost in the appeals court. Other litigation against Ashcroft with regard to the treatment of those detained is still pending.

Yet, when it looked darkest for these detainees in the United States, there was a breath of fresh air from an unexpected quarter, the Department of Justice itself. Within the department there is an inspector general, whose job is, in part, to act as a check on the department. In June and December of 2003, Inspector General Glenn A. Fine issued reports castigating the department for its treatment of the post-9/11 detainees in the United States. The reports found widespread abuses, including delays in serving immigration charges on detainees, denial of the right to an attorney, a no-bond or no-bail policy, a communications blackout including restrictive use of the telephone, and unduly harsh confinement conditions including twenty-four-hour lights in cells and shackling. The reports confirmed that detainees were beaten by slamming, bouncing, and ramming them against walls. To the extent detainees had attorneys, the meetings with the attorneys were videotaped and monitored in complete contravention of the constitutional right to counsel. These findings have apparently caused some changes at the Department of Justice and have bolstered the chances of the detainees prevailing in the lawsuit against Attorney General Ashcroft.

On other fronts the picture is not as bright. It appears that military tribunals for those at Guantanamo will begin in early 2004. These are not regularly constituted courts as required by law, but ad hoc courts set up to convict. It is likely that many of those brought before such tribunals will plead guilty. They have been in custody for almost two years without counsel or contact with family and presumably have been told that unless they plead guilty, they will be jailed in Guantanamo indefinitely.

In December of 2002, the administration appointed a four-person review panel for the tribunals. Included on the panel is Griffin Bell, a former U.S. attorney general and former appeals court judge, as well as other prominent lawyers and judges. In addition, the administration replaced Deputy Secretary of Defense Paul Wolfowitz as the "appointing authority"—the person responsible for appointing the judges for the tribunals. These new appointments are an effort by the administration to make the tribunals appear more legitimate. But they are only cosmetic. The entire system is still ad hoc: although the detainees have been questioned for two years without representation by attorneys, any statements they made can still be used against them and there is still no review by federal courts. That former judges and lawyers of some notoriety took these jobs rather than denouncing the tribunals is a sad commentary.

Meanwhile, allegations continue that the Bush administration is either using torture itself or sending detainees to other countries where torture is employed—a process called "rendering." Reports that the U.S. military was employing torture at its base in Bagram, Afghanistan, surfaced in 2002. Detainees were reportedly forced to stand or hung by their arms from the ceiling for eighteen or more hours a day, deprived of food, subjected to hot and cold temperatures, and beaten. Two of those receiving such treatment apparently died, as an examining army doctor noted, from blunt force to the body—in other words, they were beaten to death. Remarkably, to date there has been no congressional investigation of these charges.

Nor has there been attention to "rendering," wherein the United States sends detainees to countries where the security services will engage in torture as proxies for the United States. Countries such as Morocco, Jordan, and Egypt work closely with the United States to extract information from these prisoners.

The case of Maher Arar, a Canadian citizen born in Syria, has put a public face on rendering and become a cause célèbre in Canada. On September 26, 2002, Arar was returning to Canada from visiting his wife's family in Tunisia and had to change planes at John F. Kennedy Airport in New York. Upon passing through immigration there, he was detained, interrogated, shackled, jailed, and eventually rendered to Syria, without his family being informed of his whereabouts. In Syria he was imprisoned for over ten months and repeatedly tortured while being continually questioned. His rendering caused a large public outcry, particularly in Canada, and Arar was finally released in November 2002. But nothing is known of the untold others who have been rendered, tortured, and disappeared.

Many of the new laws are largely affecting noncitizens. The 660 persons imprisoned at Guantanamo are noncitizens; the 1,000 to 5,000 people detained in the United States after 9/11 are noncitizens; the tens of thousands requiring special registration are noncitizens; the thousands questioned by the FBI are noncitizens; the military tribunals only apply to noncitizens; and the refusal of courts to review detentions is limited to noncitizens. In fact, American citizens have not been asked to give up many rights, so many feel the equation is simple: someone else's rights are denied, and citizens will be secure.

But history teaches us that laws applied to noncitizens will eventually be applied to citizens. They already have in the "enemy combatant" designation of U.S. citizens Jose Padilla and Yaser Hamdi, who are imprisoned in a military brig in South Carolina without access to counsel (Hamdi recently got counsel) and only limited court review of their detentions.

And inside the United States, the attacks on free speech continue. *Equal Justice* describes how the FBI has been unleashed to spy on political and religious groups and to obtain records of citizens' reading habits from libraries, and how looser standards have led to the increased use of wiretaps and searches. New limitations on dissent include restrictions on lawful demonstrations. An early instance was New York City's refusal to permit a march protesting the war in Iraq, a refusal upheld by the federal appeals court on the grounds of national security. Wooden bullets were used to stop protests at a demonstration in Oakland, and hundreds of protesters were arrested on trumped-up charges.

Sadly, that hostility to legal street protest has continued. The October 2003 Iraq funding legislation included 8.5 million dollars to pay for law enforcement in Miami, where protesters rallied against the Free Trade Area of the Americas. Police from across Florida were called in, and peaceful protesters were beaten, teargassed, and arrested. The Steelworkers' Union, many of whose members were beaten and jailed, has called for a congressional investigation of what it calls "homeland repression in the name of homeland security."

We are in difficult times for the protection of our liberties. Nonetheless, citizens are showing an increasing willingness to resist the erosion of the U.S. Constitution. The struggle must continue. Recent victories in the courtrooms and in towns and cities across America are only the beginning of rescuing our democracy.

Michael Ratner
Director of the Center for Constitutional Rights

Preface

To those who scare peace-loving people with phantoms of lost liberty, my message is this: Your tactics only aid terrorists, for they erode our national unity and diminish our resolve.

—John Ashcroft, U.S. attorney general, statement before the
Senate Judiciary Committee questioning the patriotism
of anyone challenging the administration's antiterrorism
legal initiatives

It is precisely our deep sense of patriotism that motivated us, not only as law professors but as citizens, to write this book. The arrogance of power demonstrated by the Bush administration in its legal responses to the terrorist attacks suffered by this country on September 11, 2001, encapsulated by the notion demonstrated time and again that it holds a monopoly on the right course of action and any opposition to or fair questioning of that course amounts to treason, cannot be allowed to continue unchallenged in this, the greatest of the world's democracies.

History is littered with the remains of shattered nations whose leaders consolidated power in times of adversity while entreating the people to "trust them" to do the right thing. Crassus manipulated the Roman Senate into making him consul to defeat the revolt of Spartacus, which he engineered to threaten the city—the first step in transforming Republican Rome to Imperial Rome. Lenin implored the Russians to trust him and his provisional committee to lead them through the interim phase of socialism toward communism when the Bolsheviks took over in 1917. Stalin repeated this entreaty several years later. Hitler used it to calm the German people on his accession to power in 1933. While we may trust the current executive to lead this country's war on terror, does that mean we write a blank check? What about the next executive and the one after that? Does accumulated power get handed back when the present executive's term is over? Not likely.

The statement here by our attorney general raised hackles on Capitol Hill and beyond. Senator Patrick Leahy, chair of the Senate Judiciary Committee, responded, "This is not a question of whether you are for or against terrorists. Everyone is against terrorists. This is about whether we are adequately protecting our civil liberties."[1] Editorials proliferated against the attorney general's characterization. The *St. Petersburg Times* bristled that the Senate hearing "was a legitimate and responsible exercise of congressional oversight authority. But Ashcroft, in dismissive fashion, suggested that any inquiry into his controversial antiterrorism policies was an act of disloyalty."[2] And the *Buffalo News* issued this riposte:

> Flawed justice is flawed justice, whether or not it comes wrapped in the American flag, packaged as patriotic duty. Attorney General John D. Ashcroft, charged with upholding the Constitution and administering the American rule of law, ought to keep that firmly in mind as he wields the power of the Justice Department. And he also ought to realize that reasonable people can disagree on how far that power should extend, even in times of war. Not everyone who disagrees with the administration's new anti-terrorism powers, or its quest for more of them, should be accused of aiding terrorists by the chief lawyer of the United States. . . . Reasoned dissent is not a crime in this country. Neither is it unpatriotic. If anything is eroding national unity and respect for national leadership, it is not the loyal opposition Ashcroft blames—it is the arrogant assumption that every decision made by the administration is above question. Along that path lies the real danger.[3]

There are 537 elected leaders in our federal government—535 on Capitol Hill and 2 more down the street. They are responsible for defining the parameters of action that the hundreds of thousands of appointed unelected federal employees take in performing their assigned functions. In our republican system of governance, it is the duty of an informed citizenry to hold those 537 elected leaders accountable for this oversight responsibility. At least two such citizens are doing so by authoring this book.

The democracy that we enjoy today is not exactly the one that was created two centuries ago, although it is based on that framework. Perhaps a product of their times, our founders only empowered white landowning males in this new country, but they had the right idea about how that power should be divided. Today, every person who enjoys the mantle of "citizen" shares in the power of this democracy, and even those who are not citizens must be treated with respect and enjoy a larger set of basic rights as aliens here than they would in many cases back in their home countries. Today, also, we see that the founders' ideas about power division have endured, even if their conception of an informed citizenry has expanded beyond what they could have imagined.

That the executive should be strong but constrained, that the legislature should be representative but not beholden, that the judiciary should be independent but responsive are all the ideas we began with—and they are the ones we must continue to move forward with through the crisis presented by September 11 and beyond. To alter that delicate balance in pursuit of vengeance is to abandon the ideas we inherited. America is better than that. America is stronger than that. It is not for nothing that we are known as "the land of the free and the home of the brave."

In penning this book, we in no way wish to diminish the magnitude of what happened on 9/11 in New York, Washington, and Pennsylvania. The nearly twenty-eight hundred victims who perished that day at the hands of the al Qaeda terrorist organization deserve to be remembered, grieved, and honored. They also deserve to have their killers hunted down, apprehended, and brought to justice, as all criminals should be in a civilized society. But abhorrent to their memory would be the sacrifice of equal justice and civil liberty in pursuit of the perpetrators. That is a sacrifice that needn't be made to accomplish the task at hand. We already have legal tools adequate for the task. We must use them wisely, cleverly, and resourcefully.

Finally, we gratefully acknowledge the contribution of Michael

Ratner, our foreword author, and encourage him to continue litigating on behalf of those whose freedoms are unjustifiably threatened by the government. We also wish to extend our thanks to former attorney general Janet Reno for her detailed review of the manuscript and the many suggestions she offered during the final edits. We appreciate the help of our research assistants, Carmin Ballou, Kate Blanchard, and Rachel Alexander, and the support of Creighton University School of Law. We also thankfully acknowledge the understanding of our families, who made do without us for several days and nights while we tackled manuscript or research work. In many ways, although this book is dedicated to the author's parents we undertook it for our children—Raneta's daughter, Kandace, and Mike's son, Durham—who deserve no less a bright future in a wonderful, free, and vibrant democracy than we have enjoyed and seek now to protect.

As former president Theodore Roosevelt argued in an editorial for the *Kansas City Star*, opposing President Woodrow Wilson's crackdown on dissent upon America's entry into World War I:

> To announce that there must be no criticism of the President, or that we are to stand by the President, right or wrong, is not only unpatriotic and servile, but is morally treasonable to the American public. Nothing but the truth should be spoken about him or any one else. But it is even more important to tell the truth, pleasant or unpleasant, about him than about any one else.[4]

Raneta Lawson Mack   Michael J. Kelly
Omaha, Nebraska   Port Austin, Michigan
                                       September 11, 2002

1 Introduction
Defining the Challenge

The proposition is this: that in a time of war the commander of an armed force . . . has the power . . . to suspend all civil rights and their remedies, and subject citizens as well as soldiers to the rule of his will. . . . [I]f true, republican government is a failure, and there is an end of liberty regulated by law.

—Justice David Davis, *Ex Parte Milligan*

These are the times that try men's souls.

—Thomas Paine, *The Crisis*

Epochal events in a nation's evolution are often transforming in ways that can only be clearly assessed through the objective lens of history. The passage of time provides the necessary temporal and emotional distance, which, in turn, permits critical examination of the whole rather than piecemeal assessment of the parts while in the vortex of change.[1] Certain events, however, trigger the need for immediate assessment and debate. Such events are often characterized by the degree to which they encroach upon and threaten the fundamental principles and freedoms that we embrace, and occasionally take for granted, in a democratic society. On September 20, 2001, President George W. Bush addressed a Congress and a nation still reeling in horror and disbelief from the unimaginable acts of cruelty that the world witnessed on September 11, 2001. In his speech to a devastated nation, President Bush articulated the collective sentiment of most Americans when he said, "All of this was brought upon us in a single day, and night fell upon a different world." A different world indeed.

The tragic events of September 11, 2001, will undoubtedly be permanently etched in the memories of all Americans who were old enough to struggle with comprehending and rationalizing actions that were, by design, incomprehensible and irrational. For several weeks after the events, the surreal imagery of jetliners colliding with occupied skyscrapers on American soil played repeatedly to a stunned international audience. As with other acts of unspeakable violence throughout our nation's history, most Americans viewing the deadly imagery of September 11 will forever recall where they were the moment they first became aware of an unprecedented terrorist onslaught that, without warning, indelibly marked yet another day that will live in infamy. If the goal of these sudden and deliberate attacks was to instill fear and uncertainty in a seemingly invincible nation of people, then the attacks were an unmitigated success. For in the immediate aftermath, not only did the attacks engender a sense of vulnerability "in our own backyard," but they also induced widespread skepticism concerning America's ability to anticipate and prevent terrorism inside its own borders and within its current political, legislative, and judicial framework.

In an effort to address the myriad concerns that arose in the wake of the terrorist attacks, the government has proposed and/or implemented the following fundamental changes to America's institutions:

- Congress has enacted far-reaching legislation in record time with little or no debate.
- President Bush has issued a controversial military order without consulting Congress.
- A cabinet-level Office of Homeland Security has been created to coordinate U.S. national security efforts.
- The FBI has arrested and indefinitely detained hundreds of men of certain ethnic backgrounds while inviting hundreds more to "voluntary interrogations."
- The FBI has been given broader authority to search the Internet and other sources of public information for criminal activity—including entering public events for such purpose. This means that federal agents could, for example,

review e-mail and library patron records of those suspected of terrorist activity.

- FBI rules have been relaxed to make it easier for federal agents to get secret terrorism wiretaps.
- Attorney General John Ashcroft has proposed establishing a registry for any foreigner who might be considered an international security concern. This means that men between the ages of eighteen and thirty-five from approximately twenty Muslim and Middle Eastern countries would be fingerprinted, photographed, and required to complete a lengthy form.
- A program called TIPS (Terrorist Information and Prevention System) has been proposed to allow citizens to "help" in the antiterrorism effort by using their common sense to identify and report unusual, suspicious, and potentially terrorist activity. Although the program was scrapped in the wake of tremendous public outcry, the mere proposal of such a program is, in many respects, indicative of the government's overzealous approach to combating terrorism within its own borders.
- Ambiguous "high alert" warnings are issued periodically to serve as a constant reminder that random terrorist violence is now a part of our daily existence.
- Off American shores and presumably outside the jurisdiction of U.S. courts, hundreds of suspected Taliban and al Qaeda terrorists have been captured, labeled "enemy combatants," and are currently being "detained" at Guantanamo Bay, Cuba, without any apparent plans for implementing any type of judicial process to determine their guilt or innocence.
- Within the U.S. judicial system, American citizens suspected of or charged with terrorist-related crimes have endured differential treatment and, in the name of national security, have been denied some of the basic protections afforded criminal defendants by our Constitution.

With the current focus squarely on the undeclared war against terrorism in Afghanistan and Iraq, sweeping reforms within U.S. political and judicial systems have been effected with very little debate, consultation, or analysis. Because this unparalleled transformation impacts and, in some cases, runs roughshod over fundamental principles inherent to a democratic society, America's overall response to the 9/11 terrorist attacks has brought into sharp focus basic notions of liberty, fairness, and justice memorialized centuries ago with the ratification of the U.S. Constitution. That is, in the seemingly directionless quest to eradicate terrorism, foundational principles once considered inviolable are now being called into question or brushed aside altogether. For example, in this new era of fear, suspicion, and uncertainty, it is commonplace to question and debate whether America's criminal justice system, with all of its flaws and foibles, is an appropriate venue for the terrorists who allegedly masterminded and perpetrated the worst terrorist attack in world history. Such debate often ignores the centuries of delicate give-and-take within the American constitutional form of government that facilitated the compromises so crucial to a justice system committed to principles of equality and fairness under the law. Why is this system suddenly so profoundly inadequate that it cannot be trusted to exact fair and just punishment for terrorist defendants? The answer certainly cannot be that the United States has never charged, convicted, or punished terrorists who planned and committed deadly acts on American soil. For one only has to look at the court proceedings in the first World Trade Center (WTC) bombing and the Timothy McVeigh trial to dismiss that notion. So we are compelled to dig much deeper for a rationale that may, in the end, require confronting the unwarranted fears, suspicion, and paranoia that have no legitimate place in shaping a system committed to fairness and equal justice under the law.

However, even allowing for the sake of argument that the American justice system requires alterations to fight (and presumably win) the war on terrorism, further questions remain, such as what specific changes are necessary and how should they be proposed and implemented? Because it appears that the current restructuring trend is in the direction of piecemeal, ad hoc pronouncements and determinations that have the potential to result in differential applications and outcomes, a number of other questions that take into account historical precedent and consistency with America's guiding principles must also be considered. For example, how would this patchwork of changes comport with traditional notions of fair-play and equal justice for all? Are there lessons from America's history of wartime treatment of citizens and noncitizens that may be instructive in the current circumstances? If the U.S. justice system framework is dramatically overhauled solely to address concerns arising from the September 11 attacks, what message does this send at home and abroad? In short, the overarching question is this: Can America, a nation rooted in democracy, liberty, and justice, remain true to its commitment to equal justice under the law while simultaneously taking a leadership role in eradicating terrorism throughout the world? As this book will explain, America's strong democratic tradition, which historically manifests itself more fervently during times of crisis, not only will endure but will facilitate a balancing of interests that simultaneously protects national security while preserving fundamental principles that define America as a country committed to due process and equal justice.

A comprehensive exploration of this critical question first requires an understanding of the key concepts that define the current challenges confronting America. Because horrific acts of terrorism precipitated America's post September 11 responses, a proper introduction to the definition of terrorism is where the analysis shall begin.

Defining Terrorism: Its Aim and Infrastructure

Suffice to say that the definitions of terrorism run the gamut from highly refined and legalistic to clichéd and meaningless rhetoric. For example, international law scholar and terrorism expert M. Cherif Bassiouni observes that terrorism is defined as "a strategy of violence designed to instill terror in a segment of society in order to achieve a power outcome, propagandize a course, or inflict harm for vengeful political purposes."[2] According to this definition of terrorism, the psychology of inspiring fear is the main objective, which is accomplished when societal conditions are such that terrorist acts are perceived as perpetually imminent yet unpredictable and the citizenry as a whole feels vulnerable to attack. Bassiouni further explains that, while this strategy of psychological intimidation may be utilized by state actors against their own populations or against the population of another country, it may also be co-opted by insurgent, revolutionary, or ideologically motivated factions within the state. Regardless of motivation, however, all of the groups rely upon violence as a means to psychologically paralyze the population with fear.

Examining the different impact and outcomes of state versus nonstate sponsorship, Bassiouni theorizes that state-supported forms of terrorism have the potential to be coordinated, widespread, and easily susceptible to human rights violations. In contrast, nonstate-sponsored terrorist activity may be haphazard and sporadic in nature, although just as deadly.

Nonetheless, as Bassiouni explains:

in its common usage, the term "international terrorism" has come to exclude the activities of state actors and even insurgent and revolutionary groups. Instead it is applied to small, ideologically motivated groups, and whose strategies of terror-violence are designed to propagate a political message, destabilize a regime, inflict social harm as political vengeance, and elicit over-reactive state responses likely to create a political crisis.[3]

Another remarkably lengthy academic definition of terrorism, which attempts to encompass all aspects of terrorist motivations, rationales, and goals, explains that

[t]errorism is an anxiety inspiring method of repeated violent action, employed by (semi-) clandestine individual, group or state actors, for idiosyncratic, criminal or political reasons, whereby—in contrast to assassination—the direct targets of the violence are not the main targets. The immediate human victims of violence are generally chosen randomly (targets of opportunity) or selectively (representative or symbolic targets) from a target population, and serve as message generators. Threat- and violence-based communication processes between terrorist (organization), (imperiled) victims, and main targets are used to manipulate the main target (audience(s)), turning it into a target of terror, a target of demands, or target of attention, depending upon whether intimidation, coercion, or propaganda are primarily sought.[4]

On the governmental front, the U.S. Department of State, in its annual Patterns of Global Terrorism report, defines terrorism as "premeditated, politically motivated violence perpetrated against noncombatant targets by subnational groups or clandestine agents, usually intended to influence an audience."[5] The definition further explains that the term *noncombatant* includes civilians and military personnel who, at the time of the incident, are unarmed and not on duty. Not to be outdone, a separate U.S. governmental organization, the Department of Defense (DOD), defines terrorism as "the calculated use of violence to inculcate fear; intended to coerce or to intimidate governments or societies in the pursuit of goals that are generally political, religious or ideological."

The FBI acknowledges that there is no single, universally accepted definition of terrorism and adopts the definition set forth in the Code of Federal Regulations, which regards terrorism as "the unlawful use of force or violence against persons or property to intimidate or coerce a government, the civilian population, or any segment thereof, in the furtherance of political or social objectives." The FBI's definitional scheme categorizes terrorism as either domestic or international, depending upon the origin, base, and objectives of the terrorists.

A provision in the U.S. Code addressing immigration and nationality concerns classifies terrorist activity as

> any activity which is unlawful under the laws of the place where it is committed . . . and which involves any of the following:
>
> (I)   The highjacking or sabotage of any conveyance (including an aircraft, vessel, or vehicle).
> (II) The seizing or detaining, and threatening to kill, injure, or continue to detain, another individual in order to compel a third person (including a governmental organization) to do or abstain from doing any act as an explicit or implicit condition for the release of the individual seized or detained.
> (III) A violent attack upon an internationally protected person or upon the liberty of such a person.
> (IV) An assassination.
> (V)   The use of any—
>   (a) biological agent, chemical agent, or nuclear weapon or device, or

(b) explosive, firearm, or other weapon or dangerous device (other than for mere personal monetary gain), with intent to endanger, directly or indirectly, the safety of one or more individuals or to cause substantial damage to property.

(VI) A threat, attempt, or conspiracy to do any of the foregoing.

Finally, the USA Patriot Act defines "domestic terrorism" as activities that

(A) involve acts dangerous to human life that are a violation of the criminal laws of the United States or of any State;

(B) appear to be intended—
    (i) to intimidate or coerce a civilian population;
    (ii) to influence the policy of a government by intimidation or coercion; or
    (iii) to affect the conduct of a government by mass destruction, assassination, or kidnapping; and

(C) occur primarily within the territorial jurisdiction of the United States.

On an international level, the first attempt to gain consensus on a globally acceptable definition of terrorism dates back to 1937, when the League of Nations drafted a convention depicting terrorism as "[a]ll criminal acts directed against a State and intended or calculated to create a state of terror in the minds of particular persons or a group of persons or the general public." The convention was never ratified, and today, despite numerous efforts, there is still no internationally accepted definition of terrorism.

Indeed, as recently as February 2002, the international community struggled once again (and failed) to achieve consensus on the elusive notion of terrorism. United Nations diplomats and legal advisors at the General Assembly's Ad Hoc Committee on Terrorism meeting attempted to achieve this critical consensus as a springboard to a comprehensive treaty designed to compel all 189 UN member-states to root out and punish terrorists in their midst. As in the past, a stalemate erupted over defining terrorism strictly according to what terrorists do as opposed to what goal they are trying to accomplish. Rizwan Khan, a spokeswoman for the Pakistani UN mission, observed:

If someone's subjugating your civilians, if you're just fighting for your rights and they shoot someone in your family, you're going to have someone who's going to say, "OK, I'm going to do the same." . . . The UN must analyze the root cause and draw a line between freedom fighters, who are fighting for their piece of land, and terrorists, who are trying to impose their will, their way of thinking, by force.

Khan added that "[c]ountries like Israel or India freely label anyone who resists as a 'terrorist' in an effort to win the battle for international opinion."[6]

Others researching the subject of terrorism have agreed with Khan's observations and further contend that terrorism cannot be defined without due consideration to the political perspective of the definer. That is, the definition is purely subjective and usually reflective of a particular political goal. For instance, countries such as Syria, Libya, and Iran have promoted an international definition of terrorism that would categorize groups they sponsor as "freedom fighters," thereby giving such groups virtually unlimited permission to carry out their goals by any means necessary.

Still others in the definitional quest describe terrorism specifically as it relates to the context of war. For example, in 1992 terrorism expert Alex Schmid proposed a concise legal definition of terrorism to the United Nations Crime Branch, using the following simple equation: Act of Terrorism = Peacetime Equivalent of War Crime.[7] Similarly, contemporary novelist and military historian Caleb Carr implicated the notion of warfare when describing terrorism as the "contemporary name given to, and the modern permutation of, warfare deliberately waged against civilians with the purpose of destroying their will to support either leaders or policies that the agents of such violence find objectionable."[8]

What is patently clear from this assortment of definitional exercises is that there is no general consensus as to what constitutes terrorism. It is possible that, prior to September 11, the failure to reach accord did not generate significant hue and cry because such attempts were aimed at fostering global consensus during times of relative peace. Consequently, the lack of compromise was of little concern, and nations addressed terrorist activities using definitions that suited their own political, economic, and national security goals. For example, while Israel and the United States perceive Palestinians as terrorists, others view them as freedom fighters resisting the occupation of their homeland. Similarly, while India threatened war against Pakistan for its failure to root out terrorism, many in Pakistan regarded the "terrorists" attempting to liberate Kashmir as "freedom fighters." And, in what now seems a tragically ironic twist, the Reagan administration encouraged and financially supported the mujahaddin guerillas in their efforts to end Soviet occupation of Afghanistan. Indeed, President Reagan referred to Osama bin Laden and his cohorts as "the moral equivalent of our founding fathers." Even the United States has been characterized as a terrorist state for its military incursions into countries whose governmental policies threaten U.S. interests.

Despite such widely varying perspectives, the United States declared war on terrorism in the wake of September 11, and the corresponding threat to extend that war beyond Afghanistan and Iraq demonstrates now, more than ever, that a global consensus on the definition of terrorism is crucial to maintaining international support for the goal of rooting out terrorism worldwide. Yet, the naysayers persist. Perhaps weary from repeated stalemates in their attempts to define terrorism, or skeptical that any definition can be inclusive enough, critics still question the need to formalize the term at all. In support of this contention, they point out that criminal acts typically associated with terrorism, such as kidnapping, airplane hijacking, and bombing, are already outlawed on an international scale, thus obviating the need for a general definition of terrorism.

Whatever the final decision on the need for a global definition of terrorism, when striving for consensus, two general themes, either stated or implied, seem to permeate most characterizations of terrorist activity. First, most definitions encompass the idea of intentionally using violence against innocent victims as a means of conveying a message. Second, in the wake of such shocking and indiscriminate violence, terrorist perpetrators often utilize the threat of more unjustified mayhem as a means to psychologically paralyze individuals, causing them to act in ways that recognize and cater to the omnipresent danger. Yet, even using general themes as a reference point sometimes yields unsatisfactory results. For, as history reveals, yesterday's terrorists are today's statesmen and vice versa. Jerry Addams of Ireland's Sinn Fein and Nelson Mandela of South Africa are glaring examples of the futility of applying immutable definitions to mutable political, social, and economic realities.

The Motivations and Impact of Terrorism

Despite failing to reach agreement on a blanket definition of terrorism, scholars have not shied away from explaining "why" terrorists behave as they do, perhaps hoping to eventually arrive at a concrete definition of "who" a terrorist is. Unfortunately, attempts to delineate psychological motivations for terrorist activity has produced similarly disparate and inconclusive results. In broad terms, however, psychological factors such as hatred, revulsion, and revenge "characterize precisely the feelings and motivations of many terrorists."[9] In effect, terrorists fail to consider that their goals or objectives might be ill-conceived and obsessively characterize opponents as the epitome of evil, subject to immediate and forceful vanquishment. Such polarized "either-or" conceptions result in a striking ability to dehumanize victims of terrorist violence, which ultimately enables terrorists to perpetrate deadly activities without remorse.

Still, it is not uncommon for terrorist groups to offer strategic and seemingly logical explanations for their behavior, believing "for good reason, that any attempt to explain their motivations in psychological terms diminishes the validity of their ideas, their actions and their beings."[10] Indeed, many scholars have also eschewed the notion that terrorism is the outcome of psychological choices and, instead, portray such actions as the result of logical processes that can be examined and explained. Martha Crenshaw, in an article entitled "The Logic of Terrorism: Terrorist Behavior as a Product of Strategic Choice," posits that, when viewed analytically, "terrorism is assumed to display a collective rationality." What this means is that "the group possesses collective preferences or values and selects terrorism as a course of action from a range of perceived alternatives."[11]

Not surprisingly, according to Crenshaw, terrorist violence is often the last resort for groups failing to achieve their goals through other nonviolent or less violent methods. To illustrate, Crenshaw explains that, in the ongoing Middle East conflict, terrorist violence followed the failure of conventional methods of warfare in the Palestinian-Israeli struggle. As a result, Crenshaw concludes, terrorism may reflect the outcome of a cost-benefit analysis where the costs, although high, are perceived to be outweighed by the benefits.[12] Crenshaw further opines that, because terrorist activity is a strategic conception, "based on ideas of how best to take advantage of the possibilities of a given situation," such strategies must also define governmental responses to terrorist activities. She cautions, however, that emphasis on the strategic reasoning capabilities of terrorists must be juxtaposed against the typical stereotype of terrorists as irrational fanatics. Otherwise, we risk underestimating the dangerous capabilities of extremist groups and, perhaps more importantly, miseducate and misinform the public about the "complexities of terrorist motivations and behaviors."[13]

Although it is difficult to precisely determine what motivated the September 11 attacks, it is obvious that the various reasons posited have both strategic and psychological components. The purported justifications include a widespread belief that the United States has "colonized" the Arab world to protect U.S. access to oil; alleged U.S. support of authoritarian regimes in the Middle East; and the perception that the United States is actively assisting in the oppression of Palestinians by supporting Israel. Examining these rationales, while the strategic idea behind the attacks may have been an effort to create a large-scale Islamic fundamentalist revolution to rid the Muslim world of corrupt Western influences, the psychological factors of hatred, revulsion, and thirst for revenge were not far below the seemingly logical surface. Indeed, they were horrifyingly revealed by the indiscriminate and deadly nature of the attacks, which specifically targeted innocent victims on such a scale that tens of thousands of people could have perished.

Further evidence of a terrorist psychology or mentality can be gleaned from the fact that young men joining these militant groups are often destitute individuals in the Arab world searching for a raison d'etre. Driven by a psychological need for meaning and recognition in life, they become easy pawns for the radical, politicized religious organizations that embrace terrorism as a means to impose their will. Such is the case with al Qaeda, a network of

Islamist terrorist organizations whose main goal is to rid the Middle East of Western (and particularly U.S.) influence. By implementing a long-term strategy of attacking the United States at home and abroad, al Qaeda and its supporters are hopeful that the benefits will outweigh any costs associated with their activities. Stated differently, these highly organized and sophisticated mercenaries are using a strategy designed to instill fear in their victims and to rally their angry supporters, while simultaneously gambling that governmental responses will not be so punitive as to completely obliterate the organization and its aims. It is a deadly cat and mouse game writ large on the international landscape.

In addition to the psychological and strategic impact of terrorism, such pervasive, continuing, and unpredictable violence (or the threat of such violence) also inflicts a severe economic wound on its victims. Although terrorists rarely have as their ultimate goal the devastation of a nation's economic infrastructure, one of the inevitable consequences of large-scale terrorist violence is economic downturn and a corresponding reassessment of economic resource allocation. In the aftermath of the September 11 attacks, the United States has endured a dramatic economic upheaval in both the business and consumer markets. Widespread economic uncertainty has resulted in a declining investment market, reduced overall spending, and massive layoffs. Moreover, to fight the escalating war on terrorism, the government has radically refocused its mission to support the counterterrorism effort, which, in turn, requires equally dramatic budgetary revamping. To cite a few examples, in February 2002 Attorney General John Ashcroft requested an additional $2 billion to help the Department of Justice (DOJ) fight the terrorism battle. On the legislative front, Congress approved a $15 billion emergency assistance package to help the ailing airline industry recover from the 9/11 attacks. The bailout package included immediate cash payments to compensate for the shutdown of the airlines after the attacks and loan guarantees of $10 billion. But arguably the most devastated sector of the economy is the insurance industry, which is expected to pay out record claims to those who lost loved ones and property as a result of the attacks. Analysts predict that these claims could reach a crippling $50 billion. A draft report by NATO's Economics and Security Committee entitled *The Economic Consequences*

of 11 September and the Economic Dimension of Anti-terrorism antici-
pated that

> many of the losses associated with the [September 11] attacks
> are essentially "one-off" costs that will not endure over the
> long-term. There are, however, several important exceptions.
> Insurance [premiums], particularly against terrorist attacks,
> have probably risen permanently [and] . . . the costs of
> increased security no doubt will continue to weigh on national
> economies for the foreseeable future and will disproportion-
> ately hit certain sectors like airlines and insurance.[14]

Considering the substantial and unprecedented loss of life and
property on September 11, the continuing threat of terrorist violence at home and abroad, the omnipresent fear that more deadly
attacks are in the offing, and the ongoing economic turmoil confronting the United States, it is not entirely inconceivable that the
government would be hard-pressed to respond to the gruesome
attacks in a manner that tests its resolve and commitment as a
nation to civil liberties and principles of equal justice. America's
determination to uphold such principles has been tested during
tumultuous times throughout its history, and, sadly, it has not
always met such challenges in ways that demonstrate unwavering
dedication to its core beliefs. Indeed, there are many who advocate
that in times of war the government *must* be given a veritable carte
blanche to protect its citizens at home and abroad. While this is not
an entirely untenable position, the primary question that this book
seeks to address is whether such latitude should be ceded to the
government without also retaining some checks-and-balances
authority to protect against fear-driven legislation and policy initiatives that sharply conflict with fundamental principles of equal justice. Or, stated differently, can America respond appropriately to
the challenge of global terrorism while steadfastly remaining within
the constitutional boundaries that have defined it as a democratic
nation for well over two centuries? To begin this analysis, it is essential to define what is meant by "justice" and, more importantly,
"equal justice." That is, what precisely is expected when citizens
demand that institutions and people behave in a just manner and
that our legal system dispense justice fairly and equally?

The Equal Justice Paradigm

The term *justice* is ironically similar to the term *terrorism* in that it has also eluded a clearly defined, universally accepted meaning. Perhaps this similarity arises from the fact that, like *terrorism, justice* is a value-laden term, implicating one's beliefs, biases, and self-interest. Indeed, the meaning of justice has been debated by philosophers, legal scholars, and religious scholars from the medieval period to modern times. In Greek mythology, for example, the concept of justice is traditionally symbolized by Themis, the goddess of divine justice, who is usually depicted blindfolded, carrying the scales of justice and a sword. According to some mythology sources, Themis was the personification of justice and bore responsibility for maintaining order and keeping the moral law of gods and men.

The word *justice* itself originates from the Greek word *dike,* which, loosely interpreted, means that everything stays in its assigned place or plays its designated role according to nature.[15] Of course, this basic conception of justice suggests nothing about the "right" way to behave, and it is only in later definitions that the moral or rightness/wrongness components of justice begin to emerge. For example, St. Thomas Aquinas acknowledged that justice means "doing right" when he said "justice is a habit whereby a man renders to each one his due by a constant and perpetual will."[16] Other philosophers have similarly defined justice in terms of how one ought or ought not behave toward one's fellow citizens, thereby suggesting that justice is dependent upon a mutual network of behaviors where everyone acts in accord with certain standards. For instance, noted philosopher David Hume characterized justice as the mediator between people's essential selfishness and generosity. Similarly, political theorist William Galston described justice as

> more than voluntary agreement, [but] . . . less than perfect community. It allows us to retain our separate existences and our self-regard; it does not ask us to share the pleasures, pains and sentiments of others. Justice is intelligent self-regard, modified, by the requirements of rational consistency.[17]

The overarching ideal of enhancing justice by maintaining order and rational consistency were present at America's inception, for "not only were liberty, property and the pursuit of happiness deeply linked in the thoughts of the Framers . . . [but] they also believed in the principle that all people had a right to equal justice and to equality of rights."[18] President Abraham Lincoln in his Gettysburg Address confirmed this vision of the new nation when he spoke of a nation "conceived in liberty and dedicated to the proposition that all men are created equal." Lincoln envisioned these as founding principles and considered them interdependent concepts in that achieving equality required freedom and, in turn, freedom could not be maintained without equality.

Later, the U.S. Supreme Court, in its role as ultimate arbiter of the Constitution, endorsed the fundamental principle of equal justice under the law in several cases decided early in America's history, and reiterated throughout turbulent times, as the young nation struggled with slavery and civil rights issues. Indeed, many believe that the phrase "Equal Justice Under the Law" inscribed on the architrave above the U.S. Supreme Court building was paraphrased from a number of cases in which the Court made reference to "equal and impartial justice under the law."[19] Several decades after that inscription, in one of the key school desegregation cases, the Court eloquently explained the meaning and impact of equal justice under the law.

In *Cooper v. Aaron*, the Court rejected an attempt by public school authorities in the state of Arkansas to "postpone" school desegregation plans due to racial tensions experienced during the process. Explaining the rationale for its opinion, the Court first observed that the "federal judiciary is supreme in the exposition of the law of the Constitution." Then, illuminating one of the basic features of our system, the Court declared that "[t]he Constitution created a government dedicated to equal justice under law . . . [and] the Fourteenth Amendment embodied and emphasized that ideal." Finally, the Court ordered the school board to comply with the desegregation order because "command[s] of the Constitution are indispensable for the protection of the freedoms guaranteed by our fundamental charter for all of us. Our constitutional ideal of equal justice under law is thus made a living truth."[20]

In common parlance, the notion of equal justice probably connotes ideas of fairness and impartiality in a variety of settings. That is, like people will be treated in a like manner, whether it be a question of resource allocation or meting out punishment to a convicted criminal defendant. Traditionally, however, concerns regarding the definition and application of equal justice principles have arisen most often in the criminal justice context. This special category of justice is often referred to as "corrective justice" and is largely concerned with restoring balance to society by administering punishment to those who have created a societal imbalance through the commission of criminal acts. Of course, underlying this idea of societal balance versus imbalance are shades of the basic conception of justice, namely, maintaining order by assuring that everything is in its proper place. Corrective justice can be further subdivided into the categories of substantive and procedural justice. Substantive justice involves the concept of just deserts or how a society determines fair punishment for a criminal defendant following an adjudication of guilt. In her book *Ethics in Crime and Justice*, author Jocelyn Pollock further subdivides substantive justice into retributive and utilitarian justice. Retributive justice restores balance to society by ensuring that the criminal suffers in proportion to the pain or loss the victim was forced to endure. Accordingly, moral limits act as a restraint on retributive justice in the sense that

1. We must punish only to the extent that the loss of liberty would be agreeable were one not to know whether one were to be the criminal, the victim, or a member of the general public, and
2. The loss of liberty must be justified as the minimal loss consistent with the maintenance of the same liberty among others.[21]

Thus, the goal of retributive justice is to reinstate balance and order under circumstances of temporary imbalance. According to Pollock, this means that "the moral limit of punishment is reached when what is done to the criminal equals the extent of his or her forfeiture, as determined by the crime."[22]

Utilitarian justice, on the other hand, administers punishment to offenders primarily to deter recidivism. This formulation of substantive justice is distinguishable from retributive justice in that as long as the criminal is likely to reoffend, then punishment is justified under a utilitarian model without regard to what might be considered proportional under a retribution model. To illustrate this distinction, Pollock observes, "[i]f a criminal is sure to commit more crime, the utilitarian could justify holding him in prison as a means of incapacitation, but to hold him past the time 'equal' to his crime would be seen as injustice under a retributive system."[23]

As discussed earlier, the second subcategory of corrective justice is procedural justice, which concerns the processes utilized to ascertain who is deserving of punishment and how that punishment will be administered. In the United States, constitutionally grounded principles of due process establish the basic parameters for procedural justice. More specifically, the due process of law principle is set forth broadly in the Fifth Amendment of the Constitution and made applicable to the states through the Fourteenth Amendment. According to Leonard Levy in his book *Original Intent and the Framers' Constitution:*

> The Framers understood that without fair and regularized procedures to protect the criminally accused, liberty could not exist. They knew that from time immemorial, the tyrant's first step was to use the criminal law to crush his opposition. Vicious and ad hoc procedures had always been used to victimize nonconformists and minorities of differing religious, racial or political persuasions. The Fifth Amendment was part and parcel of the procedures that were so crucial, in the minds of the Framers, to the survival of the most treasured rights.[24]

The Fifth Amendment was thus an explicit acknowledgment by America's founding fathers that just procedures for identifying, prosecuting, and punishing offenders were indispensable to a free society. This recognition also reflected a central concern that justice, particularly in the enforcement of criminal laws, be administered fairly, impartially, and equally. It is therefore no overstatement to say that these principles have long been the underpinning of the U.S. criminal justice system and are critical to protecting individual freedoms. Indeed, the conception and application of due process and equal justice principles are so instrumental to the operation of the U.S. criminal justice system that the Supreme Court has extended these protections to citizens and noncitizens alike in a series of cases determining that noncitizens, even those who are present in the United States unlawfully, are protected by the due process of law guarantees in the Fifth and Fourteenth Amendments.[25]

To summarize, notions of due process and equal justice under the law were intentionally interwoven into the U.S. Constitution at the nation's founding. Subsequent interpretation and application of these basic principles leave little doubt that they serve as critical barriers between arbitrary and capricious governmental conduct directed against those who, for whatever reason, find themselves disfavored by the government. In fact, history has demonstrated that variance from these principles, even in times of national crisis, inevitably leads to disastrous results. Consider the case of Fred Korematsu.[26]

In 1942 Korematsu, an American of Japanese descent, was convicted for remaining in a designated "military area" in violation of Civil Exclusion Order No. 34, which directed that all persons of Japanese ancestry be excluded from that area unless detained in a designated "Assembly Center."[27] The practical effect of this order was to condemn many families to "living in horse stalls under unsanitary conditions, often by open sewers. Others occupied hastily constructed barracks. Toilet and bathing facilities were communal and devoid of privacy. Barbed wire fences and armed guard towers with guns facing toward the inmates surrounded these compounds. They were, in fact, prisons."[28]

Upon conviction, Korematsu instituted a legal challenge claiming that military detention of civilian citizens of Japanese ancestry pursuant to Order 34 was unconstitutional. The case wound its way through the courts, finally reaching the U.S. Supreme Court. In reviewing Korematsu's case, the Court began by acknowledging that legal restrictions curtailing the rights of a single racial group are immediately suspect and are therefore subject to the most rigid scrutiny. With respect to the relevant military orders issued shortly after the commencement of the war with Japan, the Court concluded that "[n]othing short of apprehension by the proper military authorities of the gravest imminent danger to public safety" can justify exclusion from an area or constant confinement.[29] Yet, the Court explained that exclusion of a specific group of people from certain areas during the war had a "definite and close relationship" to the prevention of espionage and sabotage. Furthermore, addressing the issue of "possible" racial prejudice as it pertained to the forced detention of citizens of Japanese ancestry, the Court observed:

> It is said that we are dealing here with the case of imprisonment of a citizen in a concentration camp solely because of his ancestry, without evidence or inquiry concerning his loyalty and good disposition towards the United States. Our task would be simple, our duty clear, were this a case involving the imprisonment of a loyal citizen in a concentration camp because of racial prejudice. Regardless of the true nature of the assembly and relocation centers—and we deem it unjustifiable to call them concentration camps with all the ugly connotations that term implies—we are dealing specifically with nothing but an exclusion order. To cast this case into outlines of racial prejudice, without reference to the real military dangers which were presented, merely confuses the issue. Korematsu was not excluded from the Military Area because of hostility to him or his race. He *was* excluded because we are at war with the Japanese Empire, because the properly constituted military authorities feared an invasion of our West Coast and felt constrained to take proper security measures, because they decided that the military urgency of the situation demanded that all citizens of Japanese ancestry be segregated from the West Coast temporarily, and finally, because Congress, reposing its confidence in this time of war in our military leaders—as inevitably it must—determined that they should have the power to do just this. There was evidence of disloyalty on the part of some, the military authorities considered that the need for action was great, and time was short. We cannot—by availing ourselves of the calm perspective of hindsight—now say that at that time these actions were unjustified.[30]

Several members of the Court sharply dissented from the majority opinion, and their dissenting voices warrant careful consideration because they speak specifically to the necessity of adhering to enduring constitutional principles, especially in time of war. Justice Murphy, in dissent, described the exclusion of persons of Japanese ancestry as exceeding "the very brink of constitutional power" and falling into the "ugly abyss of racism," concluding:

I dissent, therefore, from this legalization of racism. Racial discrimination in any form and in any degree has no justifiable part whatever in our democratic way of life. It is unattractive in any setting but it is utterly revolting among a free people who have embraced the principles set forth in the Constitution of the United States. All residents of this nation are kin in some way by blood or culture to a foreign land. Yet they are primarily and necessarily a part of the new and distinct civilization of the United States. They must accordingly be treated at all times as the heirs of the American experiment and as entitled to all the rights and freedoms guaranteed by the Constitution.[31]

Similarly, Justice Jackson, in a particularly strident dissent, warned of the possibility for further abuse if the Court sanctioned such a blatant constitutional violation:

Much is said of the danger to liberty from the Army program for deporting and detaining these citizens of Japanese extraction. But a judicial construction of the due process clause that will sustain this order is a far more subtle blow to liberty than the promulgation of the order itself. A military order, however unconstitutional, is not apt to last longer than the military emergency. Even during that period a succeeding commander may revoke it all. But once a judicial opinion rationalizes such an order to show that it conforms to the Constitution, or rather rationalizes the Constitution to show that the Constitution sanctions such an order, the Court for all time has validated the principle of racial discrimination in criminal procedure and of transplanting American citizens. The principle then lies about like a loaded weapon ready for the hand of any authority that can bring forward a plausible claim of an urgent need. Every repetition imbeds that principle more deeply in our law and thinking and expands it to new purposes. All who observe the work of courts are familiar with what Judge Cardozo described as "the tendency of a principle to expand itself to the limit of its logic." A military commander may overstep the bounds of constitutionality, and it is an incident. But if we review and approve, that passing incident becomes the doctrine of the Constitution. There it has a generative power of its own, and all that it creates will be in its own image. Nothing better illustrates this danger than does the Court's opinion in this case.[32]

And, indeed, the passage of time revealed that the compelling words of the Korematsu dissenters were not merely hyperbole and misplaced sympathy. In 1983 Korematsu filed a writ of *coram nobis*[33] to overturn his conviction after discovering new evidence that the government apparently suppressed in his earlier trial. The evidence strongly indicated that the government intentionally misled the court concerning its claim of "military necessity," which, during the first Korematsu case, was offered as the sole justification for exclusion and internment of Japanese American citizens.[34] In the later Korematsu opinion, the court took judicial notice of a recent report from the Commission on Wartime Relocation and Internment of Civilians, which found that, rather than military necessity, the "broad historical causes which shaped these [exclusion and detention] decisions were race prejudice, war hysteria and a failure of political leadership." Thus, upon reviewing the case, the district court determined that, while it did not have the authority to overturn the original Korematsu opinion, it could correct errors of fact and effectively vacate Korematsu's conviction. Opining about any lingering significance of the earlier Korematsu decision, the court stated:

> Korematsu remains on the pages of our legal and political history. As a legal precedent it is now recognized as having very limited application. As historical precedent it stands as a constant caution that in times of war or declared military necessity our institutions must be vigilant in protecting constitutional guarantees. It stands as a caution that in times of distress the shield of military necessity and national security must not be used to protect governmental actions from close scrutiny and accountability. It stands as a caution that in times of international hostility and antagonisms our institutions, legislative, executive and judicial, must be prepared to exercise their authority to protect all citizens from the petty fears and prejudices that are so easily aroused.[35]

In this modern "war on terrorism," as America continues to formulate legal, political, and judicial responses to the September 11 terrorist attacks, it must be ever mindful of the errors and consequences of the past, when military necessity and national security concerns were offered as scant justification for setting aside foundational principles in favor of capitulating to unfounded fears and petty prejudices. The looming shadow of the Korematsu case stands as a beacon, perpetually warning that reactions to terrorism must be prudently measured and not predicated upon ad hoc legal principles and policy initiatives driven by hatred and fear.

The goal of this book is to meaningfully analyze America's current political, legal, and judicial responses to the terrorist attacks of September 11 by critically evaluating how those responses comport with historical precedent and America's long-standing commitment to principles of equal justice. In some respects, the book's overall objective might render it controversial in light of the current national tide of patriotism. In fact, Attorney General Ashcroft essentially warned Americans that the current war on terrorism will not suffer dissenters gladly when he declared before Congress that those who challenge his wisdom only aid terrorists and give ammunition to America's enemies. Certainly he must have forgotten that more than two centuries ago popular dissent challenging a repressive English monarchy inspired the revolution that created America, a nation committed to democracy, where toleration of critical and dissenting voices is interwoven into the very fabric of its Constitution. In light of this history, we certainly do not believe that reasoned analysis and critique of America's past and present responses to terrorism equal a lack of patriotism, much less treasonous aiding of any real or imagined enemies. Indeed, the academy has often been at the forefront of furthering global understanding of complex issues that arise in times of controversy. Thus, the insights in this book are offered as a springboard to foster discussion and debate, and we hope it is received in that spirit.

This chapter introduced two of the key concepts that will be explored throughout the book: terrorism and equal justice. Chapter 2 will take a retrospective approach, examining how America has effectively responded to the challenges of terrorist violence in the past without significantly altering its political, legislative, or judicial framework. Next, chapter 3 will assess the various terrorist threats confronting America, ranging from traditional threats, such as bombings, to nuclear, biological, and chemical threats, to the twenty-first-century potential for cyberterrorism. Chapter 4 will begin the book's in-depth analysis of America's legislative, executive, and judicial responses to the 9/11 attacks by dissecting the USA Patriot Act, a lengthy and constitutionally questionable piece of legislation hurriedly enacted by Congress little more than a month after the attacks. Following this analysis, chapter 5 will explore a broad range of other legislative, executive, and judicial responses to the attacks, including the Joint Congressional Resolution Authorizing the Use of Force, legislation creating a new Department of Homeland Security, and the president's military order. Chapter 6 will examine a wide range of court proceedings and decisions arising out of the events of 9/11 and will assess the impact of these judicial measures on our justice system as a whole. Finally, in chapter 7 the book will conclude with a comprehensive review of current trends in America's legal responses to the terrorism threat and will call on America to adhere to fundamental principles of fairness and equal justice under the law as it continues to formulate responses to the emerging terrorist threat.

2 American Responses to Terrorism
A Historical Perspective

By actions which compel general attention, the new idea seeps into people's minds and wins converts. One such act may, in a few days, make more propaganda than thousands of pamphlets. Above all, it wakens the spirit of revolt; it breeds daring.

—Peter Kropotkin, Russian anarchist, *The Spirit of Revolt*

From ancient times, terrorists have resorted to acts of indiscriminate violence as a means to achieve both political and religious objectives. Ironically, many of the early terrorist atrocities were carried out in the Middle East region, which today is believed to be the primary breeding ground for much of modern-day terrorism. During the first century A.D., two Jewish groups, the Zealots and the Sicarii, sought to inspire insurrection among the oppressed Jewish populace in Judea to expunge their Roman occupiers and "purify" Jewish religious institutions from the infiltration of Roman influences. Their revolt was, in part, driven by a staunchly held belief in a messianic doctrine, which maintained that a period of unimaginable woe was the precondition for attaining paradise and divine intervention. Not content to idly wait for the precondition to arise naturally, the Zealots and Sicarii instigated conflict by perpetrating terrorist violence against their Roman occupiers to "make oppression so intolerable that insurrection was inevitable, and, subsequently to frustrate every attempt to reconcile the respective parties."[1] Hence, the Zealots and Sicarii encouraged rebellion by playing on the psychology and religious zeal of the Jewish population and by effectively manipulating "mass expectations that a cataclysmic messianic deliverance was imminent." Their deadly terrorist methods included assassination, hostage taking, and the slaughtering of prisoners; moreover, "[t]heir atrocities occurred on the most holy days to exploit the potential for publicity therein, and . . . to demonstrate that not even the most sacred occasions could provide immunity."[2]

Another early Middle Eastern terrorist group, the Assassins, also had dual objectives in mind when committing terrorist acts. The Assassins contended that Islam had been corrupted from within and murdered prominent Muslim leaders in cold blood, usually on holy days, as a means to demonstrate their outrage and to bring about publicity that they hoped "would result in attention to their cause, recognition that it was just, and the bringing about of a new, cleansed, and revitalized theological and social order."[3] As their name suggests, the Assassins' sole terrorist strategy involved "[d]ramatically staged assassinations [that drew] immense attention to a cause."[4] This was a uniquely useful strategy at a time when the basis of power was personal. Thus, when a sultan or emir fell at the hands of the Assassins, his troops were disbanded and the land was in disarray, assuring yet another victory for the purification of Islam.

Centuries later, in 1793, the terms *terrorism* and *terrorist* are believed to have officially become part of contemporary vernacular as a result of the Reign of Terror inflicted during the French Revolution. Initiated by the newly formulated French government and ostensibly designed to protect the reforms instituted during the revolution, the Reign of Terror primarily targeted those suspected of treasonous undertakings. Eventually, thousands were summarily convicted of traitorous crimes and guillotined, while hundreds of thousands were arrested and detained.

Less than a century later, Russian revolutionaries spoke of assassinations as a "destructive and terroristic activity" designed to provoke the Russian masses into revolution. Interestingly, early Russian revolutionaries eschewed the tactic of indiscriminate violence and employed their terroristic strategies in a reasonably organized fashion, mandating that they be carried out with discrimination and clear purposes in mind. Authorities were targets, not ordinary citizens. But even then the method had to be justified. And the justification was that the authorities' monopoly on power gave the revolutionaries no other choice, and that, in overturning mass tyranny, which was responsible for mass deaths, assassinations were actually life-saving and moral.[5]

From these early roots, terrorism evolved and branched out to include not only ideological objectives but nationalist goals as well. The character of its potential victims also gradually expanded to include members of the general public, especially those who were perceived to have benefited from supporting the enemy regime. The callous mind-set of nondiscrimination among victims likely finds its roots in the immortal words of French anarchist Emile Henry, who, after throwing a bomb into a crowded Paris café, proclaimed, "there are no innocents."

After World War II, as Walter Reich recounts,

> guerilla warfare related to decolonization predominated, although terrorism occurred in a number of areas. . . . [N]ationalist-separatist terrorism was prominent among the Palestinians, Basques, Armenians, Croatians, Sikhs, Tamils, and others. . . . Recently, in the 1980s, terrorism in the name of another cause, religion, reemerged with particular force and ardor in the Middle East, primarily in Lebanon and Iran, with its special characteristics and justifications, thus bringing the history of terrorism full circle to its beginnings in that convulsed corner of the world.[6]

The most recent statistics compiled by the U.S. Department of State in its annual Patterns of Global Terrorism report offer a chilling overview of terrorist exploits around the globe during the year 2001. Although the number of terrorist incidents declined from 426 to 346, the number of deaths attributed directly to terrorist activity totaled 3,547, the highest annual death toll from terrorism ever recorded. Perhaps not surprisingly, 90 percent of those fatalities occurred as a result of the September 11 attacks. In addition, despite widespread trepidation about the impending inclusion of nuclear, biological, and chemical weapons in the terrorist arsenal, the report reveals that an overwhelming number of terrorist acts are still committed using "traditional" methods and weapons, such as bombing, kidnapping, arson, and murder. Sadly, the September 11 commercial airliner hijackings stand in sharp contrast as a tragically inventive method to inflict massive harm on innocent civilians.

The Department of State report also discloses that, while declining, state-sponsored terrorism is nevertheless a source of significant concern.[7] Iraq, for example, was the only Arab-Muslim country to refuse issuing a statement condemning the 9/11 attacks. Iraqi leaders then added injury to insult by cruelly speculating that the resulting misery and death inflicted upon Americans following 9/11 was merely America "reaping the fruits of [its] crimes against humanity." Against this backdrop of hard-line anti-American sentiment, it is not at all surprising that, according to the report, Iraq provided encouragement and financial support for myriad terrorist groups, thus, perhaps, lending credence to its inclusion in President Bush's designated "axis of evil." Other countries such as Iran, Sudan, and Syria also persist in their support and sponsorship of such terrorist groups as al Qaeda, Hizballah, HAMAS, and the Palestine Islamic Jihad, despite numerous threats and sanctions from the global community.

This brief foray into the historical roots of terrorism certainly cannot do justice to its complex and abundant history. Instead, this synopsis is primarily offered to aid in understanding that terrorist attacks against governments and innocent civilians in pursuit of religious or nationalist ideologies are not a new phenomenon. Indeed, such conduct and the justifications for it have a long, rich, and sadly enduring history. The principal purpose of this chapter, rather, is to identify several significant terrorist events throughout recent history that have impacted the United States or its interests and to consider how America's governmental institutions formulated and executed responses to those unprovoked and random acts of violence. This retrospective analysis will reveal that measured responses by America's political, legislative, and judicial branches *within* the framework of its existing system have traditionally epitomized America's global stand against terrorism. Such fundamental yet calculated and decisive reactions stand as an apotheosis of how

America might fashion long-term responses to address not only the circumstances surrounding the events of September 11 but the challenges that will inevitably arise in this new age of global terrorism.

Of course, this conclusion begs the question of how the tragedy of 9/11 could have transpired if America's governmental mechanisms were, in fact, devising and implementing appropriate and effective responses to the worldwide terrorist threat. The answer to this query is threefold: First, no amount of counterterrorism planning and preparation can predict and intercept every single instance of terrorist behavior. To date, the U.S. Department of State has identified thirty-three terrorist groups as Foreign Terrorist Organizations (FTOs). Most of these FTOs are subdivided into a complex web of factions and cells that operate somewhat autonomously, although often ultimately receiving instructions from a supreme leader. These groups are tremendously successful in their efforts to recruit members from the alienated and marginalized segments of society. They aggressively prey upon gullible individuals thought to be searching for some semblance of order and meaning in their lives.[8] Hate, vengeance, and violence against a powerful oppressor afford a sense of purpose to the directionless masses, who often embrace terrorist ideologies with such zeal that many consider it an honor to sacrifice their lives to promote these beliefs. Attempting to formulate rational responses to address and prevent behavior that is so stubbornly irrational is a recipe for disaster. Indeed, although difficult to accept as a truth, martyrdom in the name of religious or political ideology is, in the end, an insidious and deadly disease without a cure.

Second, the events of September 11 do not reflexively suggest that America's political, legal, and judicial institutions failed to adequately prepare for terrorist strikes. Alternatively, the attacks could signify that U.S. counterterrorism efforts have been so effective that terrorist elements are compelled to attempt even more extreme measures to exact vengeance and to draw attention to their causes. Professor Yonah Alexander predicted such a deadly escalation in 1999, when he observed that, although ironic, "bringing terrorism under substantial control in the foreseeable future through national and international legislation, increased security and enforcement measures as well as preemptive and punitive military strikes might, in fact, hasten the advent of more daring types of terrorism."[9]

Finally, to the extent that weaknesses in America's institutions are deemed contributory factors to the 9/11 disaster, two secondary, yet critical, inquiries remain. That is, what degree of modification is required to redress any perceived inadequacies, and can such a fine-tuning process be accomplished in accordance with America's fundamental beliefs and principles as a nation? Dramatically overhauling long-standing constitutional standards and the institutions that breathe life and meaning into these ideals is ahistorical, disparages two centuries of time-honored equal justice principles, and dangerously limits America to a tunnel-vision reductionist approach that focuses on specific types of terrorism by predefined groups—a view that will eventually leave the United States unprepared for more generalized, and potentially more deadly, terrorist attacks.

Terrorism in Recent History

Shortly after the September 11 attacks, the U.S. Department of State published a document entitled "Significant Terrorist Incidents, 1961–2001." Although this compendium does not purport to be an exhaustive list of terrorist acts committed during that forty-year span, it does highlight the most noteworthy occurrences. Among the more notorious terrorist incidents are many that either implicated or directly impacted U.S. interests. They include the following:

- In January 1975 a bomb exploded in a Wall Street bar in New York City, killing 4 people and injuring 60 more. A Puerto Rican nationalist group (FALN) claimed responsibility for the explosion.
- The Iran hostage crisis began in November 1979, when Iranian radicals seized the U.S. Embassy in Tehran and took 66 American diplomats hostage. Although 13 hostages were quickly released, the remaining 53 were held until the crisis ended in January 1981.
- A four-hundred-pound suicide truck bomb exploded outside the U.S. Embassy in Beirut in April 1983. The attack,

which was initiated by the Islamic Jihad, killed 63 people and injured 120.

- In October 1983 the Islamic Jihad struck again in Beirut, this time destroying the U.S. Marine barracks and killing 241 Americans.
- The *Achille Lauro,* an Italian cruise ship, was hijacked in the Eastern Mediterranean Sea in October 1985. One wheelchair-bound U.S. passenger, Leon Klinghoffer, was murdered and his body thrown overboard. Four Palestinian Liberation Front terrorists were eventually apprehended and charged with the hijacking. As will be explored later in this chapter, the *Achille Lauro* incident sparked much international debate and military action aimed at determining the appropriate jurisdiction to prosecute the captured hijackers.
- Pan American Airlines flight 103 was blown up over Lockerbie, Scotland, by suspected Libyan terrorists in December 1988. All 259 passengers, most of whom were Americans flying home for the holidays, were killed.
- In February 1993 the WTC in New York City was badly damaged by a truck bomb planted by Islamic terrorists. Six people died and 1,000 were injured in the explosion.
- The federal building in Oklahoma City, Oklahoma, was destroyed by a massive truck bomb parked outside of the building in April 1995. Although suspicions first turned toward international terrorists, it was soon discovered that Americans Timothy McVeigh and Terry Nichols, both right-wing extremists, planned and executed what was then the largest terrorist attack on American soil. On that day 166 people lost their lives and hundreds more were injured.
- In February 1997 a sniper opened fire on tourists at an observation deck on the Empire State Building in New York City. One person, a Danish national, was killed and several others, including American visitors, were injured. The sniper, who turned the gun on himself, claimed in a note to be exacting revenge for the "enemies of Palestine."
- Two nearly simultaneous bombings occurred at U.S.

Embassy sites in east Africa in August 1998. At the U.S. Embassy in Kenya, 12 U.S. citizens were killed, along with 279 Foreign Service Nationals and Kenyan citizens, and thousands were injured. At the U.S. Embassy site in Dar es Salaam, Tanzania, 10 Foreign Service Nationals and Tanzanian citizens were killed, while 7 people were injured.[10]

What these deadly episodes of terrorism violence indicate quite clearly is that, prior to September 11, America was certainly no stranger to terrorist acts at home and abroad. These appalling statistics are also a tragic reminder that, even prior to that fateful morning in September 2001, American lives have been lost on a large scale as a direct result of terrorist assaults. Yet, none of these incidents triggered the type of comprehensive overhaul of America's governmental institutions currently being proposed and implemented in the wake of September 11. Is it possible that America's political, legislative, and judicial infrastructure in its pre-September 11 iteration was more than equal to the task of combating terrorism? The next sections will examine in further detail four of the terrorist incidents mentioned in the previous list and will explain how each was resolved within America's existing political, legal, and judicial framework, without resorting to a fundamental restructuring of the system. This analysis provides the factual foundation for a compelling argument that revamping our system in ways that ignore fundamental principles of equal justice is unprecedented and, indeed, unwarranted.

The *Achille Lauro* Hijacking

On Monday, October 7, 1985, a group of armed men took control of an Italian cruise ship, the *Achille Lauro*, in the Mediterranean Sea shortly after the ship departed Alexandria, Egypt, en route to another Egyptian city, Port Said. The hijackers identified themselves as members of the Palestinian Liberation Front and, as ransom, demanded that Israel release a group of fifty imprisoned Palestinians. The hijackers threatened to begin executing the hostages and stressed that Americans would be the first victims of their brutality if these demands were not met.[11] Because of its patently multinational scope—that is, an Italian cruise ship seized in international waters with an explicit threat to American lives— the hijacking launched crisis management initiatives among the various national security departments in both the United States and Italy. From the outset, the United States advocated a "firm stance" toward the hijackers, which meant that negotiations were quite simply out of the question. When speculation arose that an American hostage had possibly been murdered a day after the hostage crisis began, the U.S. government initiated internal discussions concerning a number of tactical approaches, including military rescue operations, designed to secure the release of the remaining hostages and to bring the terrorists to justice.

Although U.S. plans to carry out a military rescue operation on the *Achille Lauro* were squarely in accordance with a 1958 convention to the law of the sea that allowed any state to board and seize a ship "under the dominant control of pirates," the military intervention strategy nevertheless encountered a stumbling block—the involvement of the Italian government. The *Achille Lauro* was, after all, an Italian cruise ship, and, contrary to the wishes of the U.S. government, the Italian government expressed its desire to use its *own* military force to effectuate rescue, but only in case of "extreme necessity." In fact, Italy confirmed that it had already deployed forces in preparation for that possibility. To further solidify its jurisdictional dominance, the Italian government cautioned the United States against taking any action without consulting Italian officials, who, again contrary to the U.S. position, favored opening a dialogue with the terrorists so as to possibly facilitate a bloodless solution to the crisis.

Later, as the ship sailed toward Egypt, yet another sovereign nation was interpolated into an already contentious political dilemma. With the express consent of the Italian government, and *despite* America's disinclination to negotiate with the terrorists, Egyptian officials and Palestinian emissaries (assigned by Yasir Arafat) opened a dialogue with the hijackers as the *Achille Lauro* sat anchored off the coast of Port Said. Shortly after making contact with the hijackers, the negotiations evolved swiftly and the captors agreed to release the ship under two conditions: first, they demanded that five governments with direct involvement in the incident (including the United States) agree not to bring any charges against the hijackers or pursue extradition for any crimes committed aboard the ship; second, the hijackers requested that they be given safe passage and, in due course, be released to the custody of the Palestine Liberation Organization (PLO), a group that was notorious for its use of terrorist violence to accomplish its objectives.

These demands presented both political and legal conundrums for the United States due to mounting uncertainty as to whether crimes had been committed aboard the ship, despite assurances from the *Achille Lauro* captain that everyone aboard was in good health. Perhaps more importantly, however, surrendering the hijackers to the PLO granted more recognition to the terrorist entity as a legitimate governing body than the United States had previously extended in its Middle East policy.

Consideration of these critical issues was promptly set aside when it was learned, much to the surprise of the American government, that the hijackers had indeed relinquished control of the ship pursuant to a guarantee by the Italian and Egyptian governments that they would be granted safe passage. Evidently this compromise was reached without the apparent or express consent of the other sovereign nations involved in the crisis. In addition, it is unclear how much either Italy or Egypt knew about the death of American passenger Leon Klinghoffer when they offered safe passage to the terrorist hijackers.[12] What is apparent, however, is that once the United States discovered the senseless and exceptionally brutal murder aboard the ship, a collective sense of outrage erupted in the United States, which evolved into a national plea for justice, demanding that the hijackers not be allowed to get away with murder. The U.S. government agreed and declared, "there must be no asylum for terrorists." Nevertheless, recognizing the jurisdictional legal limitations of the case, the United States elected initially to take a diplomatic approach and strongly urged Italy to extradite the terrorists from Egypt to Italy, where they could face justice.

Although both Italy and Egypt acknowledged that a prosecutable crime took place aboard the *Achille Lauro*, political considerations took center stage as both countries feared that extradition of the terrorists might disrupt fragile Middle East relations and cause embarrassment for the PLO. Angered by this diplomatic rebuff and worried that the hijackers might ultimately evade justice, the U.S. government devised a plan to intercept and capture the terrorist hijackers wherever they might be and to extradite them to the United States for trial. Thus, when clandestine electronic surveillance revealed the terrorists were departing Egypt for parts unknown on an EgyptAir plane, President Reagan signed a national security directive authorizing interception of the aircraft with the expectation that the United States would obtain custody of the terrorists and return them to the United States for criminal proceedings. This strategy resulted in jurisdictional complications, however, when U.S. forces intercepted the plane and forced it to land in Italy. That is, because the *Achille Lauro* was an Italian cruise ship, as soon as the terrorists touched down on Italian soil, Italian law enforcement officials were required by law to act on information that related to criminal activity. Thus, by attempting to bring the hostages to justice in America, the United States had inadvertently forced legal jurisdiction upon Italy.

Once again, tension arose between Italy and the United States, and a standoff ensued at the Italian airport while diplomatic channels between the two countries attempted to resolve which country would retain legal jurisdiction over the terrorists.

> During these conversations . . . American officials explained their intention to take custody of the four hijackers, who were responsible for the death of a U.S. citizen. Italian officials replied that the hijackers were now on Italian soil. Italian law . . . did not allow them . . . to discard information that these hijackers had committed crimes on an Italian ship. The Italian government was obliged to entrust the matter to the Italian judicial system.[13]

After hours of tense negotiation, both countries finally agreed that Italy would assume jurisdiction over the hijackers subject to specific demands from the United States that they be punished to the full extent of the law. After securing this commitment, U.S. officials were particularly jubilant because, in the years preceding this event, it seemed that the United States could not, despite its best efforts, effectively retaliate against terrorist strikes. For the moment, the *Achille Lauro* incident represented an apparent victory over terrorism, despite the fact that the terrorists would not be prosecuted on U.S. soil. This initial enthusiasm waned over time as criminal proceedings against the terrorists languished in Italian courts, and, once again, concern increased in the United States regarding the Italian government's pledge to bring all of the hostages to justice. Indeed, pursuant to a 1984 Act of Congress, which gave the United States authority to prosecute the takers of U.S. hostages at home or abroad, proceedings were eventually instituted in the U.S. federal court to secure arrest warrants for the four hijackers and their alleged ringleader, Adul Abbas, charging each with hostage taking, piracy, and conspiracy.

Despite repeated requests from the U.S. government to keep Abbas in custody until he could be extradited to the United States, the Italian government freed Abbas, claiming to have insufficient evidence of his involvement in the hijacking scheme to detain him further. As might be expected, U.S. officials deemed this a tremendous setback in their campaign against terrorism and suspected that the Italian government's decision to release Abbas had been politically motivated and dictated by its fear of PLO reprisals on Italian soil if Abbas were arrested and extradited to the United States.[14] In due course, partial victory over terrorism was achieved when three of the four remaining hijackers were tried in Italian courts and received jail sentences ranging from fifteen to thirty years. Charges against the fourth hijacker were later dismissed when it was determined that he was a minor at the time of the criminal acts.

Although the optimal result—prosecution, conviction, and punishment of all those responsible for the *Achille Lauro* hijacking—was not achieved, the death of Leon Klinghoffer was at least partially vindicated through the persistent diplomatic efforts of the U.S. government, combined with strategically targeted military operations and criminal proceedings. In addition, Leon Klinghoffer's survivors filed a civil lawsuit against the PLO, which was settled for an undisclosed sum of money after a lengthy negotiation process.

Pan American Flight 103: The Bombing over Lockerbie

On December 21, 1988, thirty-one thousand feet above the town of Lockerbie, Scotland, a Pan American Boeing 747 was carrying 243 passengers en route from London to New York. Most of the travelers aboard were Americans flying home for the holidays. Unbeknownst to the passengers and the sixteen flight crew members, in addition to the normal luggage stowed in the plane's cargo compartment, a deadly plastic explosive known as Semtex was surreptitiously concealed in one of the suitcases. The bomb had been skillfully positioned inside a hollowed out cassette player, which was then packed in a suitcase with other innocuous pieces of clothing. No one had been alerted to anything suspicious about Pan Am flight 103, nor had anyone inspected the inside of the suitcase or the contents of the cassette player.

Shortly after 7:00 P.M., a preset timer triggered the detonator, transforming the Semtex explosive into a ball of superheated gas. Because the bomb was located near the wall of the aircraft, when it discharged its lethal payload, the blast ripped a hole in the fuselage the size of a basketball. After the explosion,

> the floor buckled and the frame cracked at a point just forward of the wings. The front of the plane—the cockpit, first-class, and the business-class cabins—was bent back to the right, and in separating, knocked off the number 3 engine, inboard on the right side. Within three seconds after the explosion, the airplane had broken open and begun spilling passengers into the air.[15]

There were no survivors of the Pan Am flight 103 bombing. In the aftermath of this horrifying tragedy, the victims' families grieved inconsolably and yet simultaneously demanded answers from Pan Am, the U.S. government, and some as yet unknown foreign government responsible for the bombing. Their main question was: How could this have happened? The U.S. government, on the brink of transition from the Reagan to the Bush administration, provided little solace to the anguished families by offering half-hearted promises to root out the responsible parties and to bring them to justice.

The first step in the investigation revealed that Pan Am, which boasted of implementing one of the tightest security programs in the industry in the wake of an earlier TWA hijacking, had, in fact, hastily assembled a security program that failed to comply with new Federal Aviation Administration (FAA) regulations in many critical respects. For example, the FAA guidelines recognized the potential for bombs being placed in unaccompanied checked luggage and, therefore, mandated that all baggage at high-risk airports be matched with passengers *actually* boarding planes. Pan Am summarily rejected that FAA regulation, arguing that it would cause unnecessary delay. Instead, Pan Am substituted an X-ray machine system at the Frankfurt airport (a high-risk facility) to screen all luggage transferring from another airline onto a Pan Am flight. Unfortunately, this seemingly innocuous deviation from the FAA regulation offered a prime opportunity for terrorists whose weapon of choice was plastic explosives, which could not be viewed through the X-ray machines.

When Pan Am's fatal security miscalculation came to light, the victims' families demanded compensation from the airline for the loss of their loved ones. The law in effect in 1988 limited recovery for airline crashes to a uniform standard of compensation, which, at that time, was $75,000. To exceed that amount, the families of the victims would have to demonstrate that the airline engaged in "willful misconduct" that led to the fatal crash. Fearing that possibility and attempting to circumvent an onslaught of civil litigation, the airline struck preemptively, offering each of the families an immediate $100,000 cash payment in exchange for the relinquishment of any rights to file lawsuits related to the crash in the future. Almost no one accepted the airline's offer, and, as expected, multiple lawsuits against the airline ensued.

On the governmental front, after mounting pressure from the families of the victims, a newly elected President Bush convened a commission to determine the exact cause of the explosion. After a lengthy investigation, the commission concluded in a 182-page report that the destruction of Pan Am flight 103 was quite likely the result of a dangerously flawed aviation security system and, thus, may have been preventable. Although the commission could not determine precisely how the explosive was placed on the aircraft, there was credible evidence that terrorists, aware of the lax airport security screening procedures at the Frankfurt airport, left extra unaccompanied luggage containing the bombing device to be loaded on the airplane by unwitting airline workers. Finally, the commission explained that it could not attribute responsibility for the deadly explosion to any particular country or group, although a criminal investigation was ongoing. What was particularly note-worthy about the commission's findings, however, was the passionate statement it made concerning America's long-term terrorism policies. The commission concluded:

> Pursuing terrorists and responding swiftly and proportionately to their acts against humanity must become U.S. policy in deed as well as in word. What is required is effective action, not simply strong rhetoric. [The United States] needs a more vigorous policy that not only pursues and punishes terrorists, but also makes state sponsors of terrorism pay a price for their actions.[16]

Nearly three years later, after a painstaking multinational investigation, the United States and Britain announced criminal charges against two Libyan intelligence officers, Abdel Basset Ali Al-Megrahi and Lamen Khalifa Fhima, for the Pan Am flight 103 bombing. The two men were indicted in a U.S. federal court on 193 felony counts, even though they had yet to be arrested and extradited to the United States. Law enforcement officials believed the suspected terrorists were in Libya and also speculated that the bombing of flight 103 had been condoned by high-level officials in the Libyan government. Using diplomatic channels, the United States immediately initiated discussions with other countries to coordinate an international response to the alleged state-sponsored terrorism. Included within the range of proposed responses was the possibility of military action against Libya. For their part, Libyan officials unequivocally denied any involvement in the bombing yet, at the same time, made it clear that surrendering the suspects to the United States for criminal proceedings was highly unlikely, thus setting the stage for a possible military showdown with the United States.

In January 1992, after Libya failed to respond to repeated requests to hand over the suspects to the custody of the United States, Britain, or France, the UN Security Council unanimously adopted a resolution urging Libya to provide a full and effective response to the demands for the suspects' surrender. The UN resolution had numerous international implications. For example, if Libya failed to comply with the resolution, its noncompliance could form the basis for a subsequent resolution calling for limited sanctions against Libya, which could include cutting off international air links and imposing an embargo on certain aircraft parts. Those countries demanding the surrender of the suspects were especially careful not to characterize their requests as an "extradition" because none of the countries had extradition treaties with Libya. Instead, the requests were expressed as urgent appeals to Libya, a known state sponsor of terrorism with little concern for the pursuit of truth and justice, to forthwith deliver the suspects to a country where they could be fully and fairly prosecuted for their crimes.

Despite these appeals for surrender, two months later the UN was compelled to impose sanctions against Libya for its continued refusal to deliver the suspects. Nearly eighteen months later, in 1993, in the face of Libya's unrelenting obstinacy, those UN sanctions were strengthened to include a limited freeze on Libyan financial assets overseas. Naturally, after such a lengthy period of time, many observers were skeptical that UN sanctions could serve as an effective tool for bringing terrorists to justice, but most nevertheless praised the international cooperative effort to effectuate a fair and just resolution to this tragic situation.

Finally, after nearly ten years of sanctions, threats, proposals, and counterproposals, the United States and Britain announced a plan to convene a Scottish court in the Netherlands to try the two Libyan intelligence officers on criminal charges in connection with the bombing. This extraordinary proposal entailed removing an entire court and legal system from one country and assembling it in another country for the sole purpose of prosecuting the suspects. If accepted, the innovative proposal would allow the Scottish courts to try the suspects using Scottish judges and law. Because the "traveling court" plan complied with the most recent demands of Libyan leader Moammar Gadhafi (who had resorted to bargaining for the suspects' surrender), it was considered the most viable resolution to the lengthy pursuit of justice. This outcome was also welcomed by the victims' families because it appeared that, after an interminable delay, justice was finally at hand. More important for the families, however, was the fact that the criminal proceedings would allow them to gain access to crucial evidence that could form the basis for civil lawsuits against Libya pursuant to recently enacted federal legislation that permitted citizens to sue foreign countries designated by the Department of State as sponsors of international terrorism.

In April 1999 Libya finally acquiesced and surrendered the suspects for trial in the Netherlands. While the commencement of the criminal proceedings was a tremendous and long-awaited victory for the victims' families, their triumph was somewhat overshadowed by concerns regarding the unfamiliar Scottish judicial process. Many were doubtful that Scottish law could provide the justice they were seeking and expressed skepticism as to whether critical evidence linking the Libyan government to the flight 103 disaster would ever see the light of day. The U.S. government allayed these concerns by reassuring the families that such evidence would not be overlooked and even made oblique references to the possibility that Moammar Gadhafi could be tried as a war criminal if the Scottish trial somehow failed to produce the just result that the families so eagerly desired.

The two suspects were duly charged in the "largest mass murder trial in Scottish legal history" with conspiracy to murder, murder, and contravention of the Aviation Security Act of 1982.[17] A three-judge panel heard the case, sitting without a jury. On January 31, 2001, more than thirteen years after flight 103 exploded over Lockerbie, the judges delivered their verdict, sentencing Al-Megrahi to life in prison and acquitting Fhima because the evidence of his involvement in the plot was deemed too speculative. Perhaps as expected, Libya denounced the guilty verdict as a "political decision," and appeals by the convicted terrorist ensued shortly after the verdict. To date, none of these appeals has been successful.

One obvious question is whether this trial and its result brought the necessary closure to the victims' families. Although many applauded the verdict, for some it was a foreign legal proceeding in a foreign jurisdiction that, when juxtaposed against the intense pain and overwhelming personal loss endured in the decade since the tragedy, was profoundly inadequate. Recognizing that the Lockerbie verdict was only a small measure of victory for the families, the current Bush administration has vowed that Lockerbie is not over and continues to press Libya to accept responsibility for the tragedy and compensate the victims' families. In the further pursuit of justice using traditional legal resources, more than two hundred families became plaintiffs in dozens of civil lawsuits against Libya. That litigation was ultimately consolidated into a single case before a federal court in New York. In total, the plaintiffs sought more than $1 billion from the Libyan government. In August 2003, Libya agreed to settle the civil litigation by paying $10 million per victim to the families. The settlement is, however, structured with $4 million being paid immediately and the subsequent amounts being dependent upon the lifting of sanctions against Libya and its removal from the U.S. State Department's list of state sponsors of terrorism. A separate civil suit against Pan Am ended in 1992, with the airline paying the families $500 million.

The First World Trade Center Bombing

In what can now be deemed the tragic precursor to 9/11, on February 26, 1993, a bomb exploded in an underground parking lot of the WTC complex in New York City, killing six people, injuring thousands, and causing hundreds of millions of dollars in damage. An investigation later revealed that the perpetrators of this attack, some of whom were "graduates" of terrorist training camps on the Afghanistan-Pakistan border, planted a homemade bomb inside a van in the parking garage of the WTC earlier that day. Further investigation into the explosion led to the discovery of a pervasive global conspiracy that aggressively promoted and encouraged terrorist activities against the United States. In this instance, although one of the conspirators, Ramzi Yousef, subsequently indicated that the terrorists had apparently planned to topple the city's tallest tower onto its twin in a cloud of cyanide gas and kill thousands of people, the cyanide gas in the bombing device burnt out in the heat, and the loss of human life was minimal and far less than expected by the deadly attackers. The apparent masterminds of this treachery, Ahmad Ajaj and Ramzi Yousef, learned how to construct explosive devices in terrorist training camps in Afghanistan and Pakistan. Upon mastering these skills, the two designed a "terrorist kit," complete with notes and manuals demonstrating bomb construction, materials describing how to plan and execute a successful terrorist operation, and videotapes advocating terrorist acts against the United States. Shortly after the blast at the WTC, one of the conspirators claimed responsibility for the bombing, explaining that the terrorist violence was undertaken in retaliation for America's support of Israel. The perpetrators also warned that future, more deadly acts of terrorist violence were being planned against the United States.

In September 1993, Ajaj and Yousef and several others were indicted on various charges related to their participation in the bombing plot.[18] The trial, which took place in the U.S. federal district court, lasted six months and involved over one thousand exhibits and two hundred witnesses. Each defendant was convicted and sentenced to 240 years in prison.

Although the loss of life in this case cannot compare to the death toll in the wake of 9/11, there are numerous other parallels that make this case ripe for comparison to the events of 9/11. For instance, the backgrounds, beliefs, and motivations of the perpetrators were similar, as was the symbolic target of their lethal attacks. The similarities cease, however, when examining America's response to these different, yet strikingly similar acts of violence. Quite simply, the first WTC bombing case illustrates how America's criminal justice system can be effectively employed to root out the perpetrators of violent attacks against American citizens, to process them fairly through the criminal justice system, and to exact punishment for their crimes. This is undoubtedly what America's founding fathers envisioned when they established a government committed to equal treatment and justice for all. The wholesale transformation of time-honored institutions and principles in the aftermath of 9/11 ignores America's long-standing tradition of working *within* its governmental framework to protect its citizens, secure its borders against the terrorist element, and bring wrongdoers to justice for their crimes. What more can be asked or expected of America's governmental institutions? Perhaps, more importantly, if more is expected, can it be accomplished without contravening cherished principles that make America a free, open, and democratic society?

The Oklahoma City Bombing

Because of the history of terrorist attacks and threats against the United States by perpetrators of Middle Eastern descent, when the

Alfred P. Murrah Federal Building in Oklahoma City, Oklahoma, was severely damaged by a massive truck bomb on April 19, 1995, suspicions ran high that this attack originated from a similar foreign source. When the smoke cleared, 168 people had perished and several hundred were injured in what was, at the time, the worst terrorist attack ever on American soil. A couple of days after the explosion, an American, Timothy McVeigh, while being detained for a traffic violation, was identified as one of the alleged bombers and eventually was charged with several capital offenses, including conspiracy to use a weapon of mass destruction with death resulting, use of a weapon of mass destruction with death resulting, destruction of government property by means of an explosive with death resulting, and first-degree murder. McVeigh's ex-army buddy, Terry Nichols, was also questioned and later indicted in connection with the bombing.

Fearing that the horrific events would preclude impartial treatment by jurors in Oklahoma, early in the trial prosecutors requested and were granted a change of venue to Denver, Colorado. In addition, because of the unprecedented loss of life on American soil and the premeditated and deliberate nature of the crimes, prosecutors elected to seek the death penalty against McVeigh, the apparent mastermind of the plot. According to the prosecutor's theory, McVeigh rented a truck, packed it with ammonium nitrate and fuel oil, and detonated this explosive combination in front of the Oklahoma City federal building. Although his motives were somewhat sketchy initially, prosecutors suspected that McVeigh, a Gulf War veteran with ties to antigovernment groups, was outraged by the 1993 FBI siege of the Branch Davidian compound in Waco, Texas, and sought revenge against the government for that debacle.

Nearly two years after the bombing, McVeigh faced trial in federal court in Denver. Following twenty-eight days of testimony, McVeigh was found guilty on all counts and sentenced to death by lethal injection. Despite the intense media scrutiny and the raw emotions surrounding the trial, by most every account McVeigh received a fair trial. After several years of legal appeals, a request by McVeigh that no further appeals be taken, and a stay of the execution occasioned by an FBI admission that several documents in the case had not been turned over to defense teams, McVeigh was finally put to death for his crimes on June 11, 2001.

It bears emphasizing that, although militant and extremist groups abound *within* the borders of the United States, upon discovering that the Oklahoma City bombing had been carried out by a "home-grown" terrorist, no military orders were issued, no constitutionally infirm legislation was enacted, and there was certainly no discussion of widespread profiling and rounding up of members of militia organizations for indefinite detention. Instead, there was a recognition that this deadly act of terrorism was a single criminal act that could be appropriately addressed by the governmental institutions already in place. Thus, the apprehension, prosecution, conviction, and execution of Timothy McVeigh represent yet another example of America's criminal justice system effectively responding to terrorism within the framework of its founding charter and, in the end, exacting the highest degree of punishment for crimes committed against American citizens.

Responses to Terrorism

The U.S. counterterrorism policy is as follows:

- Make no concessions to terrorists and strike no deals.
- Bring terrorists to justice for their crimes.
- Isolate and apply pressure to countries that sponsor terrorism to force them to change their behavior.
- Bolster the counterterrorism capabilities of those countries that work with the United States and require assistance.

Accepting this policy at face value, it does not require a great leap of imagination to recognize that each of these objectives can be accomplished within America's current political, legislative, and judicial framework. Yet, in the wake of the 9/11 terrorist attacks, the U.S. government, among other things, enacted sweeping legislation with relatively little congressional debate, engaged in military strikes that effectively toppled the Taliban regime in Afghanistan, threatened to expand military responses to the "axis of evil," indefinitely detained hundreds of "enemy combatants" at Guantanamo Bay, Cuba, and thousands of people of Middle Eastern descent in America, and proposed the creation of a Department of Homeland Secu-

rity that is, according to President Bush, the most significant transformation of the U.S. government in over half a century. In short,
America has seemingly reconstructed its system of justice to such a
degree that even U.S. citizens cannot be certain that they will receive
the protections of the Constitution upon arrest or detainment.

Without a doubt, the events of September 11 were incomprehen-
sibly tragic, but the question of great moment is whether our
responses are equally incomprehensible when critically examined
through America's historical prism. Of course, a compelling argument can be made that 9/11 was an extreme escalation of unprovoked terrorist violence warranting an equally severe rejoinder.
But, a careful assessment of America's history reveals that, in turbulent times, political, legislative, and judicial overreaction can
yield wholly unexpected results that disrupt the delicate constitutional balance established at America's founding. For instance, as
explored in chapter 1, the internment of Japanese American citizens
during World War II was a profound overreaction to the threat
posed by Japan during the war. The resulting apologies and repara-
tions, although long overdue, seemingly acknowledge this abom-
inable treatment. A similar period of American excess and overreaction is now known in history books as the era of McCarthyism.

On June 29, 1940, in response to the emerging communist threat,
Congress enacted the Alien Registration Act, which made it illegal
for anyone in the United States to advocate, abet, or teach the desir-
ability of overthrowing the government. The act also required alien
residents over fourteen years of age in the United States to register
and file a statement of their political beliefs. The act was implemented through the House Un-American Activities Committee
(HUAC), which had been established in 1937 to investigate right-
and left-wing political groups. One of the primary targets of
HUAC's scrutiny was the Hollywood motion picture industry. To
further its patently nonsensical investigation, HUAC compelled
people to "name names" of others in Hollywood who held left-wing
views and blacklisted anyone who refused to cooperate. Eventually,
over 320 people were blacklisted in Hollywood and effectively prevented from working in the motion picture industry.

The act was also used to eviscerate the American Communist
Party, as its leadership and members were routinely arrested and
jailed for violating provisions of the act. In the early 1950s, a senator

from Wisconsin, Joseph McCarthy, became chairman of the Senate's Government Committee on Operation and pledged to investigate and root out communist subversion in the government. Scores of people were questioned about their political pasts and warned that proving their absolute rejection of communism meant providing the names of others who might be communists or communist sympathizers. Thus began the communist conspiracy witch-hunt and hysteria that resulted in lost jobs, severed relationships for thousands of people, and eventually the removal of books from library shelves that were authored by communists or communist sympathizers. At the time, former president Harry S. Truman said of the Eisenhower administration:

> It is now evident that the present Administration has fully embraced, for political advantage, McCarthyism. I am not referring to the Senator from Wisconsin. He is only important in that his name has taken on the dictionary meaning of the word. It is the corruption of truth, the abandonment of the due process law. It is the use of the big lie and the unfounded accusation against any citizen in the name of Americanism and security. It is the rise to power of the demagogue who lives on untruth; it is the spreading of fear and the destruction of faith in every level of society.[19]

Is our government moving in the direction of another era of McCarthyism? Perhaps it's too early to draw any concrete conclusions, but there are some compelling indicators that strongly suggest that trend. For example, such actions as the recent expansion of powers for the executive branch via the Office of Homeland Security and the issuance of a military order, the notion of "guilt by association" that has resulted in the arrest and detention of thousands of people of Middle Eastern descent, and the expansion of powers for the FBI to pursue those thought to be connected to terrorism, even removing restrictions on the FBI for domestic spying on groups and Internet activities, all point to a country acting on fear rather than logic. All of this creates a mood of overreaction and hysteria, when calm, reasoned discourse on America's future should be the order of the day. Of course, taking immediate steps to secure U.S. borders and interests abroad from further terrorist violence continues to be a rational security response. But the failure to identify the real causes of terrorism and to, on some level, accept that no amount of planning and preparation can thwart the most determined suicidal terrorist is likely to lead to a nation where perpetual fear of the terrorist threat spirals out of control and fundamental principles of equality, liberty, and due process of law become sideline spectators in the name of security.

In an article entitled "Global Terrorism: Searching for Appropriate Responses," Majid Tehranian posits that "every major tragedy in world history has presented an opportunity for reflecting and reconstructing a more just and peaceful world order."[20] Tehranian further explains that terrorism is the weapon of choice for weak, disenfranchised individuals, motivated and driven to terrorist violence by a modern world order that constantly emphasizes the growing disparity between the haves and the have-nots worldwide. Moreover, the relative ease of communication facilitated by technological advance means that most of us now live in a global fishbowl, where social and economic gaps are graphically revealed through the global communication infrastructure. As a result, weaker marginalized groups, often with extreme fundamentalist leanings, rebel against what they perceive as postmodern elitism and excess, utilizing "shock terrorism" as a means to strike out against a more powerful, yet vulnerable enemy. Such striking inequalities breed resentment that is externalized by violently attacking icons that promote or benefit from the disproportionate distribution of wealth.

Therefore, terrorism will not be thwarted or even diminished until the proliferation of small arms; biological, chemical, and nuclear weapons; and the powerful social, economic, and political schisms that cultivate the terrorist mentality are appropriately addressed.

In the end, the 9/11 attacks were representative of a tragic, although familiar, dynamic where, according to Tehranian, the aim of terrorists is to "paralyze 'the enemy' into submission by indiscriminate violence against 'guilty and innocent,' 'civilian and soldier.' What they often achieve is a mobilization of public opinion against terrorism's indiscriminate violence. But terrorism also can polarize societies and foster security or police states infringing upon civil liberties."[21] Indeed.

America fought a public "war" on terrorism in the past with very limited success. During much of the Reagan administration, Moammar Gadhafi, the leader of Libya, was the target of our antiterrorist agenda. However, despite efforts to isolate him politically and economically, terrorist activities believed to be generated by Libyan hatred of the United States and its military actions continued to flourish. The most notable of these terrorist incidents was the previously discussed bombing of Pan Am flight 103 over Lockerbie, Scotland.

In light of these harsh realities, it is evident that combating terrorism requires much more than ratcheting up security, surveillance, and suppression. Diminishing terrorist violence entails globally examining the causes of terrorist activities and formulating remedies that specifically address those motivations. On the interrelationship of cause and effect, scholars and policy analysts have observed that there is a strong correlation between U.S. involvement (meddling?) in international situations and an increase in terrorist activity directed toward the United States. For example, in an eerie foreshadowing of events to come, the fundamentalist Islamic terrorists who perpetrated the first bombing of the WTC boldly declared that they were attempting to kill 250,000 people by collapsing the towers in order to punish the United States for its policies in the Middle East. Of course, they were not successful in destroying the towers or in taking as many lives, but, as we now know, their continued motivation inspired by hatred for American policies eventually resulted in the destruction of the towers and thousands of lost lives.

Does this mean that the United States should simply capitulate to the demands of extremists and adopt an across-the-board policy of nonintervention abroad? Absolutely not. Instead, a diplomatic multilateralist approach that takes into account the strong sense of alienation felt by large sectors of our global community might result in innovative foreign policy changes that reduce the number of attacks and lessen the number of lives sacrificed to the whims of extremists.

3 Assessing the Terrorist Threat

One fact dominates all homeland security threat assessments: terrorists are strategic actors. They choose their targets deliberately based on the weaknesses they observe in our defenses and our preparedness. We must defend ourselves against a wide range of means and methods of attack. Our enemies are working to obtain chemical, biological, radiological, and nuclear weapons for the purpose of wreaking unprecedented damage on America. Terrorists continue to employ conventional means of attack, while at the same time gaining expertise in less traditional means, such as cyber attacks. Our society presents an almost infinite array of potential targets that can be attacked through a variety of methods.

—Executive Summary, President's National
Strategy for Homeland Security (July 2002)

While terrorists' objectives may be uniform in that they tend to center on altering a government or changing its policy, the methods for carrying out the attacks designed to achieve these objectives can be as varied as the attacker's imagination allows. Thus, unpredictability is a key tool in the terrorist arsenal that boosts the chances of an attack being a success.

For instance, viewing only al Qaeda–backed attacks on U.S. interests during the past decade, we see that the first three targets were hit by trucks carrying heavy, conventional explosives: in 1993, the WTC in New York City; in 1996, the American troop barracks at Khobar Towers in Riyadh, Saudi Arabia; and in 1998, U.S. Embassies in Nairobi, Kenya, and Dar es Salem, Tanzania. Thus, while al Qaeda had achieved unpredictability in regard to the locale of its attacks (both inside and outside the United States) and the targets (business interests, military personnel, and government offices), it had failed to achieve unpredictability in regard to the method of delivery.

This changed, perhaps as al Qaeda matured, with the attack on the American Aegis-class destroyer USS *Cole* in 2000. As the ship entered the Port of Aden in Yemen for a routine stop, it was approached by a small anchoring skiff in a normal fashion. However, this skiff was guided by two terrorists and was loaded with high explosives designed to breach the reinforced steel hull of the warship. This, of course, is what happened. Then, in 2001, the method of delivery was changed yet again by resorting to hijacked, fuel-laden aircraft in the September 11 attacks that jolted the psychology of our country so profoundly.[1]

Consequently, al Qaeda eventually achieved the desired level of unpredictability in regard to delivery. Of secondary significance is the fact that not all of the attacks culminated in their desired outcome (the WTC did not collapse in 1993 and the USS *Cole* did not sink in 2000). However, government officials must now worry not only about where such attacks will occur and at what institutions they will be directed but also what avenues of delivery are open and potentially available for use. The possibilities are many, and the remedial countermeasures are both few and impracticable.

After the first WTC attack, followed by the 1994 truck-bomb explosion that decimated the Alfred P. Murrah Federal Building in Oklahoma City and the subsequent al Qaeda truck bombs, federal and military installations were ringed with concrete barricades and Pennsylvania Avenue in front of the White House was shut down and cordoned off from vehicular use. Physically limiting the proximity of ships and airplanes in a similar fashion is virtually impossible.

With regard to sea traffic, about 6 million containers arrive via ship at U.S. seaports every year, sometimes averaging over two thousand cargo containers each hour. These are taken by barge upriver or loaded onto semi-trucks or trains and then transshipped overland to their ultimate destination, be it Dallas, Salt Lake City, Atlanta, or Omaha. About 90 percent of world trade flows along international sea lanes and is carried on such cargo ships. Only 2 percent of containers arriving in the United States are checked by federal agents. It is a random sampling intended to meet the goals of fulfilling U.S. security interests and keeping would-be terrorists off-guard while not slowing down the shipping process to the point that it would harm our economy.[2]

By any measure, this process does not fulfill the first two goals but does fulfill the third. However, there are no easy solutions. We do not have the equipment to X-ray all containers entering our ports, nor do we have the financial or physical capacity to build, deploy, and operate them. And the U.S. Coast Guard, tasked with securing our country's waters, has neither the manpower, training, nor equipment to accomplish the task. As this excerpt from the *New York Times* explains, their efforts have been rewarded only with failure:

> Shortly after September 11, the Coast Guard began a program that requires every commercial ship destined for the United States to send authorities a list of crew members' names 96 hours before docking, so that they can determine if there are terrorists on board. . . . [T]he Coast Guard receives several thousand names a day. But it has no way to know whether a given name is the true identity of a crew member, or an invented one. Further, most names are sent by fax, on sheets that are frequently illegible or with notations in languages that officials cannot read.
>
> Then, because of lack of coordination among databases, the Coast Guard has no access to the most important criminal and immigrant computer files, and must rely on other agencies to run the checks on the names. . . . But even if a suspicious ship is identified, the Coast Guard crews that search it have no training to identify terrorists or their equipment, and no sensors or related detection devices that can locate chemical, nuclear or other weapons. . . . [And] as a matter of policy, the Coast Guard does not ordinarily even board container ships, since there is no way to inspect the contents of the containers [which] are often stacked six-deep and -wide, and so gaining access to many of them is impossible until they are unloaded, even though containers that may hold terrorists or weapons of mass destruction are a central concern in Washington.[3]

With regard to air traffic, emphasis has been placed on identifying and apprehending terrorists before they strike, with more serious measures implemented once the plane is airborne.

Preflight: Airport security is now regulated by government oversight, and the level of passenger scrutiny has increased markedly while the level of baggage scrutiny has increased only slightly. But the new federal agency tasked with stepping up preflight airport security, the Transportation Security Administration (TSA), has failed spectacularly in its mission. None of the congressional deadlines for action were met.

As of midsummer 2002, of the sixty-three thousand federal airport screeners needed, only three thousand had been hired, and of the 429 major airports that were to be staffed with such screeners by Thanksgiving, only three were so outfitted. And while bag-matching policies are in effect for checked luggage at all airlines now, the agency was unable to provide bomb detection machines to physically screen such luggage. In fact, most of the money earmarked for this project was instead spent on "highly paid consultants and lawyers" who were hired to advise the agency on how to meet its December 31, 2002, deadline for deploying these devices.[4]

Nor has any progress been made to date on screening air cargo containers that piggyback along with U.S. mail on passenger jets and make up 40 percent of domestic cargo in America. Thus, potential suicide terrorists can still check a bag with a time-delayed bomb and board a plane (under the current bag-matching scheme) or gain access to an air cargo container. The TSA's failure to meet any of its legislative mandates had become so apparent by the summer of 2002 that the administrator was fired and replaced with a former navy admiral.[5]

In-flight: Pilots have been issued stun guns, cockpit doors have been locked, and all flights approaching Reagan National Airport in Washington, D.C., now require passengers to remain seated thirty minutes prior to landing or the plane will detour to another airport. The debate continues on issuance of pistols to cockpit crew. On the one hand, the enhanced security offered by armed pilots cannot be denied. On the other, once a gun is fired, a missed shot could puncture a window, causing the entire cabin to depressurize at a potentially lethal altitude, resulting in the crash of another passenger jet.

Landing: President Bush has issued an order for military fighters to shoot down any suspicious, nonresponsive passenger aircraft veering off its intended flight path. For several months after September 11, F-15 and F-16 fighter jets circled the skies over most major U.S. cities, supported by refueling aircraft. These patrols were scaled back significantly in the spring of 2002. They now only operate sporadically and in a random sequence. Thus, a nonresponsive passenger jet would have to either deviate or be identified early enough in its landing pattern to allow fighters time to scramble and intercept the jet.

With regard to the attack method not yet employed by an al Qaeda group—rail—scant attention has been paid to intercity passenger or cargo lines. Most concern has centered instead on intracity subway systems, which are inherently more manageable and arguably more threatening. However, a weapon correctly placed and timed on a train entering Chicago, Philadelphia, or Washington's Union Stations; New York's Grand Central or Penn Stations; or the Amtrak stop next to Baltimore's Camden Yards baseball park could be just as destructive. Because the security focus is shifting to known transport delivery methods such as air and trucking, rail may present an easy opportunity for a group like al Qaeda to exploit in its endeavor to remain unpredictable.

This chapter focuses on the emerging terrorist threats faced by America. The threats exist both internally—from domestic sources—and externally—from foreign sources. They are not limited by geography, only capability. The traditional threats are so defined by their common usage of conventional high explosives. Systemic threats are characterized by their use of weapons of mass destruction (WMD) that often entail ripple effects beyond introduction. These include nuclear, biological, and chemical modalities of attack. Cyberthreats refer to electronic attack and/or theft via Internet, intranet, or other method. Al Qaeda's continued viability to threaten the United States and American interests abroad is also examined.

Guarding against Traditional Threats

Traditional sorts of terrorism take many forms: hijacking, kidnapping, hostage taking, ransoming, murder, and property damage. They typically also involve a conspiracy of some degree. These acts are sometimes carried out at gunpoint, but more often they occur under the threat of explosive detonation. The logic of this is fairly simple and straightforward. If one's destructive capacity is increased exponentially, then so is one's influence and thereby one's ability to coerce. Hostages are often a necessary evil in order to protect the terrorist from a military reprisal, preemptive strike, or sniper's bullet before he realizes his objective. Murder of some hostages is also deemed necessary, according to the internal logic of the terrorist mind, to demonstrate the seriousness of his intent.

Governments around the world deal with hundreds of internal and external traditional terrorist threats and attacks each year. Many of these are tied to political goals such as greater autonomy within a governing federation or outright independence from a larger state. Examples include the struggle of the Chechens in Russia, Uigirs in China, Basques in Spain, Corsicans in France, Tamils in Sri Lanka, Palestinians in Israeli-controlled territories, and Kurds in Turkey. However, other similarly violent struggles, such as that of the Irish Republican Army in the United Kingdom and the indigenous Zappatistas in southern Mexico, have been overcome through third-party overture leading to peaceful political compromise. Thus, the possibility of compromise and cessation of violence is possible if it is genuinely in the interest of both sides to engage— although political reality may dictate otherwise.

According to the U.S. Department of State, there were approximately 125 separate significant terrorist incidents around the world in 2001. *Significant* is officially defined as resulting in "loss of life or serious bodily injury to persons, abduction by kidnapping, major property damage, and/or is an act or attempted act that could reasonably be expected to create the conditions noted."[6]

Americans are not used to thinking of themselves as ready targets in the global occurrence of terrorism. Terrorist attacks statistically do not occur in North America as often as in other countries on other continents. Perhaps this is a reflection of our society; perhaps it is a reflection of our physical distance across the Atlantic, Pacific, and Caribbean from the rest of the world. Whatever the reason, the quintessential, perhaps innocent, American psyche tends to relegate images of mass death and wanton destruction confronted by it on the nightly news, Internet, or newspaper to faraway places locked in complicated cycles of conflict that are not the concern of suburban households in Cleveland or Peoria. At most, America's interests, offices, and institutions in other parts of the world have been at risk as targets of terrorism, but not Americans themselves here in the homeland.

Comparatively, until 9/11, the United States had not suffered the scourge of international terrorism to the degree the rest of the world had. Apart from the 1993 WTC attack (which was basically a failure) and the random shooting of a Danish national atop the Empire State Building in 1997, the worst terrorist act suffered by America at home in that decade was McVeigh's destruction of the federal building—an act of domestic, not international, terrorism.

This notion of immunity from foreign attack at home is buttressed by our historical experience. The terrorist acts that culminated in the destruction of the WTC and the severe damage of the Pentagon on September 11 together constituted the first major attack by a foreign entity suffered by the United States at home since Pearl Harbor in 1941 and the first in the continental United States since the British burned Washington, D.C., in 1814. All of the major wars fought by America since the end of the Civil War in 1865 have been overseas. The big problems of the twentieth century were not guarding against attack or military invasion during the cold war—which was waged by proxy abroad—but fighting domestic crime and drug addiction. However, this notion began to erode in the past decade.

The 1993 truck-bomb attack on the WTC startled us and caused us to begin thinking about our vulnerabilities at home. But Ramzi Yousef's cryptic remark to the FBI that they would return to finish the job was disregarded. Timothy McVeigh's detonation of a very simply constructed, very large fertilizer-based truck bomb in 1994, which killed 168 people in Oklahoma City, jolted us again and caused Americans to ask how such a horrible terrorist act could be perpetrated from within. The combined attacks on September 11 by Osama bin Laden's al Qaeda network—which turned four jet aircraft into human-guided missiles that killed approximately twenty-eight hundred people in three states, collapsed the WTC, and damaged the Pentagon—utterly shattered the widely held latent idea that we were immune on our continent from international terrorism.

Slowly, we in the West are starting to realize that the process of globalization (i.e., the further integration of networking capability) is a weakness as well as a strength. On the one hand, these networks provide a boost to supercharge our economies, greasing the wheels of commerce. On the other, they can be utilized by terrorists. For example, the 9/11 hijackers availed themselves of the streamlined air transit network, bin Laden spread his poisonous message to inflame anti-American passions through the television media, and the anthrax attacker who unleashed his or her deadly spores in October 2001 utilized the postal network to spread biological agents.

Highway systems, railroads, cyberspace—almost any conceivable network, be it digital, physical, or media, is susceptible to abuse by terrorists. As Yale historian John Lewis Gaddis observes:

> [I]t was held to be a good thing that capital, commodities, ideas and people could move freely across boundaries. There was little talk, though, of an alternate possibility: that danger might move just as freely. . . . It was as if we had convinced ourselves that the new world of global communications had somehow transformed the old aspect of human nature, which is the tendency to harbor grievances and sometimes act upon them.[7]

And so the question becomes, How do we guard against such attacks in the future? First, there is the physical response. Short of closing the border and cutting off the benefits of globalization, we can attempt to keep terrorism at bay through heightened awareness, security, screening, and covert intelligence. There is also the nonphysical response. This entails changing the mind-set of those who would do us harm or at least altering the equation by eliminating the latent urge in the hearts of those who can be inflamed and exploited by the clever few in pursuit of their evil ends.

Heightened Physical Security

As both the government and the public, through the news media, engaged in an appropriate and thoughtful retrospective on the events of 9/11 in the spring and summer of 2002, the myth that the federal government works as a single interlocking mechanism was laid bare. The Immigration and Naturalization Service (INS) was still processing visas of some of the hijackers and approving flight school applications. The FBI had detained Zacarias Moussaoui in Minneapolis, where he was attempting to engage in flight instruction, while an agent in Phoenix had penned a memo theorizing an attack by aircraft on the WTC that was stopped before making it up the chain of command to Washington. The CIA had been monitoring two of the hijackers for several months in Malaysia and elsewhere, following them into the United States, but did not share its information with any other federal office after losing track of them.

The problem—the reason that the 9/11 attack slipped though the cracks—is largely interinstitutional. The current system of ensuring the country's physical security sufficiently to counter a terrorist threat belies its historical piecemeal construction—the ad hoc creation of agencies with limited powers to address specific and unrelated issues. Just as it is no surprise that parts of a machine not designed to work together often fail to keep the machine running, it should come as no surprise that confusing and inconsistent interactions among the CIA, FBI, National Security Agency (NSA), Bureau of Alcohol, Tobacco, and Firearms (ATF), Drug Enforcement Administration (DEA), Defense Intelligence Agency (DIA), INS, and myriad other instrumentalities can fail to effectuate a reliable bulwark against emerging terrorist threats.

Consequently, while the government as a collective entity had several pieces of the puzzle that could conceivably have led to shutting down the 9/11 conspiracy before it went into effect, the elements of timing, nonexistence of a meaningful information-sharing system, and inability to bring the pieces together in one office worked against the puzzle ever being completed. These revelations were disturbing, even prompting the *Wall Street Journal* to call for FBI director Robert Mueller's resignation. However, they are certainly not startling.

The INS's rigid strategy of methodically handling the overwhelming workload of visa tracking, naturalization, illegal immigrant roundup, and deportation in a nonresponsive manner practically precluded the civil servants in that agency from any creative thought process. Moreover, intelligence sharing is anathema to the cultures of the CIA and FBI, both of whom enjoyed complete primacy and unquestioned power within their spheres during the cold war. Potential leaks were plugged from within and classified data jealously guarded against Soviet compromise. After the cold war, in the 1990s, both agencies were rocked by scandal and perceptions of ineptitude that seriously damaged their ability to meet their mandates while simultaneously reinforcing a defensive "bunker down" posture that made the likelihood of information sharing even less likely.

The CIA ensures America's security while operating abroad. However, its foreign and international operations were scaled back and human intelligence-gathering capacity limited in favor of technical advances in satellite capabilities. Thus, the agency was inaccurate in its assessment of the Soviet Union's ability to perpetuate itself beyond 1991 and completely failed to detect testing of nuclear devices by India and Pakistan in 1995. These errors together with the exposure of moles and double agents within the CIA caused Congress to publicly question the agency's continuing mission.

The FBI is the CIA's equivalent at home and much more. Its law enforcement arm is the most widely respected in the world. However, the FBI's own difficulties were highlighted in the 1990s by the public discovery of its own internal moles, such as Robert Hanson, together with a series of unpopular high-profile cases such as the Ruby Ridge fiasco and the Waco conflagration. However, the real weakness of the FBI—its internal culture of suspicion, secrecy, and rigidity—was not fully exposed until the September 11 attacks.

The NSA, an organization created after World War II specifically to avert another Pearl Harbor–type surprise with a $7 billion budget (twice that of the CIA), is charged with enhancing American security through electronic eavesdropping and code breaking. But its failures in this regard have been both ironic and flagrant. Of the 6,500 languages spoken around the world, this agency, which is supposed to be the center of communications sophistication, only has linguists trained in 115 of them. On September 10, 2001, the NSA intercepted conversations from Afghanistan, at least one of which was from an al Qaeda operative referring to September 11 as the "big match" and calling that day "zero hour." These messages were not translated until September 12. Moreover, the al Qaeda cell that hijacked American Airlines flight 77 from Dulles International Airport lived just blocks away from NSA headquarters in Laurel, Maryland. As the *Washington Post* put it, while "the terrorists pulled out of the Valencia Motel on Route 1 on their way to Dulles . . . they crossed paths with many of the electronic spies who were turning into Fort Meade, home of the NSA, to begin another day hunting for terrorists."[8]

In a July 2002 report to the Speaker of the House, the Permanent Select Committee on Intelligence's Subcommittee on Terrorism and Homeland Security noted that one of the common crippling weaknesses shared by the CIA, FBI, and NSA was a critical lack of Arab-speaking agents. Because of this, a backlog of documents and interceptions thousands of files deep went unanalyzed. Moreover, the NSA's technology had not developed to the point that it could track a suspect globally—only sporadically.[9]

In response to these failures, the government began retooling each of these agencies. The intent was to generate greater interaction between the FBI and CIA, to redefine the FBI's mandate, to streamline the INS's processing capability and integrate passport/customs control and border security, and to change the NSA's mission from passive information gathering to proactive targeting and hunting. However, government policymakers, especially in the DOJ, received a fair amount of criticism warning them of encroaching too much into areas of civil liberty that the public holds dear. Balancing its mission to protect Americans evenly against their legally guaranteed freedoms became the daunting and unenviable challenge.

Many of the bureaucratic and institutional reforms undertaken by the separate agencies were significant ones, such as allowing the CIA to have operational control of Hellfire missiles in the field for the first time and easing the Church Committee restrictions on it in relation to surveillance and assassinations.[10] But those undertaken by the FBI were both dramatic and public. In testimony before the House Appropriations Committee's Subcommittee for Justice and Related Agencies, FBI director Mueller explained how he has redirected that agency's mission toward focusing on counterterrorism efforts. Specifically, this entails a ten-point priority list that the director believes will put the FBI on track to fulfilling its new role:

1. Protect the United States from terrorist attack.
2. Protect the United States against foreign intelligence operations and espionage.

3. Protect the United States against cyber-based attacks and high-tech crimes.
4. Combat public corruption at all levels.
5. Protect civil rights.
6. Combat transnational and national criminal organizations and enterprises.
7. Combat major white-collar crime.
8. Combat significant violent crime.
9. Support federal, state, municipal, and international partners.
10. Upgrade technology to successfully perform the FBI's mission.

The rank order of this list reflects the new priority placed on protection, especially with regard to the first three items. This effectively puts the agency in the business of anticipation and prevention rather than evidence collection for future prosecution—its prior focus. To back up this realignment, Director Mueller has reallocated significant manpower within the FBI. He has ordered a permanent shift of 518 agents from criminal investigation to counterterrorism duty. Fully 400 agents will be removed from drug investigations to join 59 taken from white-collar crimes and another 59 from violent crimes. These new recruits in the FBI's own war on terror will be distributed directly to counterterrorism (480), security (13), and training of new special agents at Quantico (25).[11]

The FBI, under DOJ cover, has also executively increased its powers of surveillance—dropping the old standard trigger, based on "information or an allegation whose responsible handling required some further inquiry" (which did not even constitute probable cause), entirely. This move itself triggered a justified, albeit scathing, reproach from William Safire in the New York Times:

Under the police powers it operated under last year, and with the lawful cooperation of a better-managed CIA, an efficiently run FBI might well have prevented the catastrophe of Sept. 11. . . . To fabricate an alibi for his nonfeasance, and to cover up his department's embarrassing cut of the counterterrorism budget last year, Attorney General Ashcroft—working with his hand-picked aide, FBI Director "J. Edgar" Mueller III—has gutted guidelines put in place a generation ago to prevent the abuse of power by the federal government.

They have done this deed by executive fiat: no public discussion, no Congressional action, no judicial guidance. If we had only had these new powers last year, goes their posterior-covering pretense, we could have stopped terrorism cold. Not so. They had the power to collect the intelligence, but lacked the intellect to analyze the data the agencies collected. . . . Thus we see the seizure of new powers of surveillance is a smoke-screen to hide failure to use the old power.

. . . [U]nder the new Ashcroft-Mueller diktat, [the] necessary hint of potential criminal activity is swept away. With not a scintilla of evidence of a crime being committed, the feds will be able to run full investigations for one year. That's aimed at generating suspicion of criminal conduct—the very definition of a "fishing expedition."[12]

The White House has not been immune from institutional redirection either. Immediately in the wake of September 11, President Bush created the executive Office of Homeland Security, headed by former Pennsylvania governor Tom Ridge, to coordinate the efforts of the nation's dispersed and divergent federal security agencies, offices, and suboffices. Given the amorphous nature of this new office, its limited budget, and unclear jurisdiction, the degree of its effectiveness during the ensuing months was seen as problematic. The most tangible item to emerge from the office was a color-coded terrorist threat system running from green to red. Beyond this, the new presidential advisor has had closed meetings in the White House, the subjects and contents of which are denied to the public. Ridge, an advisor unapproved by Congress, like the chief economic advisor and the national security advisor, is not amenable to answering questions from congressional committees.[13]

Partly in response to congressional criticism of the Office of Homeland Security's progress, secrecy, and unamenability to oversight and partly in an effort to sew together the overlapping intelligence analysis functions of various separate agencies and the homeland security functions of others in a seamless institutional framework that is both responsive and flexible, the Bush administration proposed the creation of a new cabinet-level Department of Homeland Security.

Legislatively, Congress acted on President Bush's recommendation to create this new department, which will be separate from the Office of Homeland Security and which is envisioned as essentially an amalgam of intelligence and threat-analysis divisions from the CIA, FBI, and other agencies brought under one administrative roof while leaving the intelligence-gathering apparatus in place at those agencies. The legislation bringing this federal entity into being will be discussed in chapter 5.

The legislative branch is not wholly unconcerned about its own skin. Former Speakers Tomas Foley (D-Washington) and Newt Gingrich (R-Georgia) have suggested reforming the House of Representatives' rules for replacement of members in the event of a catastrophic attack against Congress to ensure continuity of that body:

> The executive branch has recognized just how real the danger is and has taken precautions. . . . In addition to the vice president's moving to a separate, secure location in periods of high threat . . . scores of other senior officials are on rotating assignments outside of Washington. . . . The legislative branch must take similar precautions. . . . [While] the Constitution permits governors to appoint interim senators to serve until the next election . . . each vacancy in the House . . . requires a special election. . . . [I]n recent cases, it has taken an average of 117 days to fill a vacancy. . . .
>
> The expeditious path is for the House immediately to adopt a change in its rules authorizing each member to pre-designate an interim successor who could serve for the period between catastrophic loss of House members and the election of successors. The Constitution explicitly provides that the House shall make its own rules concerning its members and shall be the judge of its members' qualification.[14]

Finally, the secretary of defense is considering the use of Special Operations Forces as hit squads to be dispatched around the globe eliminating al Qaeda operatives, disrupting terrorist activities, and foiling plots to target American interests. Delta Force and the Navy SEALS are the most likely groups to be tapped for such missions. If approved, these military units would find themselves executing many of the tasks formerly in the bailiwick of the CIA. The argument in favor of such a move is very persuasive—increasing our ability to respond creatively and quickly in a military capacity to an unpredictable opponent. However, the most troubling aspect of this idea is that the military would be able to operate clandestinely, unchecked by political or legal constraints.

Traditionally, the foreign operations by the CIA involving lethal force have been undertaken with the imprimatur of a secret finding by the president that is then monitored by closed select intelligence committees of Congress. Special Operations missions would not be subject to similar control. The covert operations under consideration at the Pentagon would involve these units in longer-term missions in countries where the United States is not currently engaged in open armed conflict and where the governments are not necessarily informed of their presence.[15]

Clearly the wisdom of employing such plans lies with executive discretion. But the possibility of doing so without the same legal constraints placed on the CIA is disturbing and goes against the grain of checking executive power. The balance in this case tips more in favor of creating conditions ripe for abuse of power. In a representative democracy, the citizens cannot simply trust the executive to do the right thing. For the system to work, the decision-making apparatus must be participatory, not exclusive and paternalistic.

Outreach to Alter Perceptions

There is some debate about why the September 11 attacks, and other al Qaeda strikes against the United States, happened. The conventional response domestically from the administration on down has been that these groups hate us and oppose what we, as Americans, stand for in the world. The alternate response dismisses this as a Western-centric point of view and, instead, this response holds that the attacks stem from strife within Islam itself about the future of that religion and its believers. The following extract from a review of Princeton professor Michael Doran's essay "Somebody Else's Civil War" encapsulates that view:

[T]he United States has been sucked into a struggle within the Muslim world. This battle pits those, such as bin Laden, who seek to re-create the era when the Prophet Muhammad ruled the Islamic lands, against those who actually govern Muslim countries today. Bin Laden used Afghanistan as a base to launch a jihad across the Muslim world, hoping thereby to bring "apostate" regimes such as Saudi Arabia within the fold of true Islam and restore the caliphate from Spain to Indonesia. By this view, the attacks on the World Trade Center and the Pentagon were collateral damage in a struggle for the hearts and minds of the *umma*—the worldwide community of Muslim believers. . . . [B]in Laden hoped that the attacks against the United States would spark uprisings by Muslims against their own American-backed regimes. As Sandy Berger [former National Security Advisor in the Clinton Administration] observes in his own essay, "bin Laden's ultimate twin towers are Pakistan and Saudi Arabia."[16]

If this is true, then bin Laden's gambit has certainly failed, at least in the short term. No such fundamentalist Islamic revolution has swept the Muslim world since 2001. However, if the terrorist threat to the United States does stem from an irrational hatred of our culture, politics, worldview, economic policies, or any other manifestation of who we are as a people, then this hatred must be addressed as part of the administration's response.

Over the ensuing weeks following the September 11 attacks, newspapers across the country began to ask, "Why do they hate us?"[17] If hatred of the West or of America in particular is indeed part of the underlying rationale supporting the efforts of al Qaeda, then in order to articulate a meaningful response, we must struggle to understand the genesis of the hatred harbored against our hegemony.

What America did to deserve such unbridled animosity is unclear. Apparently, Osama bin Laden and his colleagues were incensed about America's involvement in the Middle East on a variety of points, which led to a general amalgam of single-minded abhorrence fused with indignancy. But political hatred alone was not enough to inspire suicide terrorism; religious fervor had to be tapped. As Professor Fouad Ajami of Johns Hopkins University's

School of Advanced International Studies notes, bin Laden has managed to tap into religious zeal for political purposes:

> A sacred realm apart, Arabia had been overrun by Americans, bin Laden said. "For more than seven years the United States has been occupying the lands of Islam in the holiest of territories, Arabia, plundering its riches, overwhelming its rulers, humiliating its people, threatening its neighbors, and using its peninsula as a spearhead to fight the neighboring Islamic peoples." Xenophobia of a murderous kind had been dressed up in religious garb.[18]

Still, we must understand that these grievances change character as they are viewed through the fundamentalist lens, as presented by people like bin Laden.[19] For instance, traditional U.S. support of Israel translates into lack of sympathy for the Palestinian cause. The American-led Gulf War, intended to ensure political and economic stability in the region, translates into the dressing down of an Arab leader who presumed to defy the West. The presence of U.S. troops in Saudi Arabia for security purposes after 1991 translates into two things: reliance by the corrupt House of Saud on hired foreign mercenaries to retain power and Western assurance of continued, uninterrupted oil flow with no regard for the Arab people. Approval of American military actions abroad by the UN Security Council translates into further revelation of that body as a willing tool of American foreign policy.

How do we affect these incorrect perceptions that provide a convenient foundation for charismatic leaders to whip up into outright hatred? How can we argue against this minority Muslim view of Islam's continued humiliation and manipulation by the West? It is difficult when such perceptions are based on kernels of truth. It is even more difficult when the source of this mind-set finds its roots in religious irrationality.[20]

Historians, theologians, sociologists, and anthropologists confirm that this irrational Islamic hatred of the West cannot be easily exorcized. It was born during the Roman occupation and then reborn during the Crusades. It was inflamed after the collapse of the Ottoman Empire and the Balfour Declaration supporting a Jewish homeland in Palestine. It was further intensified after the creation of Israel in 1948 and the partition of India during independence that same year on terms perceived as anti-Muslim, pro-Hindu. Based partially in reality and partially in imagination, this attitude in the Islamic, especially Arab Islamic, world of victimization is so ingrained as to be almost unapproachable diplomatically.[21]

So if fundamentalist Islamic hatred cannot be fully eradicated, can it at least be managed and minimized to avoid further acts of terrorism? Perhaps. America has already laid the groundwork in this regard by avoiding a rash and provocative response immediately after the attacks. Although probably emotionally justified at the time, we did not launch a nuclear missile at Kabul or Kandahar. Our response was deliberate, rational, and sanctioned under international law. This is important if the response is to be viewed as legitimate by the world and especially by the Islamic world (this will be discussed further in chapter 5).

President Bush set the correct tone for allied operations in Afghanistan by stressing that we were not going to war *against* Afghanistan but *in* Afghanistan. Nonetheless, successful completion of this military mission (driving the Taliban from power and pursuing elements of al Qaeda) is only the first step in a long Afghan journey. The ensuing political aftermath is of equal importance as a demonstration of good faith. When the Soviets pulled out of Afghanistan in 1989, America ended its involvement supporting the Mujahadeen and abandoned Afghanistan to its own devices. Subsequently, the country descended into civil war and chaos.[22] We must not abandon them again. To do so would only be confirmation of the minority Islamic view that America and the West are indifferent and selfishly concerned with pursuing their own interests.

America and its allies must communicate to the Islamic world that the West actually does care about its concerns.[23] We must repeatedly point to past actions undertaken to help Muslim countries: successful intervention in Bosnia to defend Muslims against Serbian aggression; NATO bombing of Serbia despite the absence of UN Security Council authorization to protect Muslim civilians in Kosovo; and even unsuccessful humanitarian intervention in Somalia to avert famine. Then we must translate this message into reality on the ground in Kabul.

Under the aegis of the UN, the establishment of order in Afghanistan has proceeded with invisible Western guidance but with visible Western support (financial and logistic). This balance is delicate but must be maintained. As former ambassador Peter Tomsen put it, we must act "through international support for an internal Afghan dialogue leading to an Afghan regime in Kabul chosen through . . . Afghan consensus. . . . Ultimately, the multiple U.S. interests at stake in Afghanistan can only be accomplished when the majority of Afghans believe their leaders in Kabul have been chosen by Afghans and not from abroad."[24]

The most inclusive form of assemblage convened under a UN conference is the traditional Afghan Loya Jirga. This is a grand council with representatives of every Afghan ethnic, tribal, religious, and political group that historically only convenes for important national decisions. The last assembly was called thirty-eight years ago to ratify a constitution, and one has not occurred to select a new ruler since 1747. Indeed, with the sudden departure of the Taliban, with deposed presidents and lurking kings, and with temperaments fraying among Tajiks, Pashtuns, Uzbeks, and others within the country, the resort to a known and accepted form of traditional decision making could prove stabilizing. Indeed, the Loya Jirga selected interim leader Hamid Karzai as its prime minister for the immediate future.[25]

In tandem with this effort, although perhaps not simultaneously, the United States must revive the aggressive education efforts within the wider Muslim world that it used to pursue during the cold war but unwisely discontinued after the fall of the Soviet Union:

> In the 1980's, when Pakistan was considered a Cold War battleground, American cultural centers were a focus of intellectual and social life in Islamabad, Karachi, Lahore, Hyderabad and Peshawar. Each offered well-stocked libraries, discussion groups led by visiting Americans and a stream of cultural programs. In Lahore . . . singers from the Metropolitan Opera created a sensation, and there were long lines for a show of posters of American paintings. Following a series of budget cuts . . . the ideals, history and cultural vibrancy of the United States were taken off display. . . . Now, thousands of young

people live at fundamentalist academies where they learn nothing but how to chant the Koran and hate the infidel.[26]

As Allan Goodman, head of the Fulbright scholarship program, notes, "the only way we're going to reduce hatred for America is by giving people some perception of our society, some opportunity to see who we really are."[27] Moreover, we must not continue to sit passively while inflammatory stories air on Al-Jezeera television allowing radical Muslims to cast us in the role of the enemy.[28] Our Department of State must respond on that network, *in Arabic.* Domestically, our political leaders know that allowing one's opponent to define one and one's position in an election campaign cedes power to that opponent that is difficult to regain. This is no less true in our country's foreign relations. America must define itself and not leave that task to others.

In principle, just as we in the West see foreign ambassadors fluent in English defending or explaining the positions of their countries on CNN and MSNBC, our own ambassadors must take to the airwaves. However, in practice, this would be an unmitigated disaster. America's embassies around the world are staffed with ambassadors who have little or no experience in either foreign relations or the specific culture within which they find themselves. They too often owe their jobs to political patronage, measured by how much they helped the current president get elected. Ambassadors of the United States should be qualified individuals, drawn largely from the Foreign Service, familiar with the local culture, and politically astute enough to understand the subtleties of foreign relations.

Moreover, we must reopen American cultural centers and resurrect the educational arm of our public diplomacy. At the same time, we must gradually withdraw public displays of support from despotic regimes whose values are counter to our own, lest we be seen as hypocrites preaching the gospel of democratic principles on the one hand while propping up strongmen on the other. Perpetuating such a hypocritical dynamic ended in graphic failure in Iran with the overthrow of our strongman, the Shah, in 1979. Part of the problem is getting the message through to the masses, perhaps bypassing the state-controlled media through Internet and underground radio usage. As the *Economist* notes:

If America fails to export a much better side of its culture, its model of freedom—including the freedom to be devout in whatever way you choose, so long as nobody else is hurt—that is mainly because most traditionally Muslim states, including pro-American ones, will not take the risk of opening their air-waves and their printing presses to genuinely plural-ist debate. In practice, this has often left the way clear for the message of people . . . like Mr. bin Laden. . . . [H]is kind may be sloppy historians and faulty interpreters of their own faith, let alone others. But even now he could win the propaganda war.[29]

In short, America must engage to set the story straight, espous-ing our values and ideals, but in a nonthreatening, inclusive man-ner. We can no longer afford to let our Constitution speak for itself to those who bother to pick it up. The United States must make an effort to display it to the world. But we cannot expect that our ver-sion of representative democracy will be adopted wholesale upon presentation, considering anything short of that a failure. Islamic society, especially Arabic society, is ill-suited for immediate democ-racy. So even limited progress, such as that by Bahrain this year to open parliamentary elections to women, must be encouraged and not criticized because no women were ultimately elected.

From the viewpoint of religion, which of course dominates at least Arabic Muslim culture, Islam, in its classical sense, allows for no separation of church and state. Islamic law, or *sharia,* is not secu-lar; rather, it is law that is ordained by God as interpreted by the clergy. Therefore nonclerical Islamic men who propose framing their own laws, what democracy would consider representatives or parliamentarians, are technically apostates. And historically, the Arab states that emerged from the destruction of the Ottoman Empire inherited borders, like much of Africa, that were drawn in London or Paris for administrative convenience rather than to reflect cultural associations or nationhood. Thus, because the people of these artificial countries identify more strongly with their local tribe or clan and with pan-Arab or the wider Islamic fellow-ship than with the state, strongmen with strong armies provide the glue that holds the system in place.[30]

As former diplomat Charles Hill explains in his essay "Myth and Reality of Arab Terrorism," there is a

single approach to the political ordering of [Arab] society. In Oman, a sultan; in Yemen, a military "president"; in Saudi Arabia, a king . . . ; in Jordan, a king . . . ; in Egypt, a president and a parliament only nominally connected to the original Western meaning of these institutions. Beneath all these styles a single form is discernible. Power is held by a strongman, surrounded by a praetorian guard. . . . Every regime of the Arab-Islamic world has proved a failure. Not one has proved able to provide its people with realistic hope for a free and prosperous future. The regimes have found no way to respond to their people's frustration other than a combination of internal oppression and propaganda to generate rage against external enemies. Religiously inflamed terrorists take root in such soil. Their threats to the regimes extort facilities and subsidies that increase their strength and influence. The result is a downward spiral of failure, fear and hatred.[31]

Hill concludes that the impact of this disenfranchisement in Arab society has been undergirded by the "deeply rooted conviction that virtually every significant occurrence is caused by some external conspiracy. Every societal shortcoming is attributed to a foreign plot."[32] Anecdotal evidence of this dynamic is not hard to come by. One of the more persistent rumors circulated and believed by many Arabs—including Mohammad Atta's own father, an Egyptian lawyer—holds that the destruction of the WTC was actually not carried out by Muslims but was rather a plot by Mossad (Israeli intelligence), which is supposedly supported by the fact that four thousand Jews did not come to work at the WTC on September.[33]

Both Russia and America supported these corrupt, despotic systems during the cold war when it suited their purposes. So, the question is, Did that system become more intolerable in the 1990s because the stifling repression by corrupt governments in Arab society increased dramatically or because that system no longer suited the purpose of the great powers, whose forty-year geopolitical chess match had ended and who no longer required obedient pawns—which were much easier to deal with in dictatorial form than in democratic form? The latter is more likely, and the Arabs know it, which is why the argument must shift from one of right and wrong governance (which leads to the dead end of hypocrisy as we condemn dictatorial Iraq, Syria, and Libya while supporting equally antidemocratic Kuwait, Egypt, and Saudi Arabia) to one of a better life offered to the man on the street.

America cannot change the Arab world at a stroke. It will not risk knocking the legs away from longstanding allies such as Egypt and Saudi Arabia. In wars hot and cold, great powers have collected allies where they can, without too much scruple. But the struggle against forces unleashed by Mr. bin Laden is a most unusual war. Because his aim was to lure the West into an internal quarrel about the future of the Muslim world, it is in large part a struggle about values. The West must not impose its values, but needs to say out loud that its own achievements of religious tolerance and liberal democracy are not just luxuries to be consumed at home. They are universal ideals that can, and should, be welcomed by Arabs too.[34]

Indeed, part of this message could entail simply pointing to the millions of Muslims who live peaceful, contented, religiously fulfilling lives in the West that are often simultaneously economically advanced, politically active, and academically secular. From Hamburg to London to Detroit, Michigan, knowledge of Islamic citizens who have adopted the Western model of democratic freedom but who remain devout might work to ameliorate some of the inaccurate hyperbole directed at the "decadent West" by small-minded fundamentalist clerics seeking to control their own little enclaves of a repressed population.[35]

But in order for this message to resonate, the United States and its allies in the West must avoid government actions that unnecessarily stigmatize Muslims who live in the West or seek to visit. Specifically, the DOJ must issue a detailed statement justifying (in a nondefensive manner) its detention of hundreds of, mostly Muslim, individuals for several months without legal representation. This statement should explain the action, discuss the bases for detention (mostly INS and visa violations), recount the outcome of individual actions (release, deportation, continued detention, etc.), and offer something approaching credible regret about the offensive and discriminatory way in which the action was carried out.

Attorney General Ashcroft must also rethink his proposal to fingerprint and photograph anyone from Iran, Iraq, Libya, Sudan, and Syria who enters the United States, regardless of their prior individual activities. By virtue of the fact that they come from those states, they will be treated as security threats. Beginning in the fall of 2002, this applies to anyone from those countries who holds a nonimmigrant visa over the age of fourteen. And for those who remain in the United States longer than thirty days, they must register with the INS and provide proof of employment, school enrollment, or information on their residence. Moreover, if they fail to register each year, they will be fined, jailed, or deported.[36] This ruling affects about 100,000 visitors annually.

The official justification for creation of this state list is that these are five countries "where terrorists are known to operate."[37] While all of these Muslim states have undeniable terrorist connections, so too do Egypt and Saudi Arabia, which furnished fifteen of the nineteen September 11 hijackers. Yet even though these two countries are more directly linked to the attack on the United States than are the five listed states, they are not included. Presumably, this is due to their current friendly relations with our government.

If Ashcroft's reasoning were in fact valid, then any five countries "where terrorists are known to operate" would qualify for the initial spots on his list—Spain, Russia, Ireland, Colombia, and France (none of which are majority Islamic). However, he selected only Islamic states for his list. What message does this send to the Muslim world? It only reinforces the incorrectly perceived anti-Islamic sentiment by the West. These are exactly the type of wrong-headed government actions that must be tempered to help alter such perceptions. The relatively low benefits gained from such pronouncements pale in the balance against the damage they do to our image in the eyes of average Muslims around the world.

We must remember that the real enemy is hatred, and hatred is not defeated on the battlefield. It is conquered in the hearts and minds of the people who harbor it. On September 11, the hearts of most of the world, including the Islamic world, were with us. Now the task is capturing the minds as well.[38] Today's active, reinvigorated education together with multiple tangible demonstrations of empathy in place of yesterday's sentiment of indifference and pervasive arrogance are essential components of attacking the real enemy. Equally essential is treating the Muslim population at home with due respect. That takes a different kind of mind-set on our part and a more advanced strategy.

There appears to be a recognition of this on the part of the administration. A month after the attacks, President Bush remarked, "How do I respond when I see that in some Islamic countries there is a vitriolic hatred of America? I'll tell you how I respond: I'm amazed. I'm amazed that there is such misunderstanding of what our country is about. We've got to do a better job of making our case."[39] Let's hope that we do. As the respected internationalist cold warrior J. William Fulbright once said, "In the long course of history, having people who understand your thought is much greater security than another submarine."[40]

The Problem of the Suicide Bomber

Obviously, the irrationally disturbed mind cannot be easily reached even with the most aggressive and persistent educational efforts, which we in the West have yet to adequately mount. These are the candidates who are ripe for conversion into suicide bombers. They are perhaps the most devious of delivery devices and the most difficult to stop. Short of building a fence around the intended target, as Israel is now doing around the city of Jerusalem, those bent on destroying themselves along with their prey will use any resource and all their human capacity to achieve their result.

Martyrdom is a tricky business, both for the would-be martyr and the leader who recruits, indoctrinates, trains, and releases him or her. However, the idea of self-sacrifice is a powerful one with long historical antecedents that can be used in the indoctrination effort. The Old Testament, considered holy text in the Jewish, Christian, and Islamic faiths, recounts the compelling story of Samson asking God for revenge against the Philistines and placing himself between two giant pillars supporting a building that he forces apart, burying himself and his intended victims in the ruins:

And Samson took hold of the two middle pillars upon which the house stood, and on which it was borne up, of the one with his right hand, and of the other with his left. And Samson said, "Let me die with the Philistines." And bowed himself with all his might; and the house fell upon the lords, and upon all the people that were therein. *So the dead which he slew at his death were more than they which he slew in his life.*[41]

The example in that biblical story could not be clearer. By destroying oneself in a heroic way, one's cause may be furthered beyond what one is capable of accomplishing as an individual while alive. This principle is a key element in the strategy of suicide terrorism. Although perhaps a truism, this teaching nonetheless resonates with the right personalities whose hatred has more value to them than their own lives. Moreover, history shows that governments respond to such tactics.

In 1983 a series of suicide car bombings was unleashed by Syrian-backed fundamentalist Shi'ites in Beirut, Lebanon. On April 18 the U.S. Embassy was attacked, wounding 120 and killing 63; on October 23 the U.S. Marine headquarters was hit, killing 241; on that same day the French paratrooper headquarters was attacked, wounding 15 and killing 58. Shortly thereafter French and American forces were withdrawn from Lebanon[42] and the area was left to descend into a decade of chaos and religious internecine warfare occasionally interrupted by overlapping periods of Israeli occupation and Syrian military dominance.

Given such salient religious and historic examples, what base factors come together to create a suicide terrorist? Dr. Ariel Merari, a psychologist and the director of the Project on Terrorism at Tel Aviv University's Jaffe Center for Strategic Studies, has identified four constituent elements: cultural factors, indoctrination, situational factors, and personality traits.[43] When these elements are present and combined correctly, the suicidal mind-set can be exploited for any purpose.

The first element, cultural factors, includes religious motivators. As Merari notes, "All monotheistic religions promise life after death. Hypothetically, they may thus encourage suicidal behavior, especially if the suicidal act is carried out for a righteous cause."[44] And although suicide is formally forbidden in the Jewish, Christian, and Islamic faiths, a clever leader can twist religious teachings to allow that which is forbidden. In Islam, a believer who is killed by the enemy in jihad (holy war) is guaranteed a place in paradise—clearly a tempting alternative to life in the hellish refugee camps of the West Bank, for example. But there is no paradisal place for suicides.

Knowing this, an educated leader may capitalize on the dual hatred nursed in the bosom of the downtrodden together with the potential suicide's lack of doctrinal religious teaching to convince him or her to attain a place in paradise (and also for their family) by joining the falsely named jihad against the West. Thus, martyrdom can be packaged and sold as a one-way ticket to everlasting happiness in the afterlife. In this way, the cultural factors lay the foundation for suicide terrorism to manifest itself.[45]

The second element, the indoctrination itself, occurs on two levels. The first is an educational process whereby the person is "convinced of the importance of the cause and of the means necessary for its implementation."[46] Parents, teachers, writers, and others are participatory agents of influence. The second level is the brief, mission-oriented persuasion task, usually performed by a charismatic political, military, or religious leader, shortly before the attack is to be carried out. The person conducting the indoctrination of the would-be suicide terrorist strengthens already existing convictions laid by the cultural factors and the influence wielders during the education process but adds the element of personal commitment to the cause.

The third element, situational factors, includes the conditions and circumstances surrounding the commission of the attack. If the opportunity (geography, proximity, timing, target awareness, etc.) does not exist, then the situational factors are not contributory in a significant way. But situational factors also include those surrounding the suicide terrorist, such as the possibility of group suicide and the effect of an audience.[47] Group suicide tends to strengthen the resolve, through peer pressure and other mechanisms, to carry the task through to completion. Moreover, the effect of an audience is practically guaranteed in the age of instantaneous electronic media coverage.

Another element that could perhaps be included in situational factors is the prospect of tangible benefit. One of the more interesting components to arise during the Palestinians' second *intifada* against Israeli occupation has been the financial reward bestowed upon the families of successful suicide bombers. Saddam Hussein's Ba'ath Party regime in Baghdad, maybe recalling the unmitigated support it received from Palestinians during the Gulf War, sent cash to family members of dead terrorists. Each family that suffered the loss of a son or daughter in a suicide mission against Israel received twenty-five thousand dollars. In the world of the refugee camp, this dynamic could provide a twisted motivation in itself.[48]

The fourth element, personality traits, is an amalgam of the internal psychologic condition of the potential suicide and the effects of the environment upon him or her. Consequently, it is exceedingly difficult to construct a dependable profile of personality traits that is uniform for potential suicide terrorists. This is made more complicated by the fact that successful ones are consumed in their own attacks, and their personal histories are often not available.

Nonetheless, with respect to the first three of Merari's constituent elements, al Qaeda's success in producing such devastating weapons as suicide bombers in the first WTC attack, the Khobar Towers bombing, the USS *Cole* attack, the bombing of the American embassies in Africa, and then the September 11 attacks inside the continental United States is self-evident. That organization's mastery at exploiting the constituent elements cannot be denied. The cultural factors existed for the indoctrination to take place on both levels. Osama bin Laden provided the charismatic leadership for the second level of indoctrination. Group suicide and the access to a global audience stimulated the nongeographic situational factors, and mobility of the suicide terrorists mitigated the geographic ones.

What can we do to defend against that which cannot be stopped by concrete barriers or intercepted by law enforcement or destroyed by military action? What can we do to defend against those people who are bent on destroying themselves in the process of destroying their perceived adversaries? We must reach out and alter that perception of America as the enemy. Only by taking ourselves out of the role of adversary can we protect ourselves, our interests, and our way of life from suicide bombers.

Thus, we must aggressively proceed on the path laid out in the preceding section to educate the Muslim world about our American values and our support of Islam. Only by defining ourselves and what we stand for can we undermine the power of charismatic Islamic leaders to define us in a distorted manner. In this way, the cultural factors will dissipate over time. Once that foundation evaporates, the first level of indoctrination (through influence-wielding parents, teachers, and writers) becomes more difficult and may dissipate as well, thereby making the job of the charismatic leader in the second level of indoctrination all the more difficult and unsuccessful.

Biological, Chemical, and Nuclear Threats

WMD conjure up scenarios and destructive forms that not only capture the literary imaginations of authors such as Tom Clancy (*Sum of all Fears*) and Stephen King (*The Stand*) but provide many sleepless nights for those in government charged with guarding against their use. Biological, chemical, and nuclear weapons are the WMD most often cited as areas of concern should they fall into the hands of anti-American terrorists.

Historically, such weapons have a long, but limited track record. Biological weapons have been around since the Middle Ages, when commanders laying siege to cities would catapult dead bodies over city walls to spread Black Plague and other forms of pestilence.[49] Chemical weapons were employed by artillery and used in World War I on both the Eastern and Western fronts by the Germans and later in response by the Allies. The nuclear device has been used twice, both times by the United States against Japan during World War II.

Employment of such weapons by states against other states in the latter half of the twentieth century was rare, due largely to the deterrent effect of like retaliation coupled with treaties outlawing their use. Consequently, the emerging threat today is not from other states so much as from terrorist organizations who are immune from deterrence and do not belong to the treaties designed to control WMD. A report by the National Research Council released in the summer of 2002 found that the United States was ill-prepared to deal with a terrorist WMD attack and lacked a "coherent overall strategy."[50] The government is now working to develop one.

Harvard University's Jessica Stern, Senior Fellow at the Belfer Center for Science and International Affairs, has studied terrorist groups in their quest to acquire WMD. She notes that "[c]andidates for employing these weapons are found at the intersection of three subsets: terrorists who want to use the weapons despite formidable political costs, terrorists who are able to acquire or produce them, and terrorists who have the ability to deliver or disseminate them covertly. . . . [T]he area created by the intersection of these sets is small but growing."[51]

At least in the case of Stern's first criterion, religious fanaticism may provide such motivation. The Library of Congress's report to the National Intelligence Council—entitled "The Sociology and Psychology of Terrorism: Who Becomes a Terrorist and Why?"— found that for the most fundamentalist of groups

[t]heir outlook is one that divides the world simplistically into "them" and "us." . . . The religiously motivated terrorists are more dangerous than the politically motivated terrorists because they are the ones most likely to develop and use weapons of mass destruction in pursuit of their messianic or apocalyptic visions. The level of intelligence of a terrorist group's leaders may determine the longevity of the group. . . . [Osama bin Laden is] the prototype of a new breed of terror-ist—the private entrepreneur who puts modern enterprise at the service of a global terrorist network.[52]

In the case of the second criterion, where can such highly deter-mined groups access the WMD in a form that can be easily con-verted to later use in a terrorist attack? While isolated incidences outside of Eurasia occur, such as the South African biological weapons scientists who offered their expertise to Libya,[53] the main fear rests with the former Soviet Union. When the USSR collapsed in 1991, its massive arsenal of biological, chemical, and nuclear weapons and facilities was inherited by fifteen suddenly struggling independent states that were not only new custodians of WMD but also in dire economic straits. Many of them remain so.

Moreover, the chaotic new legal and political environment in these fledgling democracies (Russia included) remains rampant with corruption and heavily influenced by organized crime, whose networks have provided willing purchasers of WMD material and scientific expertise backed with much needed hard currency.[54] According to Stern, the resulting black market is now offering these items along with their delivery technology. But the danger remains. For example, although "law enforcement authorities have seized hundreds of caches of stolen nuclear materials,"[55] it is impossible to know for certain how many transactions were culminated.

As for the third criterion, covert delivery, small or isolated organizations may find this hurdle insurmountable. However, groups with large, perhaps clandestine followings, such as Japan's Aum Shinrikyo, or groups with widely dispersed networks operating in individual cells with separate destructive capacities, such as bin Laden's al Qaeda, could clear such a hurdle. The possible delivery scenarios are what policymakers have some control over; consequently, the troubleshooting, border and security systems testing, threat analysis, and debates about resource allocation tend to focus on this area. The result is an unsettlingly long catalog of hypothetical doomsday scenarios about which little can be done, but preventative measures must nonetheless take place.[56]

Biological Weapons

The first challenge for governments developing a defense to biological weapons is facing the mental hurdle of segregating that defense from the tendency to lump it together with a coordinated response to other WMD such as chemical and nuclear devices. As Christopher Chyba, codirector of Stanford's Center for International Security and Cooperation, points out, biological, chemical, and nuclear weapons

[d]iffer greatly in their ease of production, in the challenges they pose for deterrence, and in the effectiveness of defensive measures against them. The post-September 11th focus on WMD and whether they are in the hands of enemy states or groups risks overlooking these complexities. Put simply, biological weapons differ from nuclear or chemical weapons, and any biological security strategy should begin by paying attention to these differences.[57]

Indeed, the unique character of bioweapons is self-evident: they can be secretly introduced to a population through an unknowing carrier (or a knowing one if he or she is a suicide terrorist) without warning; they have the ability to self-perpetuate—widening the circle of destruction exponentially upon introduction; and in many instances there is no known vaccination, treatment, or cure. Moreover, the terror factor, derived from the panic that inevitably ensues from a biological attack, can be an ancillary form of injury as populations scramble to escape the effects of the bioagent. This factor could claim lives too, as accidents occur, hospitals are overrun, evacuations or quarantines spin out of control, or troops are forced to fire on civilians.

Another unique characteristic of biologic weapons that could draw religiously fanatical terrorist organizations to seek them is their metaphoric use as divine retribution. In the Book of Exodus, the fifth plague used by God to punish Pharoah is believed to be murrain—from the anthrax family. And in the Book of Samuel, God unleashes a pestilence on the Philistines that medical historians correlate to bubonic plague. There are other examples, but it is the symbolism and religious connotation of employing a living organism to destroy other living organisms that sets bioweapons apart from chemical or nuclear agents.[58]

These biologic killers come in mainly three forms: bacteria, viruses, and toxins. Bacteria are single-celled living organisms. They are tiny (measured only in micrometers) and range in shape from the spherical cocci to the long, rod-shaped bacilli. The single cell contains DNA, cytoplasm, and the membrane. Some bacteria can transform themselves into spores. If this happens, they lie dormant, like plant seeds, until conditions are right to germinate. Bacteria cause disease in humans by directly invading the tissue, producing toxins, or both. Examples of deadly bacteria that can be utilized for bioterror purposes include anthrax, cholera, and plague, with mortality rates upon contraction of almost 100 percent, 50–80 percent, and 50–100 percent (depending on whether bubonic or pneumonic plague is used), respectively.[59]

Viruses are even smaller than bacteria. They are composed of DNA or RNA and require living cells in order to replicate. They are not self-contained and cannot metabolize on their own. The host cells they need to live and multiply can be human, plant, animal, or bacteriological—but each type of virus requires a specific type of host cell. Normally, this parasitic relationship kills the host cell. The most dangerous viruses include smallpox; a wide variety of hemorrhagic fevers ranging from the most lethal Ebola, Marburg, and Crimean-Congo strains to the less lethal Q fever and yellow fever; and the generally nonlethal Venezuelan Equine Encephalitis.[60]

Toxins are any naturally occurring poisonous substances. Their origin could be animal, plant, or microbe. They are typically not infectious and therefore do not have the potential for a ripple effect that bacterial and virological agents have. Delivery can enhance or constrain the toxin's effect. Some toxins are more toxic when sprayed by aerosol while others can only be delivered orally or via blood-to-blood contamination. The toxins most commonly considered dangerous for bioterror purposes include botulinum, against which humans have no natural defense and which can be converted to powder, aerosolized, and sprayed; ricin, derived from the widely available castor plant and against which antibiotics cannot be used due to the rapidity with which it causes respiratory failure (36–72 hours) when inhaled or vascular collapse if ingested; and the much less lethal *Staphylococcus aureus* toxins, most commonly associated with food poisoning.[61]

Of the three, the United States has the most recent experience with anthrax, which was unleashed domestically through the U.S. mail system after the September 11 attacks by an as yet unknown assailant. When inhaled, spores from this bacterial agent can penetrate deep into the lungs. While the spores are vulnerable to treatment by ciprofloxacin (Cipro), penicillin, and tetracycline, getting the treatment soon enough is problematic.[62] The attacks came in the form of a fine white powder in letters sent to Democratic members of Congress and elsewhere. Experts estimate that the original letters contained one trillion spores.[63]

But four of the five deaths that resulted from the mailed letters were not direct recipients. Rather, they were postal workers and unfortunate individuals who received one of the five thousand letters that were cross-contaminated during the postal routing and handling process.[64] The postal service has used money earmarked by Congress to counter such powdery anthrax attacks in the future. Specifically, they are installing PCR systems at 292 sorting facilities that collect air samples sucked from the mail and test for eight different biohazards (anthrax plus seven that will not be disclosed) and retrofitting their high-speed sorters with vacuums that feed air out of the system and into filters.[65] Whether such measures prove sufficient remains to be seen. Shortly after the September 11 terrorist attacks, the United States and Uzbekistan signed an agreement to clean up an island in the rapidly disappearing Aral Sea, where the Soviet government had dumped tons of weaponized anthrax spores from its illegal biological warfare program in 1988.[66]

The only other time anthrax claimed a larger number of lives in weaponized form in an industrialized nation was when a Soviet military experiment went dangerously awry in 1979 in Sverdlovsk, claiming sixty-four lives according to Soviet sources or thousands according to U.S. intelligence.[67] Anthrax and botulism were used alternately from 1990 to 1995 by the Japanese religious cult Aum Shinrikyo to attack subway systems, the Diet, the Imperial Palace, and the naval headquarters of the U.S. Seventh Fleet in Yokosuka in mist form. However, due to a combination of ineptitude, repentant followers, and insufficiency of the biological agents' virulence, no one was killed; indeed, neither the Japanese nor U.S. governments became aware of the attacks until years later, after the cult had switched to chemical attacks (sarin gas), which proved much more successful.[68]

Nevertheless, the importance of the attempt by the Japanese terrorist group remains significant because it points to the fact that states and their militaries are no longer the sole actors in biowarfare. This, in turn, reinforces the importance of government measures to limit access to these contagions. William Patrick, a former germ warfare expert for the U.S. government, considers limited access the key to protection. He notes that because a specific type of microbe could come in hundreds of subvarieties, but only one strain might pose lethal risks to humans, for bioterrorists "getting the most infectious and virulent culture for the seed stock is the greatest hurdle."[69]

But small organizations, not typically regarded as terrorist, can convince themselves to use the less virulent varieties of germ in order to further their political ends. A nonlethal toxin attack was mounted by followers of the Bagwan Shree Rajneesh in 1984 by sprinkling salmonella typhimurium onto restaurant salad bars in Oregon in an attempt to sway an election. More than 750 people fell ill as a result.[70] Thus, apocalyptic visions of divine retribution can at times give way to achieving more mundane objectives as a motive for use of bioweapons by a fringe group.

Beyond bacteria and toxins, the virus smallpox is emerging as a deadly alternative agent. Eradicated by the World Health Organization as a naturally occurring disease in 1980 and confined to two frozen vials (one in the United States, the other in the USSR), it is apparent that Iraq and North Korea now also have the virus and that China, Libya, South Africa, Israel, and Pakistan are believed to possess it as well. Consequently, the containment policy did not work. During the twentieth century alone, smallpox killed more than 300 million people—more than all the wars of that period combined.[71]

The symptoms of smallpox are unmistakable. Ten days after infection, headache, backache, vomiting, and fever manifest themselves. Then the fever wanes, and the individual begins to feel better. Consequently, one might mistakenly believe that it is the flu. Shortly thereafter, the first red spots appear evenly spaced on the face and extremities. This rash spreads as the spots turn to lumps and fill with fluid that seeps from capillaries, making them hard, like BBs embedded under the skin. Sheets of skin begin to separate and slough off as the disease quickly progresses, which can lead to death within sixteen days from organ failure, pneumonia, or overreaction by the immune system. There is no treatment, only the possibility of vaccination prior to infection. The mortality rate is around 50 percent.[72]

Computer modeling, hypothesizing a not unreasonable single bioterrorism outbreak of one hundred smallpox cases in a typical American city, predicts that the resulting disease "would become a worldwide conflagration in as little as a year" unless an aggressive, large-scale immunization campaign were undertaken to stop it— which is not currently possible. As of 2001, there were only 60 million doses of smallpox vaccine in the world, of which the United States had 8 million. Containment of the outbreak hypothesized in the computer scenario would require 30 to 40 million doses.[73] In response, the Department of Health and Human Services began purchasing enough vaccines for every American, the military innoculated 480,000 personnel, and 38,000 emergency health workers were vaccinated by 2003.[74]

Another viral superbug with exponential ripple-effect capability that government officials worry about is Ebola, strains of which do not even have vaccinations. Graphically recounted in Richard Preston's reality-based novel *The Hot Zone* in 1994, Ebola Zaire and Marburg strains emerged from Africa and through Europe to the United States undetected, living in monkeys kept at a laboratory in Reston, Virginia. The virus jumped from the animals to humans, and, of course, chaos and cycles of human death ensued.[75] Ebola does have that transmutational capacity, as well as the ability to become airborne, which makes it so deadly and unpredictable.

Ten days after infection of Ebola, the flu-like symptoms common to most viruses emerge: fever, vomiting, and achiness. However, the second phase moves more quickly and gruesomely. The virus attacks all organs and tissues except bone and muscle in the body, most of which is progressively turned into "a digested slime of virus particles," as the BBC's Tom Mangold and Jeff Goldberg describe in their documentary book *Plague Wars:*

> As the virus storms through the body making copies of itself, small blood clots appear in the bloodstream, the blood thickens and slows, and the clots begin to stick to the walls of the blood vessels. Eventually, the skin develops red spots . . . which are haemorrages under the skin. Subsequently, spontaneous tears appear and join up, the skin goes soft and pulpy, and can tear off. Soon every orifice in the body begins to bleed. The skin of the tongue can slough off causing indescribable pain. The heart bleeds into itself, the eyeballs fill with blood. And it gets considerably worse before death.[76]

The horrific scenarios by which such attacks can be carried forth are limited only by the imagination, the stability of the biological agent, and the virulence of the strain. Luckily, the latter two actually function as limits on most forms of attack. Only militaries typically have the scientific expertise, discipline, and foresight to successfully mount such attacks. Few terrorist groups would have the know-how to control stability when the agent is converted to delivery form, as well as the proper use of an effective delivery mechanism coupled with the reliability of the agent and its continued potency.[77]

However, this does not solve the problem of former military members with mercenary streaks joining forces with terrorist organizations seeking their guidance—for a price. Delivery can be aggressive: using crop-dusting airplanes, dispersing it in building ventilation ducts, injecting it clandestinely into drinking water aquifers, depositing it into postal systems, or simply tossing a glass vial onto the tracks of an oncoming subway train, whose trailing air vacuum would send the spores dashing through tunnels and onto platforms.

Delivery can also be subtle. Jose Padilla, an al Qaeda operative instructed to scout out targets for a radiologic "dirty bomb" attack, flew from Pakistan to O'Hare Airport in May 2002, where he was apprehended by waiting law enforcement officials. Federal agents patted themselves on the back for effecting his capture, and Attorney General Ashcroft made a valedictory statement from Moscow in that regard. From the government's perspective, the case was closed upon apprehension, and the job remaining to handle Padilla was for lawyers.

But suppose Padilla had been exposed to delayed-effect virological agents like smallpox or an Ebola strain (knowingly or unknowingly) prior to boarding his plane in Karachi. During the thirty-six hours it takes to get to Chicago, he could have contaminated those around him and those who used the washroom after him through fluid contact and could have contaminated the other four hundred passengers and crew breathing the same recirculated air as he was (if airborne contact transmits, as in the case of Ebola). In that time, the flu-like symptoms would not yet have become apparent. Consequently, upon landing, his capture would not matter much. No one else on the plane had been detained—there was no reason to do so.

By the time Padilla's symptoms appeared, perhaps two days before anyone else who was on that plane, those four hundred souls would have driven into their Chicago suburbs or boarded other flights for a hundred other destinations within the United States. They could not be tracked using the flight lists before they died and had infected others. The agents making Padilla's arrest would likely themselves be infected, as well as their families and fellow law enforcement officers and their families. Indeed, by the time patients wandered into hospital emergency rooms around the country with red dots covering their faces, in the case of smallpox, or spewing blood from their eyes and ears, in the case of Ebola during what is called a "bleedout," containment would be impossibly difficult (perhaps requiring martial law) and treatment not an option for those already infected.

So what have we done to respond legally to this threat? Domestically, the unauthorized manufacture, trade, sale, or public exposure of such biological agents is illegal under Titles 18, 22, 42, and 50 of the U.S. Code and several executive orders. This web of laws also criminalizes attempts and conspiracy. Moreover, shipment of deadly bioagents has been monitored since 1997; however, no development of a gene library creating a national inventory of these diseases or consolidation of facilities with the most dangerous strains has been undertaken. According to Stanford's Dr. Chyba, had these efforts been in place in the fall of 2001, "the anthrax investigation could have proceeded more quickly."[78]

Internationally, deterrence through the threat of massive retaliation has been the key strategy relied upon to prevent the use of these agents. However, deterrence won't work against a terrorist organization that does not care if it is eradicated (or martyred) or that has dispersed by the time the United States figures out the biological agents' point of origin. The 1972 Biological and Toxin Weapons Convention prohibits production and stockpiling of the agents, and the 1925 Geneva Protocol prohibits their use. However, the Bush administration rejected the compliance and verification protocol to the treaty in July 2001, arguing that it would "jeopardize U.S. [pharmaceutical] companies' proprietary information, did not provide sufficient protection for U.S. biodefense programs, and would not improve verification capabilities."[79]

Nonproliferation is a related but separate concern from noncompliance. The goal of nonproliferation is less easily reached in the context of deadly biological agents than it is in the context of nuclear weapons. Scientists can come by potentially lethal germs or toxins in the course of otherwise legitimate, perhaps university-backed or federally funded research. Naturally occurring disease outbreaks are another source of these organisms—witness the continual recurrence of the Ames strain of anthrax in eastern Texas.[80]

Artificial construction of such diseases is yet another possibility. In the summer of 2002, the *New York Times* reported the success of scientists at the University of Buffalo–Stony Brook in their quest during a Pentagon-funded study to create a synthetic version of polio from chemicals and publicly available information:

The scientists constructed the virus using its genome sequence, which is available on the Internet, as their blueprint, and genetic material from one of the many mail-order companies that sell made-to-order DNA. Dr. Eckard Wimmer, professor of molecular genetics and microbiology at Stony Brook and leader of the project, said they made the virus to send a warning that terrorists might be able to make biological weapons even when they could not obtain a natural virus. "You no longer need the real thing in order to make the virus and propagate it." The work immediately set off a debate over whether the same technique might be applied to other viruses. The genetic codes for many dangerous pathogens, including smallpox and ebola, are freely accessible on the Web. And the team relied on technology that is generally available in molecular biology labs around the world.[81]

It is also unclear whether bioweapons technology has remained contained by the superpowers since the end of the cold war. Indeed, the Soviets flagrantly violated the terms of the 1972 treaty for two decades prior to their country's collapse—a fact we in America did not become aware of until 1989. The man who ran the Russian bioweapons program as deputy chief of Biopreparat from 1988 to 1992, Ken Alibek, defected to the United States in 1992 and is now a citizen. He discloses in his book *Biohazard* the extent to which Russian efforts to capitalize on their scientific expertise in this area continue:

In July 1995, Russia opened negotiations with Iraq for the sale of large industrial fermentation vessels and related equipment. The model was one we had used to develop and manufacture bacterial biological weapons. Like Cuba, the Iraqis maintained the vessels were intended to grow single-cell protein for cattle feed. What made the deal particularly suspicious was an additional request for exhaust filtration equipment capable of achieving 99.99 percent air purity—a level we used only in our weapons labs.

Negotiations were called off by the time reports of the deal surfaced in the Western press, but a United Nations employee told me Iraq obtained the equipment it needed elsewhere.

United Nations Special Committee Inspection Teams, established after the Gulf War to monitor the dismantling of Iraq's chemical and biological weapons programs, had not been able to find this equipment by the time they were ejected from Iraq in late 1998. Many similar deals have gone undetected. . . . In 1997 Russia was reported to be negotiating a lucrative deal with Iran for the sale of cultivation equipment including fermenters, reactors, and air purifying machinery. The equipment was similar to that which was offered to Iraq.[82]

Given the failure of states to comply with the treaty prohibitions, the increased realization that bioagents are widely available, and the first biological attack on the United States last fall, Congress passed legislation, signed by the president in June 2002, to provide $4.3 billion for drugs, vaccines, training, and other initiatives to prepare for further biological attacks. This includes tightening security at water plants, improving food inspections, and increasing stockpiles of smallpox and other vaccines. Another $1.6 billion is earmarked for distribution to states and localities—recognizing the fact that such attacks must be initially identified and tackled by first responders at the local level.[83]

Localities will spend the money on new protective gear, mobile laboratories, pathogen testing equipment, traffic control (new lights and video technology), and hazmat equipment for fire departments. After decades of neglect, these disbursements amount to the first step on the part of the federal government to build a robust biodefense system centered on the key elements of quick response, containment, treatment, and panic control. But it is expected to take years for the system to ramp up to where it needs to be to prove effective.[84]

Chemical Weapons

Chemical weapons have been used more extensively than biological weapons. Although tried on the Russians six months earlier, the first large-scale chemical attack came during World War I when the Germans released a five-mile-wide cloud of chlorine gas against the French in Belgium on April 22, 1915. There were fifteen thousand casualties and five thousand deaths. By 1918 both sides employed the technology and one in four artillery shells fired contained a gas component. Adolph Hitler, a corporal in the German army, was temporarily blinded by a British gas attack in Flanders—which many believe led to his decision not to employ it as a weapon in military operations during World War II. In fact, no major power has employed the use of chemical weapons in combat since that time.[85] This, of course, does not rule out the possibility of their future use, either by corrupt regimes of rogue states or by terrorist organizations.

Chemical weapons come in three types of agents based on the area of the body they affect: choking, blistering, and nerve agents. Choking agents include chlorine and phosgene gases. They attack the respiratory tract, destroying pulmonary capacity in about four hours, leading to death. Blistering agents include the family of mustard gases and lewisite. These agents cause blisters on the skin and destroy substances within living cells—attacking the eyes, mucous membranes, internal organs, and respiratory tracts. They are slower acting (taking effect twelve to twenty-four hours after exposure) and less deadly, although death can result from lung injury. Nerve agents include sarin, tabun, somoan, and VX. They disable enzymes that transmit nerve impulses, the incapacitating effects of which are felt within ten minutes. Death invariably occurs within fifteen minutes unless VX is used, which has a longer mortality (and suffering) time line of four to forty-two hours.[86]

These agents can be dispersed as liquids, vapors, gases, and aerosols; however, the effectiveness of the attack can be compromised by the method of dispersal, which is closely linked to the chemical used. In the case of munitions, the explosive device must be constructed such that it does not destroy the chemical intended for deployment. In the case of sprayers or liquid dispersal, the delivery media must be carefully measured such that it does not dilute the chemical to the point of impotence. Scientific and engineering accuracy are the keys to success.

Chemical weapons were used by both sides in the Iran-Iraq War from 1980 to 1988, and Saddam Hussein used them to devastating effect against his own countrymen to put down the 1987–88 Kurdish rebellion in the north. However, Iraq did not employ them against American-led coalition forces or against Israeli SCUD rocket targets during the Gulf War in 1991, largely in response to a specific threat by the United States that such an attack would be met with an overwhelming nuclear response. Prior to the recent regime change in Iraq, Iraq and Iran continued to have an antagonistic relationship; thus, they continued to manufacture and stockpile chemical weapons despite negative international pressure (and UN Security Council prohibition in the case of Iraq) due to strategic concerns vis-à-vis each other.[87]

Sarin gas was the weapon used by the apocalyptic Aum Shinrikyo religious/terrorist group in its 1995 attack on the subway system in Tokyo. The cult's followers carried frozen packets of sarin onto the trains during the morning rush hour, poked holes into the packets with sharpened umbrella tips, and then exited the subway as the packets began to thaw and poison the commuters. Over five thousand people were injured by the nerve agent, and eleven people who were in closest proximity to the exposure died. The Tokyo attack followed an earlier sarin attack that year on the Japanese city of Matsumoto, about one hundred miles north, where seven people were killed and six hundred sickened.[88]

This was the culmination of the group's ineffective attempts during the prior five years to use biological weapons. Technical difficulties controlling the strain and the dissemination method led to repeated failures. Aum Shinrikyo also tried but failed to obtain usable nuclear weapons. Consequently, chemical weapons were the third and last choice of WMD that the group finally used with limited success. Had the group been able to use a purer form of sarin and a more effective, focused delivery device, the 1995 attacks would have been far worse. Consequently, while the failures of the group are instructive, its "success" supports the theory that such organizations may continue to acquire WMD and that WMD usage is no longer limited to governments and militaries.[89]

So how is this material controlled so it will not fall into the hands of such organizations? The Chemical Weapons Convention (CWC), formally adhered to by 143 nations but not always in practice, prohibits the production, testing, and use of chemical weapons and is designed to eliminate already existing stockpiles—mostly through incineration. The United States joined the CWC with its ratification in 1997. Through inspections and supervision, the Organization for the Prohibition of Chemical Weapons (OPCW) deploys more than two hundred experts to accomplish its task.[90]

Battlefield evidence gathered by American forces in Afghanistan, however, indicates that al Qaeda had some chemical weapon capability and was working on perfecting and expanding that capability.[91] This raises the question of where such organizations can obtain this material. If the CWC is working, then terrorist groups should not be able to acquire it. Actually, the CWC is not working all that well.

The OPCW has been underfunded since its inception, forcing them to cut back from 98 to only 42 military inspections and from 132 to only 61 industry inspections in 2001. Key countries with known or suspected stockpiles and delivery capability, but questionable security, either have not joined the CWC, as in the case of Egypt, Syria, Iraq, North Korea, and Lebanon, or have signed but not ratified the treaty, as in the case of Israel and Libya.[92] But even for those that sign or ratify the treaty, compliance is often not a high priority—as is the case with Russia.

Russia solemnly pledged in the spring of 2001 to begin destroying forty thousand tons of lethal chemical weapons from its massive stockpile (the largest in the world) at three new destruction plants designed for that purpose. After more than a year of noncompliance and dithering, Russia still had forty thousand tons of chemical weapons on its hands. By the summer of 2002, the Group of Eight industrialized nations agreed to match the $10 billion earmarked earlier by the United States to speed the process along.[93]

But even if terrorists cannot get the chemical materials they need from "leaky" states like Russia or one of the former Soviet republics that inherited abandoned testing, storage, and production facilities and that continue to worry the West, they can take advantage of sitting ducks. By targeting a chemical processing facility close to a population—850,000 dot the American landscape and thousands more are scattered across Canada and Europe—when it happens to be running a particularly lethal and explosively gaseous substance, the terrorists' job is made all the easier.[94]

For example, the 1984 accident at the Union Carbide plant in Bhopal, India, killed seven thousand people when cyanide was leaked into the surrounding community.[95] And that was only an accident. Clearly, security must become a top priority at private industrial facilities. Otherwise, terrorists seeking to employ chemical agents in their destructive plans may be able to avail themselves

of both the lethal substance and the delivery device simultaneously—without spending vast sums of money on scientific or engineering know-how, chemical acquisition, storage, or transportation.

Nuclear Weapons

At an undisclosed location near Kabul, on a cold November night
with the sound of antiaircraft guns booming in the distance, Osama
bin Laden confided to Hamid Mir, editor of the Urdu newspaper
Ausaf, during an interview that "we have chemical and nuclear
weapons as a deterrent and if America used them against us, we
reserve the right to use them." The White House responded that
they took this threat seriously.[96] To date, nuclear weapons have not
been utilized by the United States or al Qaeda. Nonetheless, shortly
after September 11, the United States rerouted low-altitude planes
around nuclear facilities and the National Guard was activated to
protect them. European countries also secured their nuclear arse-
nals and power stations, some such as France and Hungary posi-
tioning surface-to-air missiles near them.[97] So far all is quiet.

Indeed, nuclear weapons have not been successfully employed
by a state or substate group since the United States dropped two
atomic bombs on Japan to end the Pacific conflict and World War II.
Not even the recent dust-up between India and Pakistan that took
those rival nations to the nuclear brink over the disputed province
of Kashmir resulted in the use of these weapons. It is the finality of
a nuclear explosion that causes one to pause and think before
employing it as a weapon. As technology progressed from atom to
hydrogen to plutonium to neutron bombs, the devastative capacity
of nuclear weapons increased exponentially. Consequently, their
use by rational actors remains a remote possibility, while simultaneously their acquisition remains a priority for security and status
reasons.

Most states are rational actors, influenced by such notions. But
are terrorists rational actors? It is impossible to answer that question. Thus, states conservatively must assume the worst—that they
are not and that if they obtain the technology they will use it. The
threat derived from terrorist nuclear capacity is of two types. First is
the extremely unlikely, but far more devastating possibility of a ter-

rorist successfully detonating a nuclear weapon. Second is the more likely, but less destructive radiological attack—exploding a conventional bomb laced with radioactive material (known as a dirty bomb) or sabotaging a nuclear facility. In either case, the nuclear avenue of attack was reluctantly admitted by Office of Homeland Security director Tom Ridge to be the most worrisome of all the WMD options.[98]

As for the first type of threat, there are only eight countries known to have nuclear weapons: Russia, America, China, Britain, France, Pakistan, India, and Israel—all of which have supported America's war on terrorism after the September 11 attacks. However, despite assurances to the contrary and the existence of the Nuclear Non-Proliferation Treaty, there is worry that one of the world's twenty-five thousand nuclear warheads could find its way into the wrong hands. And it only takes one. Russia and Pakistan have the poorest records in this regard.

Russia currently maintains the largest nuclear arsenal—fifteen thousand warheads (both strategic and tactical). A recent treaty with the United States commits Russia to reduce its strategic missile-tipped arsenal by about thirty-eight hundred, still leaving it in charge of the largest stockpile of nuclear material. But the caretaker of this heavy responsibility has been described as a country with "sloppy accounting, a disgruntled military, an audacious black market and indigenous terrorists." All of the high-profile arrests in Munich, St. Petersburg, Vienna, and Prague during the early 1990s were of smugglers attempting to escape with Russian nuclear material. But as one official of the International Atomic Energy Agency (IAEA), which tracks these arrests, noted, "Are we seeing half the iceberg or only the tip?" For comparison, drug enforcement officers only consider their police seizures to represent 10–20 percent of what is actually shipped.[99]

Since European controls have tightened, Turkey has emerged as the favorite route for smugglers to get nuclear material out of Russia. In the last eight years, Turkey has intercepted 104 attempts to smuggle mostly uranium, but sometimes plutonium (non–weapons grade), across its frontier. The country is slightly bigger than Texas and has 120 border posts that include crossings to neighboring Iraq and Syria in the south, Bulgaria in the north, and Iran, Georgia, and Armenia in the east. Only two of those posts are outfitted with radioactive detection devices—both donated by the United States.[100] Thus, Russia continues to leak nuclear material; it is just the direction that has changed. According to the Department of Energy, after ten years and millions of dollars in American subsidies, only 41 percent of Russia's weapon-usable nuclear material has been secured.[101]

Pakistan, which built its own nuclear weapons program by using the black market to obtain expertise and material, is the other member of the nuclear club that presents some worry. However, Pakistan stores its nuclear weapons disassembled in different locations; so a smuggler would typically only be able to obtain several parts at a time. Even so, the close relationship between members of the Pakistani military, government, and nuclear research division and elements of the Taliban and al Qaeda give the West reason to worry. Pakistan, however, remains reluctant to accept security assistance from the West, as Russia has done, for fear that India would learn its nuclear secrets. But while the Pakistani option remains a largely unexplored one, the small size of its nuclear program (only twenty-five to forty weapons) means that there is less material available.[102]

Assuming terrorists did manage to secure a nuclear weapon, the technological hurdles they would face to cause a detonation are considerable. American warheads are rigged with multiple permissive action links, which are codes and self-disabling devices meant to keep an unauthorized person from detonating the warhead. Russian weapons are similarly rigged. General Eugene Habiger, formerly in charge of the American strategic weapons unit, explained that a terrorist would have to take the weapon apart to make it work, and the failsafes are so complex that it would be easier to extract the plutonium or enriched uranium from the core and build an entirely new weapon.[103]

This is reassuring in the context of the big strategic weapons, but how about the smaller tactical weapons—nuclear torpedoes, depth charges, mines, and artillery shells? Their antiuse devices are less sophisticated because these weapons are meant to be used on the battlefield—and the older tactical weapons have no such devices. That element, coupled with their smaller size, greater number, and lack of coverage by a formal treaty regime (which means they are not counted or inspected), as opposed to their larger strategic cousins, makes them prime targets for theft. Consequently, we must rely on the inherently unreliable border, surveillance, and facility security.

Beyond ready-made weapons, the second option for a terrorist seeking to employ a nuclear method of attack is radiological dispersion using a dirty bomb—which is actually not a nuclear bomb at all. Rather, it is a conventional bomb made of traditionally widely available explosives (TNT, fertilizer, plastique, etc.) and laced with radioactive material, which is equally abundant. Three types of such elements—cobalt-60, americium, and cesium-137—are commonly used in food processing to kill bacteria, in hospitals for medial gauges and radiotherapy machines, and in items such as smoke detectors and equipment for oil prospecting, in addition to the many academic and industrial research laboratories across the country.[104]

This solves the problem of terrorists having to import their tools of destruction. They can simply find them in the United States. The Nuclear Regulatory Commission (NRC) reported in 2002 that U.S. business, industrial, and medical facilities lost track of almost 1,500 pieces of radioactive equipment since 1996. Of this, about 660, or 44 percent, had been recovered, but the rest remain "missing." Penalties and fines have been issued against some of the institutions, very little of which has been collected. Similarly, a 1995 Department of Energy inventory determined that "tens of thousands" of the agency's radioactive elements could not be accounted for. Many of the items are thought to have ended up in dumps and scrap yards—posing additional contamination risks to workers there.[105]

The actual disaster following detonation of a dirty bomb would flow not from the explosion itself, which would kill hundreds, or from the radiation that ensued, which would contaminate hundreds more, but from the mass panic that would result. A report issued by the Center for Strategic and International Studies (CSIS) for the Metropolitan Washington Council of Governments found that a four-thousand-pound dirty truck bomb detonated on Washington, D.C.'s National Mall in a bus would contaminate about 20 percent of downtown but would present a long-term risk of increased cancer or cataract rates in people exposed only a few blocks around the blast site.[106]

However, the psychological effect on the surrounding population would be catastrophic. The responses elicited by a group from local government and emergency response workers at a workshop indicated that a dangerous spontaneous mass evacuation of the Virginia–D.C.–Maryland metro area could not be contained. The report said that "the presence of radioactivity was an issue that the participants were clearly not prepared to deal with." Unlike their local counterparts, federal authorities have taken some preventative action, deploying radiation sensors around the capital, placing a commando unit on standby, and testing various delivery scenarios using boats on the Potomac River and trucks on Interstate 95.[107]

Poorly guarded nuclear waste at weapons facilities and power plants also poses tempting targets for terrorists to exploit in their search for radiologic material. Moreover, if acquisition, stabilization, transport, and detonation present insurmountable technical or logistical problems for the terrorist group, then it has the same option that the terrorist group seeking to utilize chemical weapons has—bypass those issues by exploiting an already existing nuclear facility located near a population center. The Three Mile Island meltdown of 1979 in Pennsylvania demonstrated the panic scenario that would ensue if a reactor were attacked, regardless of success. And the Chernobyl meltdown in the Ukraine graphically demonstrated the contaminative capacity that poorly contained radiologic material has if such an attack were indeed a success.

Internationally, although the IAEA attempts to coordinate threat assessment and security, it is ultimately up to each country to determine its own security needs. Even transnational shipping could be a target. For example, in July 2002, a ship set sail from the Japanese port of Takahama with 550 pounds of almost weapons-grade plutonium for reprocessing in Britain—an eighteen-thousand-mile voyage. It relied for security on several deck-mounted 30-millimeter guns manned by a crew of thirteen British officers employed by the U.K. Atomic Energy Authority Constabulary and on a second vessel similarly outfitted. There was neither official naval escort, as was common practice in the 1980s, nor radar-controlled defenses to guard them from attack by small aircraft or fast boats.[108] No international legal regime is currently in place to require further security measures.

Domestically, America's 103 nuclear power stations are supervised by the NRC. However, for the most part they are on their own to hire private security. Disturbingly, many nuclear facilities routinely fail security breach scenarios designed by the NRC to weigh in favor of defense. In these mock drills, typically only three assailants are allowed with one person working inside, and any variation from the rules, such as improvising the use of a wheelbarrow to cart off material, while successful, disqualifies the study. Some plants even have a less than 50 percent success rate of withstanding a breach in security by ground agents. This does not take into account the lax security under the Department of Energy at the nation's ten nuclear weapons research facilities or the horrific potential of a plane crashing into such a facility or plant—a scenario for which no drill exists.[109]

To counter the effects of a meltdown resulting from an attack, the NRC has offered free potassium iodide pills to thirty-four states that have populations living within ten miles of nuclear power plants. Thirteen have accepted. The pills are to be distributed at homes, schools, and workplaces because immediate administration is critical; however, people are only supposed to be instructed to take the pills if health authorities predict that radiologic exposure is high enough to destroy their thyroid.[110] But not all of the government responses have been adequate or permanent.

In the spring of 2002, the secretary of energy requested $397.7 million to increase security guarding the nation's nuclear weapons, materials, and radioactive waste—as he put it in his letter, "a critical down payment to the safety and security of our nation and its people." However, the White House's Office of Management and Budget cut that request by 93 percent (only $26.4 million) when the executive's budget was sent to Congress.[111] Moreover, temporary measures implemented in the aftermath of 9/11, such as rerouting flight paths around nuclear facilities and placing police and National Guard units at those sites, are expiring. As the extra measures disappear, none has emerged on the horizon to replace them, despite the suggestion from some experts to federalize nuclear plant security forces.[112] Perhaps the new Department of Homeland Security will provide new measures, but until that happens a critical gap in coverage now exists.

Cyberterrorism: The Twenty-first-Century Threat

In August 1999 the Center for Study of Terrorism and Irregular Warfare issued a detailed report analyzing the threat of cyberterrorism. Based upon its analysis, the center concluded that "the barrier to entry for anything beyond annoying hacks is quite high, and that terrorists generally lack the wherewithal and human capital to mount a meaningful operation." The report effectively dismissed cyberterrorism as a real threat, noting that it was a prospect far into the future, although it could be used as an ancillary tool to other physical attacks. Fast-forward to June 2002. The FBI began examining a suspicious pattern of surveillance emanating from the Middle East and South Asia exploring digital systems used to manage Bay Area utilities and government offices. Upon further investigation, the FBI learned that these activities were part of a much larger reconnaissance effort and eventually traced multiple instances of Internet Web browsers routed through Saudi Arabia, Indonesia, and Pakistan, apparently studying emergency telephone systems, electrical generation and transmission, water storage distribution, nuclear power plants, and gas facilities.[113] Thus, where cyberterrorism is concerned, *the future is now,* and, indeed, some government experts have concluded that "terrorists are at the threshold of using the Internet as a direct instrument of bloodshed."[114]

What Is Cyberterrorism?

According to Professor Dorothy Denning, cyberterrorism is

> the convergence of terrorism and cyberspace . . . [and] is generally understood to mean unlawful attacks and threats of attack against computers, networks, and the information stored therein when done to intimidate or coerce a government or its people in furtherance of political or social objectives. Further, to qualify as cyberterrorism, an attack should result in violence against persons or property, or at least cause enough harm to generate fear.[115]

To illustrate her point, Denning further circumscribes the categories of violence against persons or property necessary to rise to the level of a cyberterrorism attack. For example, terrorists gaining access to and tampering with an air traffic control system resulting in a plane crash would be deemed cyberterrorists, as opposed to those disrupting nonessential services, such as defacing a corporate Web page, which results in little more than a costly nuisance to the company involved.

Ironically, the type of cyberterrorism described by Denning is an emerging threat precisely because the global digital revolution has achieved unparalleled success in bringing the world closer together politically, socially, and economically. High-technology tools and services such as the Internet, e-mail, and e-commerce enable people to communicate and transact business across global boundaries, often with the simple click of a button. Thus, while the advent of the technological revolution has been a boon to worldwide social and economic development, it is also very susceptible to manipulation by criminals, who can quickly and effortlessly research and perpetrate harmful deeds across the communications infrastructure. As might be expected, the vulnerabilities inherent in this immensely complex global interconnection of networks have not escaped notice by those bent on exploiting technology for their own terroristic objectives. Indeed, "[t]here is no shortage of terrorist recipes on the Internet . . . [and] step-by-step cookbooks for . . . cyberterrorists."[116]

Consequently, if technologically open societies such as the United States do not take steps now to address this nontraditional threat, which analysts have termed "information warfare," then they could be confronted with cyberterrorism on the scale of an "electronic Pearl Harbor" in the immediate future.[117] Although the United States has yet to experience cyberterrorism on a widespread basis, there are certainly telltale signs that such destructive behavior could be in the offing. Unfortunately, there are also indications that many private and government entities would be ill-prepared to contend with such an eventuality. Consider the following documented cases of cyberterrorism around the globe:

- In the spring of 1999, during the Kosovo conflict, "hactivists" protesting the NATO bombings deluged NATO's computers with "ping attacks," which effectively occupied their computers with a flood of requests and denied service to others seeking legitimate access to the NATO Web site.
- In February 1998 an Israeli hacker, Ehud Tenebaum (aka "The Analyzer"), in collaboration with two California

youths, launched attacks against Pentagon systems, the NSA, and a nuclear research lab. Their handiwork successfully disrupted troop deployments to the Persian Gulf, leading Deputy Secretary of Defense John Hamre to conclude that the cyberterrorists executed "the most organized and systematic attack on U.S. defense systems ever detected."[118]

- Also in 1998 ethnic Tamil guerillas inundated Sri Lankan embassies with eight thousand e-mail messages a day for two weeks, with statements that read, "We are the Internet Black Tigers and we're doing this to disrupt your communications."

- In March 2000, the Japanese Metropolitan Police Department unwittingly procured a software system from the Aum Shinrikyo cult, which was responsible for releasing the deadly sarin gas in the Tokyo subway five years earlier that killed twelve people and injured six thousand more. The software was used to gather classified tracking information on police vehicles, including unmarked cars.

In the United States, according to various reports, almost every Fortune 500 company has experienced at least one unauthorized digital intrusion, many resulting in the theft of data, with an estimated cost of $10 billion per year to companies and consumers. Unwilling to shatter consumer confidence in technology and concerned about potential liability to shareholders, many companies intentionally forego reporting these intrusions and instead choose to silently enhance their security systems, accepting any financial losses as a cost of doing business in this age of technology. Similarly, on the governmental front, tens of thousands of probing attacks are launched against Pentagon systems every year, and information warfare specialists at the Pentagon estimate that a "properly prepared and well-coordinated attack by fewer than thirty computer virtuosos strategically located around the world, with a budget of less than $10 million, could bring the United States to its knees."[119] In fact, there is already some evidence that technology infrastructure attacks apparently originating in countries hostile to United States have been perpetrated against critical government hardware and software systems.

In 1996 the Defense Science Board, in a document entitled "Report of the Defense Science Board Task Force on Information Warfare," identified one of the key impediments to fighting the battle against cyberterrorism:

> Within this rapidly changing, globally interconnected environment of telecomputing activities it is not possible for a person to identify positively who is interconnected with him or her or know the exact path a message and voice traffic takes as it transits the telecommunications "cloud." It is not possible to know . . . how the various software components . . . interact together [or] . . . if the various components installed in computer hardware only do what is asked of them. . . . In sum, we have built our economy and our military on a technology foundation that we do not control and which, at least at the fine detail level, we do not understand.[120]

The task force report also observed that the United States is an information and information systems society, with interconnected and interdependent systems and networks that form the foundation for critical economic, diplomatic, and military functions.

In addition to the exposure occasioned by the interconnection of vital systems, three additional factors exponentially increase the vulnerability of U.S. systems: globalization, which encourages worldwide information exchange and interdependence; standardization, which, although cost-effective, standardizes vulnerabilities across the spectrum; and regulation/deregulation, which often mandates open network architectures, thereby increasing possible points of access to critical infrastructure systems. Taken together, all of these seemingly innocuous features make the United States one of the most vulnerable nations to a variety of cyberattacks, ranging from rogue hackers for hire to state-sponsored attempts designed to gain economic, diplomatic, or military advantages.

According to the Defense Science Board, the overall risk of such an attack upon the U.S. information infrastructure is considerable and best captured in the following equation:

$$\text{Risk} = \frac{\text{Threat} * \text{Vulnerabilities}}{\text{Countermeasures}} * \text{Impact}$$

The threat is very high, as evidenced by persistent probes and attacks against critical governmental systems. The success of many of these attacks indicates that the vulnerabilities are numerous and are a function of the interconnected and interdependent network infrastructure. Although America is lumbering toward designing and implementing solutions to its technology security conundrum, current countermeasures are woefully inadequate to respond to the potentially overwhelming cyberterrorism threat. Consequently, the impact of a targeted attack on America would be catastrophic, prompting the overall conclusion that America is confronting a vast, and potentially deadly, risk that critical infrastructure systems could be devastated and rendered inoperable unless effective countermeasures are initiated and executed posthaste.

What Is Information Warfare?

Even before the digital revolution, information was a choice commodity in the sense that its creation and exchange were essential to building bridges of communication between families, communities, states, and nations. Because the means to convey information in an open society are almost always universally available, they are often taken for granted, and it is generally expected that such capabilities will be reliable and regularly accessible. In other words, whether consciously or not, the United States is a society that depends heavily upon the ability to receive and convey information across the communications infrastructure.

Information warfare takes advantage of this inherent dependency and "is attractive to many because it is cheap in relation to the cost of developing, maintaining, and using advanced military capabilities."[121] Indeed, potential terrorists can utilize the vast and readily available information resources to "suborn an insider, create false information, manipulate information, or launch malicious logic-based weapons against an information system connected to the globally shared telecommunications infrastructure."[122] For example, many Web sites today offer detailed information concerning governmental and corporate structures and systems. Often these data are provided in digital form to enhance the government-citizen and corporate-consumer relationships by maximizing the flow of critical information, while simultaneously lowering the costs of providing such information on an individual basis. But just as this glut of information is readily available to those with benign purposes, it is also easily co-opted by those with criminal intentions. In fact, investigators found that one al Qaeda laptop discovered in Afghanistan had repeatedly visited a French Web site run by the Societé Anonyme, which advertised a two-volume on-line "Sabotage Handbook" complete with tips on planning a digital "hit," computer switch gear, and implementation and antisurveillance methods.

State-of-the-art encryption technology also makes it easier for terrorists to conspire and plan their attacks across international boundaries with little or no detection. For example, Ramzi Yousef, who is currently serving a life sentence for the first WTC bombing, is said to have used his computer to develop and secretly communicate with others concerning a plot to destroy at least a dozen American airlines over the Pacific Ocean. Likewise, it is commonly acknowledged that Osama bin Laden's al Qaeda network frequently uses sophisticated technology devices, such as satellite uplinks and cryptography, to plan and perpetrate their terrorist activities across the globe.

Although information warfare generally connotes using information to one's tactical advantage, the ease of access to information and the means of communication can also facilitate information warfare attacks on the infrastructure itself. Such attacks may arise from within or without the communication network, ranging from physically destroying the system to rendering it useless by disrupting or denying legitimate access. Moreover, depending upon the magnitude, an infrastructure assault may result in the loss of sensitive or critical information or services. In these instances, while the cyberterrorism activities may not directly harm anyone, they might well be a supplemental aspect of a much broader attack. Terrorists might, for example, use information warfare to disrupt or disable a 911 emergency system in conjunction with a traditional bombing assault.

Regarding the tools of the trade necessary for information warfare, cyberterrorists utilize a variety of technology weapons (all readily available on the Internet) to accomplish destructive acts, including Trojan horses, viruses, worms, and denial of service attacks. Such nontraditional weapons and methods of attack are uniquely appealing to the terrorist mentality because individuals and groups can effectively challenge the defensive capabilities of more powerful countries without physically crossing sovereign borders or owning a single traditional warfare weapon. In that sense, information warfare might be considered the "great equalizer."

Like most modern-day terrorist attacks, information warfare designed to further violent agendas is unlikely to be haphazardly planned and carried out. Instead, to maximize harm and increase fear, true cyberterrorism is usually the manifestation of well-organized planning against strategically selected targets. Because the intent is to inflict considerable physical or psychological damage, such attacks are generally leveled against high-profile infrastructure apparatuses. Such detailed planning and implementation, expressly designed to increase the magnitude of harm, is typically referred to as strategic information warfare and is distinguished by the fact that terrorists elect to tactically use information warfare over an extended period of time to accomplish a very specific set of goals. According to a CSIS task force report entitled "Cybercrime, Cyberterrorism, Cyberwarfare: Averting an Electronic Waterloo," strategic information warfare adds a modern gloss on the historical notion of strategic warfare, which "deduced that it was often more effective to attack an opponent's factories, cities and transportation centers, than to defeat its armies on the battlefield." Moreover, "strategic information warfare offers the ability to target an opponent's information infrastructure directly in order to achieve a decisive victory or competitive edge. . . . Strategic information targets are . . . selected for their ability to cause the systematic collapse of an opponent's capabilities and ability to resist."[123]

For example, one implementation of strategic information warfare might utilize sophisticated technology to surreptitiously evade trade embargoes and sanctions imposed upon disfavored countries. That is, in an effort to skirt the restrictions, a country might develop and implement software to infiltrate banking systems worldwide, skimming money over time from targeted accounts. The purloined funds could then be used to sustain the embargoed government and build its military arsenal, possibly including the acquisition of biological or chemical weapons and technology.[124] In other iterations, terrorist organizations determined to embarrass corporate elitists while simultaneously broadcasting the group's propaganda message to a worldwide audience might deface an e-commerce Web site, causing economic loss to the company arising from the inability to receive and process orders as well as reputational loss from the apparent security system breach that permitted the Web site vandalism. Finally, strategic information warfare might be executed to alter the strategic balance in an ongoing conflict. "A determined adversary could undertake a comprehensive, systematic effort to undermine U.S. military forces by compromising the commercial technologies and services that support them. Such an adversary could be ambitious and aim at nothing less than changing the strategic balance."[125]

Defending against Information Warfare

Mounting an effective defense to information warfare is a particularly daunting task because the apparatuses to carry it out are already widely available, and, indeed, many of the tools are employed daily for entirely legitimate purposes. In addition, these technology devices can be easily manipulated to perpetrate hostile attacks while leaving very little in the way of "fingerprints" to detect the origin of the attack and the responsible parties. For example, in many denial of service attacks, the individual originating the attack usually "spoofs" the source of the intrusion, giving the appearance that it was initiated in a different location. Therefore, because knowledge truly is power in the digital age, the first step in any defense planning against information warfare is educating the public about the very real dangers that exist with these new technology weapons. Although this seems a straightforward solution, observers speculate that the biggest obstacle to averting information warfare will be actually convincing individuals, governments, and industries to examine critical functions and processes with an eye toward securing them against information warfare attacks. Current practices in each of these segments virtually invite attacks due to

> poorly designed software applications; the use of overly complex and inherently unsecure computer operating systems; the lack of training and tools for monitoring and managing the

telecomputing environment; the promiscuous inter-networking of computers creating the potential for proliferating failure modes; the inadequate training of information workers; and the lack of robust processes for identification of system components.[126]

In its task force report, the CSIS recommended that, after explaining the threat in terms that clearly articulate and emphasize its seriousness, the United States should develop national security policies designed to address the unique systemic vulnerabilities that arise from an interconnected and interdependent network infrastructure. According to the CSIS, this national policy should take the form of an executive order that precisely characterizes the nature and likelihood of strategic information warfare and that requires

a top-down review of existing [governmental] organizations assigned responsibilities related to [information warfare], information security, security policy, and cybercrime. The review should result in recommendations ensuring that organizations' roles are consistent, do not overlap, and do not leave gaps and specifying how and under what conditions they will interface with each other.[127]

The CSIS also recommended that incentives be offered to the private sector to encourage the development and implementation of measures that improve security against strategic information warfare and simultaneously provide a benefit to the global networked community.

Finally, U.S. military and intelligence policies must now be refocused on the new threat of strategic information warfare. Because America's military and intelligence strategies have historically been oriented toward traditional weapons of war, the new focus must take into account that the modern threat will likely be launched over buried fiber-optic cables rather than experienced as land- or sea-based assaults. This revamping will require additional personnel with the requisite technical expertise, as well as significant collaboration with the private sector, whose participation will be critical to the creation and coordination of a national defensive approach to protect against strategic information warfare.

Congressional initiatives will also play an instrumental role in the battle against cyberterrorism, and, indeed, Congress has already acknowledged its responsibility to establish laws that take a proactive approach to this innovative form of terrorism. For instance, in January 2002, Senator John Edwards introduced two pieces of legislation designed to increase security and overall protection for the U.S. technology infrastructure. The Cyberterrorism Preparedness Act of 2002 would create a nonprofit consortium of academic and private sector experts to establish a set of "best practices" for the technology industry in an effort to effectively guard against cyberterrorism. According to the proposed legislation, *best practice* means

a computer hardware or software configuration, information system design, operational procedure, or measure, structure, or method that most effectively protects computer hardware, software, network, or network elements against an attack that would cause harm through the installation of unauthorized computer software, saturation of network traffic, alteration of data, disclosure of confidential information, or other means.[128]

Contemplating that government implementation of best practices security systems will be the archetype for private industry and citizens alike, the act proposes that, after an initial assessment period, a report be created that identifies appropriate cybersecurity best practices that are reasonably susceptible to adoption by departments and agencies of the federal government over a two-year period. Such practices must permit customization or expansion of hardware, software, and network infrastructure, while taking into account the risk and magnitude of harm threatened by potential attack, the cost of imposing security protection, and the rapidly changing nature of the technology. Based upon that report, demonstration projects will be initiated to test the efficacy of the practices, and those deemed "security-enhancing, missions-compatible and cost-effective" will be implemented by the government forthwith. A separate but related bill, the Cybersecurity Research and Education Act of 2002, contemplates funding new Information Assurance fellowships to attract and train more researchers and teachers of cybersecurity.

On the international front, a draft report by NATO's Science and

Technology Committee entitled "Information Warfare and International Security" recommends that, due to the open and global nature of the Internet, laws regulating infrastructure protection and security should involve computer security experts and legislators internationally. The report also stresses the need for a symbiotic relationship between public and private entities because "[o]ften the private sector can better identify, understand and evaluate threats" and the exchange of information could be instrumental in detecting and preventing attacks on the infrastructure. Finally, the report raises a number of perplexing questions concerning the future impact of information technology on existing weapons systems, military organization, and strategy. For example, would it be possible to respond to an attack upon critical information systems with conventional forces and weaponry? Also, under what circumstances could a country deploy "offensive information warfare?"[129]

Ironically, during the Clinton administration, two Pentagon leaders proposed an "aggressive campaign of covert action against financial accounts and centers owned by al Qaeda." This clandestine operation called for U.S. operatives to acquire the necessary authentication to make valid withdrawals from terrorists' accounts, potentially "raining electronic havoc on a business or financial institution as a whole." However, then Treasury Secretary Robert Rubin vociferously opposed the plan, arguing that "as the world's preeminent financial center . . . the United States has the strongest interest in maintaining a global norm that cyberattacks on banking systems are acts of war. The United States could not defend that principle if it engaged in such attacks, and its own vulnerabilities would be substantial."[130]

In the short term, the threat of strategic information warfare as the preferred method of facelessly engaging and potentially destroying the enemy in modern times raises one key question for the United States: "Should [we] invest [our] shrinking defense dollars exclusively in additional fighter-bombers, carrier battle groups, and 70-ton tanks if the nation's most pressing vulnerabilities lie in its commercial information systems?"[131] Whether the United States can successfully defend against strategic information warfare depends upon its ability to spread the message that the threat exists and to marshal resources nationally and internationally to develop cost-effective polices to protect national security. Until then, the risk persists and evolves in dangerous lockstep with the global digital revolution.

The Continuing al Qaeda Threat

It remains unclear as of this writing, two years after the September 11 attacks, whether Osama bin Laden is dead or alive. He has not been apprehended. Mullah Omar, the former leader of the Taliban, has also escaped capture. However, after the decisive defeat of his forces by the coalition of Northern Alliance, American, and British troops and the evaporation of his Taliban during the Afghan campaign, he no longer poses the continuing threat to the United States that the remnants of the al Qaeda terrorist network do.

Although al Qaeda's headquarters and training camps have been destroyed and many of their top- and mid-level leaders captured, the group is still very active and carrying out terrorist strikes, reorganizing cells in the West and Middle East, and even negotiating new contacts with other terrorist organizations such as Lebanese-based, mostly Shiite Hezbollah. The Bush administration recognizes this continuing threat.[132]

Almost one thousand al Qaeda operatives have been arrested in sixty countries around the world, seriously disrupting its network; however, the threat continues. In testimony before Congress, CIA director George Tenet warned that "[o]perations against U.S. targets could be launched by al Qaeda cells already in place in major cities in Europe and the Middle East. Al Qaeda can also exploit its presence or connections to other groups in such countries as Somalia, Yemen, Indonesia and the Philippines. I must repeat that al Qaeda has not yet been destroyed."[133]

Nor are the various components of al Qaeda and their allies completely isolated incommunicado. They make use of a Codan radio network, like that used by UN and foreign aid workers in remote places. The recount of how an American rocket attack against al Qaeda forces in 2001 failed illustrates this radio network's importance:

One night at the end of October, Osama bin Laden and 120 bodyguards came to spend the night at the camp of Beni

Hissar, near Kabul. He told the camp boss that he would leave at eight the next morning. But he got up at five, prayed and then left. After that, everyone else was ordered out on the news that a missile attack was imminent. The rockets struck at eight. Since missile strikes happen with little or no warning, Mr. bin Laden evidently has some very reliable sources of information. The best of these, operated by his legion of foreign supporters, is linked by a sophisticated Codan radio network. . . . Arab and Afghan residents of Beni Hissar were given frequent warnings, via this network, of possible strikes by aircraft.[134]

Domestically, al Qaeda remains a threat as well. According to Attorney General Ashcroft, al Qaeda operatives posing as tourists, businessmen, and students are actively attempting to penetrate our borders. This is in addition to the already present "sleeper" cells that are plotting future attacks. Ashcroft explains:

Today the United States is at war with a terrorist network operating within our borders. Al Qaeda maintains a hidden but active presence in the United States waiting to strike again. . . . There remain sleeper terrorists and their supporters within the United States who have not yet been identified in a way that will allow us to take pre-emptive action against them.

Federal officials say that many of these people are to be found in large cities, using the local Muslim community for support, to recruit sympathizers, and for cover.[135]

Table 1 illustrates foiled al Qaeda or al Qaeda–sponsored missions undertaken after September 11. Thus, we are faced with an enemy that not only continues to haunt us in our darkest nightmares but also continues to manifest itself through violent acts against civilians. The fluidity of its actions, flexibility of its remaining organization, secrecy of its planning and operations, and boldness of its deadly strikes make al Qaeda one of the toughest adversaries this country has faced. Nonetheless, it is, like every other adversary, defeatable in the end.

While America must reorganize its government, retool its mili-

TABLE 1. Foiled al Qaeda or al Qaeda–Sponsored Missions after September 11, 2001

Sept. 13, 2001	A Frenchman of Algerian background arrested in Paris said he had been part of a plot by Osama bin Laden to destroy the U.S. Embassy in Paris.
December	A Sudanese man with possible links to al Qaeda fired a Stinger missile at a U.S. warplane near Prince Sultan Air Base in Saudi Arabia.
December	Authorities in Singapore arrested thirteen suspected al Qaeda operatives and said they were part of a sleeper cell preparing to blow up several embassies.
December 22	Passengers and crew aboard an American Airlines flight from Paris to Miami subdued Richard C. Reid, who had the explosive C-4 in his shoes. Reid was linked by French authorities to Zacarias Moussaoui and al Qaeda.
January 2002	*Wall Street Journal* reporter Daniel Pearl was killed by Islamic militants, who kidnapped him in Karachi, Pakistan. The architect of the plan, Ahmad Omar Saeed Sheikh, has been linked to al Qaeda. He was arrested by Pakistani police, tried for the murder, and sentenced to death.
January	U.S. and Bosnian intelligence agencies captured an al Qaeda suspect who had planned attacks on U.S. bases, including Eagle Base outside Sarajevo.
February 20	The Italian police arrested four Moroccans with nine pounds of cyanide and a map pinpointing the location of the water pipes that lead to the U.S. Embassy in Rome.
March 17	Five worshipers, including an American embassy employee and her daughter, were killed when a man detonated a bomb in a Protestant church in Islamabad, Pakistan.
April 1	Seventeen people, including twelve German tourists, were killed in a synagogue bombing in Djerba, Tunisia. German and French investigators blamed al Qaeda, a spokesman for which, Sulaiman bu Ghaith, later claimed responsibility.
May 8	U.S. authorities arrested Jose Padilla, an American citizen who had trained in al Qaeda camps, as he traveled from Pakistan to the United States. Officials said he planned to detonate a radioactive bomb in the United States.
May 8	A Toyota Corolla exploded outside the Sheraton Hotel in Karachi, killing fourteen people, including eleven French citizens. French officials were "80 percent" certain al Qaeda was behind the attack.
June 11	Moroccan authorities announced they had broken up an al Qaeda cell that was planning to target NATO ships in the Strait of Gibraltar.
June 14	A vehicle loaded with explosives crashed into a guard post outside the U.S. Consulate in Karachi, killing eleven people and wounding twenty-six. American and Pakistani officials have yet to draw an al Qaeda connection, which they consider likely.
July 27	Mohammed Mansour Jabarah, an al Qaeda member and Canadian citizen, is arrested in Oman. He admitted directing his cell's unfulfilled plots to blow up the U.S. Embassy in Singapore as well as to attack other Western embassies, naval vessels, companies, and shuttle buses.

Source: New York Times. Data from FBI, CIA, and the Associated Press. Additional information compiled from *Time,* CNN, ABC News, MSNBC, *Financial Times, Chicago Tribune, Washington Post, Boston Globe,* and *Omaha World-Herald.*

tary, and reenergize its intelligence capability to fight this war, it can still be won without sacrificing our cherished way of life, basic freedoms, or fundamental civic convictions. The United States need not upset the balance of power nor sacrifice its democratic principles to win. It is precisely *because* we are America that we, perhaps uniquely in the world, can do both.

4 The USA Patriot Act
A Challenge to Equal Justice?

[A] man has property in his opinions and the free communication of them. He has a property of peculiar value in his religious opinions, and in the profession and practices dictated by them. He has property very dear to him in the safety and liberty of his person. He has an equal property in the free use of his faculties and free choice of the objects on which to employ them. In a word, as a man is said to have a right to his property, he may be equally said to have a property in his rights.

—James Madison, *Essay on Property*, 1792

The true danger is when liberty is nibbled away, for expedients, and by parts. . . . the only thing necessary for evil to triumph is for good men to do nothing.

—Edmund Burke

A quarter-century ago, the Senate Select Committee to Study Governmental Operations issued its final report with respect to intelligence activities within the United States. Named after its chairman, Senator Frank Church, the Church Committee was charged with conducting a wide-ranging investigation into governmental intelligence activities in the wake of the Watergate scandal. To effectuate this mandate, the committee interviewed hundreds of individuals and pored through voluminous documents generated by the FBI, CIA, NSA, and IRS, as well as many other federal agencies with intelligence-gathering responsibilities. In its painstakingly detailed final report, the committee found, among other things, that domestic intelligence activity has been overbroad in that (1) many Americans and domestic groups have been subjected to investigation who were not suspected of criminal activity and (2) the intelligence agencies have regularly collected information about personal and political activities irrelevant to any legitimate government interest.[1]

The committee further determined that although the government had a responsibility to act in the face of legitimate national security concerns, including intelligence efforts by Nazi Germany, Japan, and the Soviet Union,

appropriate restraints, controls, and prohibitions on intelligence collection were not devised; distinctions between legitimate targets of investigations and innocent citizens were forgotten; and the Government's actions were never examined for their effects on the constitutional rights of Americans, either when programs originated or as they continued over the years.[2]

Typical of these investigative techniques, for example, was an Army Domestic Surveillance program developed in the late 1960s, which permitted the armed forces to collect information on and scrutinize the behavior of "dissidents," "instigators," "group participants," and "subversive elements." Later, these already vague criteria were broadened even further to include "prominent persons who were friendly with the leaders of the disturbance or sympathetic with their plans." In a vain attempt to add some semblance of specificity, the program suggested that likely targets for rooting out such dissidents might include the "civil rights movement" and the "anti-Vietnam/anti-draft movements," two very prominent political factions of the 1960s.[3]

Applying these nebulous standards, the Army created intelligence files on nearly 100,000 innocent American citizens, including clergymen, attorneys, authors, athletes, and business executives whose "crime" was nothing more than their constitutionally protected participation in political protests or association with those who engaged in such activities. The Church Committee concluded that this wholly unjustified intrusion into the lives of Americans was a direct result of the inexplicable and unpardonable failure of the legislative branch to *"enact statutes precisely delineating the author-ity of the intelligence agencies or defining the purpose and scope of domes-tic intelligence activity."*[4]

As if time stood still and the lessons of history were fleeting, the recently enacted Uniting and Strengthening America by Providing Appropriate Tools Required to Intercept and Obstruct Terrorism Act, best known by its acronym, the "USA Patriot Act," offers yet another glimpse of an America tragically surrendering her demo-cratic principles to the whims of contemporary fears and prejudices. At this writing, America is approaching the second anniversary of a terrorist attack so unimaginable that even two years later the images remain as incomprehensible as the day they were first broadcast to a disbelieving national audience. Over time, disbelief turned to dismay, which eventually gave way to passionate demands that the government act promptly to avenge the senseless tragedy. A mere six weeks after the attacks, with the nation still struggling amid overwhelming emotional and political turmoil, the USA Patriot Act was signed into law by President George W. Bush, ostensibly signaling to the global community that although Amer-ica's resolve had been severely tested she was nevertheless ready to meet the challenges ahead.

Reviewing its brief history in Congress, the Patriot Act origi-nated in the House of Representatives as H.R. 2975 (the Patriot Act) and in the Senate as S.1510 (the USA Act). The House subsequently passed H.R. 3162 (under suspension of rules), which resolved criti-cal differences between 2975 and 1510. The resulting 342-page leg-islative tome, which amends more than fifteen different statutes and grants sweeping new powers to law enforcement and intelli-gence officials to combat terrorism at home and abroad, then passed by overwhelming margins in both the Senate—98–1—and the House of Representatives—356–66. In an unprecedented abrogation of long-standing legislative process, prior to its passage the Patriot Act was not carefully analyzed, studied, or debated; no testimony from experts or impacted parties was solicited or heard; and no con-ference or committee reports were issued. In short, the normal leg-islative vetting process was almost completely abandoned in an attempt to fast-track the legislation to passage. Not surprisingly, the process (or lack thereof) surrounding passage and the substance of the legislation were met with immediate and withering criticism from civil liberties organizations.

Apparently undaunted by the blistering attacks, the Bush administration hailed the legislation as a resounding blow against terrorism, which is not entirely surprising given that many of the more controversial portions of the Patriot Act are based, in part, upon a DOJ counterterrorism "wish list" submitted to Congress little more than a week after the devastating 9/11 attacks. The DOJ memorandum to Congress proposed that appropriate legislation be enacted or amended to bolster the government's aggressive new counterterrorism initiative. Specifically, the DOJ proposal called upon Congress to authorize:

- the unprecedented sharing of confidential grand jury information with the U.S. intelligence community;
- the weakening of standards for obtaining court authorization for surveillance activities under the Foreign Intelligence Surveillance Act (FISA) by removing the "agent of a foreign power" requirement;
- the restoration of presidential power to confiscate and vest in the U.S. property of enemies during times of national emergency;
- the broadening of the definition of terrorist to include "anyone who affords material support to an organization that the individual knows or should know is a terrorist organization, regardless of whether or not the purported purpose for the support is related to terrorism";
- the attorney general's office to detain those illegally in the United States who, as determined by the attorney general, pose a threat to national security, whether or not the alien is eligible for or is granted relief from removal from the United States;
- the removal of any statute of limitations for "terrorism offenses" committed before or after the effective date of the statute; and
- the institution of lengthier periods of postsupervision release for persons convicted of a crime, including the possibility of lifetime tracking and terrorist oversight.[5]

Although the Patriot Act as enacted did not incorporate all of the modifications proposed by the DOJ, the list is a compelling reminder of the hard-line, constitutionally questionable stance espoused by an administration seemingly ignorant of the historical reminders that excess in times of national upheaval is a recipe for disaster.

As enacted, the USA Patriot Act consists of ten separate titles, each containing a multitude of sections. Substantively, the act enhances many existing crimes, creates new crimes, extends statutes of limitation, toughens penalties, and grants unparalleled power to the executive branch, with correspondingly minimal judicial or congressional oversight. Perhaps most importantly, in the rush to passage, Congress failed to critically evaluate whether these statutory tools are even necessary to fight the so-called war on terrorism, apparently either ignoring their fact-finding authority or ceding it to the executive branch. However, assuming such a legislative overhaul is essential to the antiterrorism agenda, then Congress also neglected its constitutional responsibility to oversee and limit, if necessary, the executive's power to abuse its new authority, a startling yet patent indication of excessive deference to the executive branch.

Indeed, in an apparent acknowledgment of these failings, on October 25, 2001, during a debate session that leaned more toward the appearance of procedural propriety than substantive analysis, Senator Patrick Leahy conceded that such a weighty piece of legislation required meaningful congressional debate and discussion but insisted that "there is no question that we will vote on this piece of legislation today and we will pass this legislation today." Moreover, recognizing that the haste with which the bill was produced might result in questionable legislation, Leahy delivered an ominous prediction: "I do believe that some of the provisions contained . . . in this bill . . . will face difficult tests in the courts, and that we in Congress may have to revisit these issues at some time in the future when the present crisis has passed, the sunset has expired or the courts find an infirmity in these provisions."[6]

Interestingly, Leahy's determination to upend legislative process in favor of swift resolution was in sharp contrast to his demeanor during the glaringly superficial debate on another piece of counterterrorism legislation, the Combating Terrorism Act (CTA). The CTA was proposed just two days after the 9/11 events and was subsequently passed by the Senate in the middle of the night on the same day it was submitted.[7] Leahy scathingly criticized the Senate's haste to enact the CTA, offering the following observations:

> Somewhere we ought to ask ourselves: do we totally ignore the normal ways of doing business in the Senate? If we do that, what is going to happen when we get down to the really difficult questions? Maybe the Senate wants to just go ahead and adopt new abilities to wiretap our citizens. Maybe they want to adopt new abilities to go into people's computers. Maybe that will make us feel safer. Maybe. And maybe what the terrorists have done made us a little bit less safe. Maybe they have increased big brother in this country. If that is what the Senate wants, we can vote for it. But do we really show respect to the American people by slapping something together, something that nobody on the floor can explain?[8]

Despite Leahy's adamant remarks concerning adherence to process and legislative precision during the Senate's consideration of the CTA, Senator Jon Kyl's passion-filled comments echoed the raw sentiments of the majority of those present and ultimately carried the day:

> Let me be very clear about the intent of this legislation. This country has just suffered the worst terrorist attack in its history. All of us are focused on the victims. We are focused on the terrible devastation and the individual lives impacted. But, as policymakers, we have also been asked some hard questions by our constituents and those questions include things such as: Why can't our Government do something about these horrible crimes? As policymakers, we have to respond to that. Our constituents are calling this a war on terrorism. In wars, you don't fight by the Marquis of Queensberry rules. The time to be overly punctilious about who you get to work with you to get information from the enemy ought to come to an end.[9]

Assuming *arguendo* that, as Senator Kyl urges, Americans are pleading with the government to "do something" about the horrific events of 9/11, can such a demand be taken to blithely cede authority to the government to disregard constitutional values in pursuit of vengeance? As British statesman and political philosopher Edmund Burke observed two centuries ago, a free people "augur misgovernment at a distance; and snuff the approach of tyranny in every tainted breeze."[10] Consequently, if history is indeed an accurate indicator, then the call for governmental action in the wake of 9/11 is not intended as carte blanche authorization to annihilate the constitutional underpinnings of America's democratic society.

At its inception, America was a relatively free country with a zealous adherence to the social compact theory. This philosophy, grounded in the predominant political thinking of the times, mandated that every citizen in the prepolitical state possessed God-given or natural rights, and the constitutional system of government originated as a consensual mechanism designed to protect and ensure those natural rights. This limited conferral of power meant that government existed solely by the consent of the governed, which necessarily implied that governmental authority could be constrained so as not to impinge upon natural rights and individual liberties.

To memorialize these tenets and appropriately define governmental powers and constraints, the Founding Fathers reasoned that the basic charter for the new government must incorporate standardized procedures known and applicable to all so as to avoid arbitrary and capricious governmental behavior. Precolonial experiences in England taught the drafters that "[v]icious and ad hoc procedures . . . [could be] used to victimize religious and political minorities [and] . . . [o]ne's home could not be his castle or his property be his own, nor could his right to express his opinion or to worship his God be secure, if he could be searched, arrested, tried, and imprisoned in some arbitrary way."[11]

The Bill of Rights evolved as the vehicle to simultaneously preserve these natural rights and impose limitations on governmental power. Originally omitted from the Constitution, the Bill of Rights added ten substantive amendments to the Constitution and became the unlikely basis for ratification compromise after a relatively short but contentious political struggle. Ultimately, its inclusion in America's founding charter represented a triumph of individual liberty against government power, which is, as Leonard Levy points out, "one of [American] history's noblest themes."[12]

Over time, the Fourth Amendment emerged as the chief constitutional means for preserving personal liberties and restraining the unreasonable exercise of governmental power in the criminal justice context. Although notably brief—a mere fifty-four words—the amendment articulates the fledgling nation's abhorrence for arbitrary and capricious governmental intrusion into specific zones of personal privacy. As ratified, the Fourth Amendment states:

> The right of the people to be secure in their persons, houses, papers, and effects, against unreasonable searches and seizures, shall not be violated, and no Warrants shall issue, but upon probable cause, supported by Oath or affirmation, and particularly describing the place to be searched, and the persons or things to be seized.

Prior to the ratification of the Fourth Amendment, early settlers in America, newly freed from an oppressive English monarchy, professed a fierce belief in the "home is castle" ideology. However, the laws and corresponding actions of government officials in the new world were the antithesis of these sentiments. As Levy describes, in colonial America a man's home was hardly his castle, and general searches, which were commonplace occurrences in England, became the norm on the American continent. To facilitate these intrusions, magistrates issued warrants based upon mere suspicion, as the modern notion of probable cause was nonexistent. Use of such illimitable search and seizure practices continued during the Revolutionary War, when they were primarily implemented to banish those of questionable loyalty or those who refused to take an oath of allegiance to the country. Having thus experienced the scourge of unchecked governmental search and seizure authority, postrevolutionary America was eager to institute governmental systems that effectively reined in law enforcement excess while still permitting searches to be utilized as a tool in the crime-fighting arsenal.

One of the earliest reported cases challenging the legality of the general warrant was *Frisbie v. Butler*.[13] In that case, the complainant, one Josiah Butler, suddenly discovered missing "twenty pounds of good pork" and suspected the defendant, Benjamin Frisbie, of stealing the cache. Butler made application to the local magistrate for a general warrant to search for meat. The warrant, directed to the appropriate authority, was issued with the following language:

> By authority of the state of Connecticut, you are commanded forthwith to search *all* suspected places and persons that the complainant thinks proper, to find his lost pork, and to cause the same, and the person with whom it shall be found, or suspected to have taken the same, and have him to appear before some proper authority, to be examined according to law.[14]

Upon conviction, Frisbie appealed, arguing, among other things, that his arrest was effected pursuant to a general search warrant, commanding *all persons and places* throughout the world to be searched, at the discretion of the complainant. The warrant's unnecessarily broad parameters, Frisbie contended, were illegal and, therefore, void. The court, in its opinion, concluded that, because the warrant imposed no limitations on its execution and authorized officers to search all places and arrest all persons whom the complainant should suspect of purloining the pork, it was patently illegal. In a further attempt to provide future guidance to issuing authorities, the court observed that "it is the duty of a justice of the peace granting a search warrant (in doing which he acts judicially) to limit the search to such particular place or places, as he, from the circumstances, shall judge there is reason to suspect; and the arrest to such person or persons as the goods shall be found with."[15]

The Frisbie case and others of its ilk sowed the seeds for a constitutional amendment that solemnized the sentiments expressed in the Frisbie court's opinion. Yet, according to Levy, the Fourth Amendment was no panacea. While it articulated specific areas of privacy immune from unreasonable government intrusion and represented a swift and decisive liberalization of the law of search and seizure, it provided no remedy for violations of its dictates and introduced vague concepts such as "probable cause," which ultimately became the determinative factor for deciding whether a search or seizure was constitutionally reasonable.

Yet another avenue for governmental intrusion exists because the core foundation upon which the Fourth Amendment rests—the right to privacy—finds no express support within the four corners of the Constitution. That is, although Fourth Amendment protections are constitutionally grounded in "reasonable expectations of privacy," the framers did not explicitly articulate such a right, much less define its parameters. Instead, the U.S. Supreme Court later recognized that the right to privacy emerges from the "penumbras" of specific guarantees of the Bill of Rights. Expounding on this right to privacy, the Court, in the ground-breaking case of *Griswold v. Connecticut,* observed:

> specific guarantees in the Bill of Rights have penumbras, formed by emanations from those guarantees that help give them life and substance. Various guarantees create zones of privacy. The right of association contained in the penumbra of the First Amendment is one, as we have seen. The Third Amendment in its prohibition against the quartering of soldiers "in any house" in time of peace without the consent of the owner is another facet of that privacy. The Fourth Amendment explicitly affirms the "right of the people to be secure in their persons, houses, papers, and effects, against unreasonable searches and seizures." The Fifth Amendment in its Self-Incrimination Clause enables the citizen to create a zone of privacy which government may not force him to surrender to his detriment. The Ninth Amendment provides: "The enumeration in the Constitution, of certain rights, shall not be construed to deny or disparage others retained by the people."[16]

Speaking more specifically to Fourth Amendment protections, the Court noted that, where innocent citizens are concerned, it is not the breaking of doors or the rummaging through of drawers that constitute the essence of a Fourth Amendment violation, for these are minor annoyances. Instead, the injury arises from the invasion of the "indefeasible right of personal security, personal liberty and private property, where that right has never been forfeited by . . . conviction of some public offence."[17] These are the very rights that are in grave jeopardy of perishing under the weight and breadth of the USA Patriot Act.

The USA Patriot Act increases governmental authorization for practically every surveillance apparatus currently available to the government. To date, these tools consist of an extensive variety of mechanical, digital, and legal devices, including wiretaps, pen registers, trap and trace devices, the Carnivore system, subpoenas, and search warrants. In conjunction with this newly expanded authority, the Patriot Act also broadens the definition of terrorism, thereby exponentially increasing the possibility of surveilling more categories of people with these myriad investigative instruments. If historical precedent is an important teacher, then unfettered governmental authority to spy on its citizens can be quickly transformed into an absolute license to invade the privacy of innocent individuals (especially disfavored groups) in the name of national security.

Early in the twentieth century, legislation circumscribing the government's domestic clandestine investigative techniques became necessary as the feasibility of surreptitiously capturing private conversations expanded with the inventions of the microphone, telephone, and dictograph recorder. Initial court challenges to evidence obtained through such covert means were largely unsuccessful, however, as the U.S. Supreme Court interpreted the Fourth Amendment to narrowly protect property rights from unwarranted *physical* trespass into protected places. Thus, as long as the recording device could be placed without physically invading private areas, then the Fourth Amendment was inapplicable. The Court also strictly defined property as tangible assets, thus barring the inclusion of mere "information" obtained by eavesdropping. Later, in a series of opinions, the Court reversed direction and dispensed with both unpersuasive rationales for supporting such unwarranted governmental intrusions, observing in *Katz v. United States* that

> [o]ver and again this Court has emphasized that the mandate of the [Fourth] Amendment requires adherence to judicial processes . . . and that searches conducted outside the judicial process, without prior approval by judge or magistrate, are per se unreasonable under the Fourth Amendment—subject

only to a few specifically established and well-delineated exceptions.[18]

According to the Court, "bypassing a neutral predetermination of the scope of a search leaves individuals secure from Fourth Amendment violations only in the discretion of the police."[19] The Court, however, left open the possibility that safeguards other than review by a neutral magistrate might be constitutionally permissible in situations involving national security, thereby laying the groundwork for a secret court system dedicated to authorizing surveillance when national security issues are implicated.

Accepting the Court's implicit invitation in *Katz* and its progeny to craft a federal statute delineating government surveillance practices, Congress enacted Title III of the Omnibus Crime Control and Safe Streets Act of 1968, a far-reaching piece of legislation authorizing the procurement of warrants for electronic surveillance but imposing strict judicial oversight throughout the process.[20] Title III provides, for example, that the attorney general or other specifically designated officials may apply for wire or oral interception for certain enumerated felonies.[21] To limit the possibility of arbitrary determinations based on vague and shifting criteria, Title III applications must be in writing and describe with particularity the alleged criminal offense and the location and place of the proposed electronic interception. Moreover, because Title III electronic surveillance is considered a "last resort" investigative technique, the application must discuss specific alternatives to interception and explain why those options are not equally practicable under the circumstances. Finally, the application must identify the proposed time frame for the interception in light of the circumstances of the underlying criminal investigation.

Based upon this information, the court reviewing the Title III application must find probable cause that electronic interception will yield evidence of criminal activity before issuing an order authorizing the surveillance. In that order, the court must carefully instruct law enforcement officials regarding the scope and content of the interception, the type of communications sought, and the duration of the order. Specifically, Title III requires that the order indicate:

(a) the identity of the person, if known, whose communications are to be intercepted;

(b) the nature and location of the communications facilities as to which, or the place where, authority to intercept is granted;

(c) a particular description of the type of communication sought to be intercepted, and a statement of the particular offense to which it relates;

(d) the identity of the agency authorized to intercept the communications, and of the person authorizing the application; and

(e) the period of time during which such interception is authorized, including a statement as to whether or not the interception shall automatically terminate when the described communication has been first obtained.[22]

Perhaps most importantly, however, when executing the court's order, law enforcement personnel are required to make every effort to limit indiscriminate or arbitrary eavesdropping unrelated to the focus of the investigation to protect the privacy interests of innocent third parties. In practice, of course, this requires agents to listen, at least momentarily, to every conversation transmitted over a particular line to determine its relevance, thereby diminishing the privacy interests of all who converse via that medium, even if only in a *de minimus* fashion.

Title III did not encompass every mode of surveillance technology, and as more sophisticated methods for eavesdropping were developed, Congress dutifully enacted statutes governing the use of those tools in criminal investigations. For example, the pen register, a device that decodes electronic impulses enabling the identification of a telephone number dialed, and trap or trace devices, which decode impulses to discover incoming telephone numbers, are among the surveillance tools requiring judicial authorization prior to implementation. However, because the information obtained by use of these devices is negligible (mere telephone numbers and no conversation content), law enforcement personnel need only demonstrate to the court that the records likely to be obtained by the installation and use of these tools is relevant to an ongoing criminal investigation.

As noted earlier, the U.S. Supreme Court allowed for the possibility that domestic national security investigations directed toward foreign agents or powers might fall outside the parameters of Fourth Amendment protections and, once again, invited Congress to enact standards governing such investigations. Wary of accusations of legislating from the bench, the Court cautioned that, while not attempting to guide congressional judgment in these matters, it was patently obvious that the same type of standards and procedures prescribed by Title III are not necessarily applicable to cases where national security concerns are implicated. Indeed, the Court expressly recognized

> that domestic security surveillance may involve different policy and practical considerations from the surveillance of "ordinary crime." The gathering of security intelligence is often long range and involves the interrelation of various sources and types of information. The exact targets of such surveillance may be more difficult to identify than in surveillance operations against many types of crime specified in Title III. Often, too, the emphasis of domestic intelligence gathering is on the prevention of unlawful activity or the enhancement of the Government's preparedness for some possible future crisis or emergency. Thus, the focus of domestic surveillance may be less precise than that directed against more conventional types of crime. Given these potential distinctions between Title III criminal surveillances and those involving the domestic security, Congress may wish to consider protective standards for the latter which differ from those already prescribed for specified crimes in Title III. Different standards may be compatible with the Fourth Amendment if they are reasonable both in relation to the legitimate need of Government for intelligence information and the protected rights of our citizens.[23]

Consistent with the Court's implicit direction, the executive branch sought legislation establishing a "separate track" for electronic surveillance directed to national security concerns, and Congress acceded to that request by enacting legislation loosening electronic surveillance standards when foreign intelligence matters were implicated. FISA fashioned guidelines for the collection of foreign intelligence information without regard to whether any criminality was involved. According to the DOD, FISA facilitates the U.S. counterintelligence mission by permitting electronic surveillance, which is critical to detecting espionage, sabotage, terrorism, and related hostile intelligence activities in order to deter, neutralize, or exploit them.

Generally, under FISA, electronic surveillance is permissible if there is probable cause to believe that the target is a foreign agent or foreign power and the "primary purpose" of the investigation is collection of foreign intelligence information. The FISA statute also established a special secret court composed of federal district court judges to review applications for electronic surveillance orders for purposes of foreign intelligence gathering. As will be discussed more completely later in this chapter, until recently, the FISA court operated under a shroud of secrecy, revealing no public information concerning electronic surveillance, with the exception of an annual report detailing the number of requests made and the number granted. The court had never refused a request in its twenty-one-year history until its recent head-on collision with FISA requests arising under the seemingly boundless USA Patriot Act.

Upon obtaining a FISA court order, the government is permitted to use electronic surveillance methods similar to those implemented for domestic purposes, for example, wiretaps, pen registers, and trap or trace devices. Government agents may also make covert physical entries onto premises to acquire foreign intelligence information. Notably, because of the FISA statute's foreign intelligence orientation and less restrictive guidelines for securing court orders, it draws a distinction between "U.S. persons" and "non-U.S. persons" for purposes of classification as "foreign agents or powers."[24] Specifically, U.S. persons may not be the target of a FISA order unless there is probable cause to believe that they are acting on behalf of a foreign power and engaged in or about to engage in activities that violate U.S. criminal laws. However, mindful of the potential chilling effect on constitutionally protected behavior, the FISA statute directs that, as it pertains to U.S. persons, activities protected by the First Amendment may not form the sole basis for determining foreign agent status. Finally, FISA authorizes the DOJ to engage in electronic surveillance to collect foreign intelligence information without a court order for periods of up to one year, with one caveat: There must be no "substantial likelihood" that the intercepted communications include those to which a U.S. person is a party.

As explained, the USA Patriot Act significantly expands the government's power to utilize a variety of devices to surreptitiously intrude into protected private areas of citizens and noncitizens alike. For example, the implementation of pen register and trap and trace devices is no longer limited to telephone technology. Section 216 of the act now authorizes the use of pen registers and trap and trace devices to capture "dialing, routing, addressing and signaling" information from computer conversations "anywhere within the United States, if the court finds that the attorney for the Government has certified to the court that the information likely to be obtained by such installation and use is relevant to an ongoing criminal investigation."[25] The government is, however, prohibited from tracking the *contents* of wire and electronic communications with these devices, and therein lies the critical difference. For while the use of these surveillance tools on traditional telephone technology is fairly noncontroversial because of the minimal amount of information revealed, the expansion of this investigative resource to digital communications, primarily e-mail, is particularly troublesome. Unlike telephonic communications, where such electronic surveillance devices can only capture numbers dialed to or from locations, routing and addressee information encoded in digital exchanges can contain a plethora of additional revelatory information, thus potentially granting the government access to private information that is well beyond the scope of its investigation. Key to the potentially confusing implementation of this section and consequent invasions of privacy is the lack of definitional precision. While the term *content* is clear in the context of telephone communications, the digital landscape does not lend itself to such unambiguous distinctions. For instance, Web site addresses may technically fall within the category of "addressing information," yet such addresses clearly reveal a wealth of content once accessed, and some Web addresses may even disclose information simply by virtue of their name designations. The potential ability of governmental authorities to track and catalog Web site addresses raises the frightening specter of database warehousing and profiling of targets using composite information that is exponentially more revealing than a mere catalog of telephone numbers dialed or calls received.

The use of the Carnivore system, a controversial computer tracking program capable of capturing *all* communications on any network where it is installed, is also authorized by Section 216. While the government is required to maintain specific records associated with Carnivore's installation and use, such record keeping does little to quell suspicions of governmental overreaching and, ironically, likely increases public apprehension concerning the government's ability to compile private information for purposes of covert profiling.

The Patriot Act also grants the DOJ's request to modify the already lenient standard for implementing pen register and trap and trace devices under FISA. Section 214 now permits the government to obtain orders for electronic surveillance under FISA if sought as part of "any investigation to obtain foreign intelligence information not concerning a United States person or to protect against international terrorism or clandestine intelligence activities, provided that such investigation of a United States person is not conducted solely upon the basis of activities protected by the first amendment to the Constitution." Previously, FISA pen register and trap and trace device standards required that the telecommunications device be "used to contact an agent of a foreign power engaged in international terrorism or clandestine intelligence activities." The new powers under this amendment potentially subject American citizens to the vagaries of a secret court system, which, with its Kafkaesque implications, is the absolute antithesis of the U.S. accusatory system of justice. Similar to the expansion under Title III, FISA orders can also now be obtained to capture computer source and addressing information, again with the caveat that such orders cannot be directed against American citizens based solely upon activities protected by the First Amendment.

With respect to stored electronic communications, Section 209 of the act mandates that recorded voice mail messages shall now be treated the same as stored e-mail and communications records held by third parties for purposes of governmental access. That is, law enforcement personnel may obtain a search warrant to access the content of a stored communication, and if the communication has been in remote storage for more than 180 days, the application may be made and the warrant issued without notice to the subscriber. If probable cause to secure a search warrant is lacking, the government may obtain a court order (with prior notice to the customer or subscriber) "if the governmental entity offers specific and articulable facts showing that there are reasonable grounds to believe that the contents of a wire or electronic communication, or the records or other information sought, are relevant and material to an ongoing criminal investigation." However, notification to the customer may be delayed for up to ninety days if it is determined that such notice could, among other things, endanger lives, cause the destruction of evidence, seriously jeopardize an investigation, or unduly delay a trial. Another seemingly mundane, but ultimately intrusive, amendment to this section adds credit card and bank account numbers to the list of information that may be demanded from the service provider. The DOJ wish list offered the following explanation for requesting that Congress impose this further requirement:

> In fast-moving investigation[s] such as terrorist bombings—in which Internet communications are critical methods of identifying conspirators in determining the source of the attacks—the delay necessitated by the use of court orders can often be important. Obtaining billing and other information can identify not only the perpetrator but also give valuable information about the financial accounts of those responsible and their conspirators.[26]

Section 215 of the act now permits the director of the FBI or his designee to make an application for an order requiring production of tangible things for investigations to protect against terrorism or clandestine intelligence activities. Once again, if the request is directed toward a U.S. citizen, the act mandates that the investigation may not be based solely upon activities protected by the First Amendment. The act also cloaks this surveillance conduct in the utmost secrecy, requiring that the order not disclose that it is issued for purposes of a foreign intelligence investigation. In addition, "[n]o person shall disclose to any other person (other than those persons necessary to produce the tangible things under this section) that the Federal Bureau of Investigation has sought or obtained tangible things under this section." The deleterious effect of Section 215 has already been demonstrated. According to a national survey conducted by the University of Illinois at Urbana-Champaign's Library Research Center, law enforcement officials had approached at least eighty-seven libraries for patron records by January 2002, and the actual numbers of requests are believed to be much higher. Many libraries, in turn, have begun purging their patron files every week instead of every couple of months in an effort to protect the privacy of their patrons. Similar "protest" activities by libraries include shredding the computer use sign-up sheets and posting signs warning patrons about the federal government's ability to review their patron records without their knowledge. As Leigh Estabrook, director of the center, observed:

> Public libraries are one of the last public spaces in our com-
> munity and so there's a sense that officials want to get at that
> public behavior. . . . For me and a number of my colleagues,
> we are quite worried about the chilling effect to use public
> libraries and the differential effect on the poor who don't have
> Internet access except at the public library. We know that
> librarians are really worried about it, but because of the gag
> order we don't know how many librarians are cooperating
> with [requests] and I can't, in good conscience, ask them. I
> don't think we will know unless someone is successful in a
> request through the courts.[27]

As to the ultimate impact of this section of the act, Estabrook strikes a decidedly resigned, although cautiously hopeful, tone, conclud-ing, "It's really a judicial issue now." Indeed.

The act also amends the FISA statute in a number of ways that grant the government more authority to exchange information with domestic law enforcement personnel during the course of foreign intelligence investigations. More specifically, Section 218 eliminates the requirement that foreign intelligence gathering be the sole or primary purpose of the investigation and now only requires that it be a "significant purpose." Thus, it is now possible for law enforce-ment agents to obtain court orders for electronic surveillance and physical searches upon showing "that a significant purpose of the search is to obtain foreign intelligence information." This amend-ment represents a radical departure from the reasonably bright line separating domestic criminal investigations and foreign intelligence gathering and has far-reaching implications in terms of its potential to eviscerate due process standards and trample the rights of innocent individuals.

Three decades ago, when the U.S. Supreme Court acknowledged the potential for different investigative standards, and Congress responded by establishing the separate foreign intelligence investigation track under FISA, the apparent basis for permitting more relaxed standards under FISA was the understanding that foreign intelligence gathering operations were not criminal investigations and, therefore, did not require the same judicial oversight. Allowing foreign intelligence investigations to proceed as long as gathering foreign intelligence information is a "significant reason" confers wide latitude on law enforcement officials to conflate criminal investigation purposes among the reasons for obtaining court orders under FISA. Not only does this amendment sanction end runs around traditional Fourth Amendment standards, but it fosters an environment where privacy standards are subject to the whims and creativities of the executive branch, an absolute, although unfortunately not unprecedented, affront to the core principles of democracy. The question that looms large is whether the courts will once again intercede to rescue the Constitution from the current executive stranglehold before history, with all of its tragic consequences, repeats itself.

Complementing the broader authority to obtain court orders under the FISA "significant purpose" standard, Section 203 of the Patriot Act dramatically increases the possibility that information gleaned from unrelated criminal investigations will be shared with the intelligence community. As a launching point to encourage this unbridled exchange of information, the act now permits disclosure of grand jury material "when the matters involve foreign intelligence or counterintelligence . . . or foreign intelligence information . . . to any Federal law enforcement, intelligence, protective, immigration, national defense, or national security official in order to assist the official receiving that information in the performance of his official duties." This sharing of traditionally secret proceedings represents a shocking departure from compelling historical precedent emphasizing and respecting the sanctity of the grand jury process. This development is particularly disturbing because of the role the grand jury plays in the American criminal justice system. The familiar maxim that "a grand jury would indict a ham sandwich" is indicative (albeit cynically) of the fact that its role is to review the *government's* evidence and to determine whether an indictment will issue. To aid in its search for the truth, the grand jury has extensive subpoena authority and may compel witnesses to appear and provide testimonial and/or documentary evidence. However, because the government's evidence is largely unchallenged in most instances, only the flimsiest of cases fail to attain indictment status, and even then the government may convene another grand jury in hopes of achieving a different outcome. It certainly does not require a great leap of imagination to envision the eventual unfettered sharing of one-sided evidence that lacks indicia of criminality but nevertheless subjects targets to continual surveillance and investigatory tactics by various branches of the law enforcement bureaucracy.

Historical justifications for enshrouding grand jury proceedings in secrecy include encouraging witnesses to speak freely and truthfully without fear of negative repercussions and avoiding the unfair stigmatization of targets of criminal probes in the event that an indictment is not issued. Disclosure, even for purposes of aiding national security, defeats each of these justifications and converts the grand jury into a largely unrestricted ancillary investigatory tool in the war on terrorism. The only statutory veneer of protection against rendering grand juries as "witch hunting" venues for foreign intelligence investigations is the requirement that *after* the disclosure the "government shall file under seal a notice with the court stating the fact that such information was disclosed and the departments, agencies, or entities to which the disclosure was made."

In accordance with the Patriot Act's implicit goal of conjoining criminal investigations with foreign intelligence gathering, Section 203 also provides that information gathered through electronic means under Title III is subject to disclosure to the extent that the contents pertain to foreign intelligence information.

Yet another addition to the invasive arsenal already at the government's fingertips arises out of Section 213, which authorizes so-called sneak and peek search warrants. Unlike traditional search warrants, where execution of the warrant generally results in notice, seizure, and the inventory of evidence, sneak and peek warrants permit law enforcement officials to enter protected areas, either physically or virtually, to merely search for evidence of a criminal offense without prior notification to owners or other interest holders if the court "finds reasonable cause to believe that providing immediate notification of the execution of the warrant may have an adverse result." According to the statute, such adverse results might include the risk of destruction of evidence, bodily injury, and the potential to jeopardize an investigation or to delay a trial proceeding. Thus, while sneak and peek warrants limit the government to conduct that does not physically deprive the owner of property, such intrusive investigation practices can nevertheless facilitate the compilation of an abundance of information concern- ing a target simply by entering a premises to observe, take mea- surements or pictures, copy documents, or download computer files.

Section 213 directly contravenes the spirit of Rule 41(d) of the Federal Rules of Criminal Procedure and myriad legal precedents establishing notice of government intrusion into private spaces as a preeminent requirement of the Fourth Amendment. Specifically, the rule stipulates that

> the officer taking property under the warrant shall give to the person from whom or from whose premises the property was taken a copy of the warrant and a receipt for the property taken or shall leave the copy and receipt at the place from which the property was taken. The return shall be made promptly and shall be accompanied by a written inventory of any property taken.

As written, the rule imposes no limitations on the nature of "property" and is arguably applicable even if the "property" taken is intangible information, such as in the case of a sneak and peek warrant. Moreover, the U.S. Supreme Court has determined that "we have little doubt that the Framers of the Fourth Amendment thought that the method of an officer's entry into a dwelling was among the factors to be considered in assessing the reasonableness of a search or seizure . . . [and] in some circumstances an officer's unannounced entry into a home might be unreasonable under the Fourth Amendment."[28] In practice, this reasonableness standard generally means that, barring exigent circumstances, law enforcement personnel desiring entry onto the premises must knock and verbally announce their presence and purpose so as to provide adequate notice to the occupants. Such a requirement protects both officers and citizens because it signals the initiation of a presumptively legal encounter with law enforcement agents and individuals opening their doors with notice of this fact are presumed to submit to that lawful authority. Obviously, reasonableness does not require knock notice when exigent circumstances prevail, such as the likelihood that evidence may be destroyed or when a threat to the officer's safety exists. Overall, the reasonableness of most searches and seizures conducted under the Fourth Amendment appears to be predicated upon timely notice to affected parties.

A further concern arising under this section and premised on Fourth Amendment jurisprudence is, even if covert entry for purposes of mere investigation falls through a loophole in the Constitution, to what extent does the Fourth Amendment nevertheless require timely notification *after* surreptitious entry? In the case of *Dalia v. United States*, the U.S. Supreme Court determined that there was "no basis for a constitutional rule proscribing all covert entries" and made explicit what had long been implicit in their decisions addressing this issue: "The Fourth Amendment does not prohibit per se a covert entry performed for the purpose of installing otherwise legal electronic bugging equipment."[29] Although relevant, the *Dalia* case holding is seemingly limited to circumstances involving covert entries for purposes of placing electronic devices pursuant to Title III electronic surveillance orders. In considering this issue, the Court reasoned that "absent covert entry . . . almost all electronic bugging would be impossible,"[30] a compellingly rational conclusion given that the entire purpose of wiretapping would be defeated if law enforcement officers were required to advise targets prior to implementing the electronic surveillance devices.

Several appellate courts have considered the issue of whether timely notice after surreptitiously executing a warrant is constitutionally required. For example, in the case of *United States v. Freitas*, the court determined that a warrant failing to explicitly provide for notice to the target at a reasonable time after the covert entry was constitutionally defective. According to the court, surreptitious searches and seizures of intangibles strike at the very heart of the interests protected by the Fourth Amendment. The mere thought of strangers walking through and visually examining the center of our privacy interest, our home, arouses our passion for freedom as does nothing else. That passion, the true source of the Fourth Amendment, demands that surreptitious entries be closely circumscribed.[31]

Section 213 of the Patriot Act authorizes delayed notice to targets of sneak and peak warrants, but rather than incorporate a definite time period for notification, it permits "such notice within a reasonable period of [the warrant's] execution, which period may thereafter be extended by the court for good cause shown." Again, in this setting, the lack of definitional precision renders potential targets captive to the whims and creativities of law enforcement officials. The imagery of government officials surreptitiously entering private dwellings and rummaging through homeowners' personal possessions is one that Americans have viewed in countless movies depicting the travails of everyday life under oppressive governmental regimes. Because of a strong constitutional foundation supporting personal privacy and limited governmental intervention, Americans hardly imagine that such outrageous conduct could occur in the United States. However, Section 213 of the Patriot Act threatens to convert remote film images into real cinema vérité on American shores.

When notice of covert entry into protected areas is delayed, Fourth Amendment protections are compromised in ways that can result in irreparable harm to the innocent and guilty alike. It is virtually impossible to challenge the scope of a search if one cannot meaningfully recreate the circumstances existing at the time of the search, particularly if no tangible items were seized. Moreover, notification long after the fact precludes targets from pointing out obvious deficiencies (e.g., wrong address) to law enforcement personnel at the scene. Perhaps most importantly, though, because sneak and peak warrants are not limited to investigations regarding terrorist activity but rather apply to *all* criminal investigations, every person within the jurisdictional reach of the statute now has reason to fear being victimized by these invasive techniques in an age of overzealous law enforcement purportedly aimed at fighting a war on terrorism.

Threats to Due Process

The first several clauses of the Fourteenth Amendment of the U.S. Constitution state:

> All persons born or naturalized in the United States and subject to the jurisdiction thereof, are citizens of the United States and of the State wherein they reside. No State shall make or enforce any law which shall abridge the privileges or immunities of citizens of the United States; nor shall any State deprive any person of life, liberty, or property, without due process of law; nor deny to any person within its jurisdiction the equal protection of the laws.

Because this language inexplicably categorizes protections for "citizens" as well as "any person," the U.S. Supreme Court has on myriad occasions interpreted this language and defined its applicability to various classes of individuals. In the case of *Zadvydas v. Davis*, for example, the Court began by elucidating the general guidelines of Fourteenth Amendment protection, namely, that certain constitutional protections available to persons inside the United States are unavailable to noncitizens outside of its geographic borders.[32] The Court then explained, however, that once a noncitizen is within the United States his or her legal status changes along with safeguards provided under the Fourteenth Amendment. More specifically, the Due Process and Equal Protection Clauses apply to "all persons" within the United States and make no distinction based on citizenship or the legal status of one's presence in the country. Similarly, in the case of *Yick Wo v. Hopkins*, the Court emphasized that

> The Fourteenth Amendment to the Constitution is not confined to the protection of citizens. It says: "Nor shall any state deprive any person of life, liberty, or property without due process of law; nor deny to any person within its jurisdiction

the equal protection of the laws." These provisions are universal in their application, to all persons within the territorial jurisdiction, without regard to any differences of race, of color, or of nationality; and the protection of the laws is a pledge of the protection of equal laws.[33]

Numerous provisions of the USA Patriot Act threaten the values inherent in these fundamental notions of due process and equal protection. For instance, Section 806, a new forfeiture provision, authorizes confiscation of all assets, foreign or domestic, of any individual, entity, or organization engaged in planning or perpetrating any act of domestic or international terrorism against the United States or their property. Furthermore, any property acquired, maintained, or derived from involvement with domestic or foreign terrorism activities is also subject to forfeiture to the U.S. government. To extend the act's global reach, Section 319 provides for forfeiture of funds in interbank accounts. Essentially, any funds deposited in a foreign bank that has an interbank account with a U.S. bank are treated as if deposited in the United States for purposes of forfeiture rules. Presumably to reduce any unfairness and hardship that might result from this provision, the attorney general is authorized to suspend forfeiture proceedings when the "interests of justice" obviate the need for applying the "U.S. deposit presumption." Traditionally, forfeiture is a tool utilized by the government to remove the economic underpinnings of criminal activity. The theory is, quite simply, that crime should not pay, and, therefore, to the extent that unlawful activities result in proceeds of any kind, those tainted profits are forfeitable to the government.[34] This remedy is exclusive of and in addition to any criminal sanctions that might be imposed. Over the years, numerous defendants stripped of their economic resources have challenged the constitutionality of criminal forfeiture. More specifically, defendants have alleged that, in some instances, the total dollar amount of the mandated forfeiture is excessive and, therefore, violative of the Eighth Amendment prohibition against excessive punishment. Moreover, because forfeiture is a separate remedy, often in addition to a period of incarceration, it is alleged to directly contravene the Fifth Amendment double jeopardy ban on multiple punishments for the same offense.

The U.S. Supreme Court has consistently rejected the double

jeopardy argument, noting that civil forfeiture sanctions assessed in conjunction with criminal penalties and based upon the same underlying events have been employed against criminals since the earliest days in America. According to the Court's reasoning, civil forfeiture proceedings do not violate double jeopardy standards because civil sanctions target the proceeds of the crime rather than the defendant, thus not exacting another personal punishment from the convicted person. However, with respect to the excessive punishment argument, the Court has determined that, when the case proceeds under a criminal forfeiture provision, the Eighth Amendment's Excessive Fines Clause limits the government's power to extract payments as punishment for an offense. Expressed differently, this means that the designated forfeiture must be proportional to the criminal conduct, a basic tenet of criminal law. The proportionality requirement is also applicable to civil forfeitures if it is determined that effectuation of the forfeiture imposes a punitive sanction in addition to the civil remedial component.

Section 806 of the USA Patriot Act is troublesome because it mandates forfeiture for conduct that is arguably at the outer limits of historically defined notions of criminality, if not completely outside the bounds altogether. For example, Section 806 authorizes forfeiture for any act of domestic or international terrorism. The newly enacted definition of *domestic terrorism* as set forth in Section 802 of the act describes domestic terrorism as activities that

(A) involve acts dangerous to human life that are a violation of the criminal laws of the United States or of any State;
(B) appear to be intended—
    (i)   to intimidate or coerce a civilian population;
    (ii) to influence the policy of a government by intimidation or coercion; or
    (iii) to affect the conduct of a government by mass destruction, assassination, or kidnapping; and
(C) occur primarily within the territorial jurisdiction of the United States.

On its face, this definition is far-reaching and consistent with other sections of the act lacking in precision. As such, application of Section 806 could result in the classification of legitimate political dissent as terrorism, thereby subjecting participants to possible criminal convictions and forfeiture of assets for such conduct. Another basic tenet of criminal law requires that statutes be drafted in a manner that gives citizens fair notice of prohibited conduct, so that they may conform their conduct to the dictates of the law. As Nancy Chang, senior litigation attorney at the Center for Constitutional Rights, observes of Section 802:

> Because this crime is couched in such vague and expansive terms, it may well be read by federal law enforcement agencies as licensing the investigation and surveillance of political activists and organizations based on their opposition to government policies. It also may be read by prosecutors as licensing the criminalization of legitimate political dissent. Vigorous protest activities, by their very nature, could be construed as acts that "appear to be intended . . . to influence the policy of a government by intimidation or coercion." Further, clashes between demonstrators and police officers and acts of civil disobedience—even those that do not result in injuries and are entirely non-violent—could be construed as "dangerous to human life" and in "violation of the criminal laws." Environmental activists, anti-globalization activists, and anti-abortion activists who use direct action to further their political agendas are particularly vulnerable to prosecution as "domestic terrorists."[35]

Also of particular note with respect to Section 806 is its failure to include a conviction requirement prior to imposition of its draconian forfeiture standards. Thus, an indictment or even perhaps an arrest for "domestic terrorism" can arguably trigger the application of the forfeiture statute. As a final example of the stringent nature of Section 806, it entirely omits the typical requirement that forfeited assets be tied to criminal or terrorist activity. Instead, it is sufficient if the property was owned or possessed by the alleged terrorist at the time of the suspected illegal conduct. The very fact that these proposed forfeitures are, on their face, inexact and excessively punitive negates any conclusion that they are designed to serve an underlying remedial purpose and creates a constitutional conundrum that may, before long, require judicial intervention. In the end, to quote the fateful words of Senator Patrick Leahy, "Congress may have to revisit these issues."

Indefinite Detention and Deportation

Prior to the enactment of the USA Patriot Act, immigration legislation provided that noncitizens could be excluded from the United States for a number of reasons, including having prior criminal activity and exhibiting behavior that may pose a threat to the health or safety of others. Section 411 of the Patriot Act expands the grounds for exclusion to include categories such as being a representative of a political, social, or other similar group whose public endorsements of terrorist activities undermine U.S. efforts to reduce or eliminate terrorism; being a spouse or child of an inadmissible alien associated with terrorist activity within the past five years; and being an alien who uses a position of prominence within *any* country to endorse or espouse terrorist activity. Those who associate with terrorist organizations and intend "while in the United States to engage solely, principally or incidentally in activities that could endanger the welfare, safety or security of the United States" are also inadmissible. The determination of whether one has associated with a terrorist is left to the discretion of "the Secretary of State, after consultation with the Attorney General, or the Attorney General, after consultation with the Secretary of State." Section 411 of the act also defines "engage in terrorist activity" to comprise such a broad category of conduct that it is difficult, if not impossible, to meaningfully distinguish legitimate and constitutionally protected political dissent from unlawful terrorist activities. For example, one such clause, which is hopelessly mired in ambiguity, defines "engaging in terrorist activity" to include committing

> an act that the actor knows, or reasonably should know, affords material support, including a safe house, transportation, communications, funds, transfer of funds or other material financial benefit, false documentation or identification, weapons (including chemical, biological, or radiological weapons), explosives, or training . . . to a terrorist organization . . . unless the actor can demonstrate that he did not know, and

should not reasonably have known, that the act would further the organization's terrorist activity.

The use of phrases such as "reasonably should know" and "material support" grants wide latitude to the executive branch to declare open season upon disfavored immigrants for conduct as innocent as lending money or a means of transportation to a friend who is later determined to be affiliated with a terrorist organization. Moreover, even if an immigrant has knowledge of a friend's association with a terrorist organization, the statute provides no reasonable yardstick for measuring when the critical "material support" threshold has been crossed. Thus, this clause looms like a dark cloud over the legitimate associations and private friendships of legal immigrants in America, potentially resulting in unnecessary self-monitoring and limitations on lawful conduct lest it be taken as "material support."

But the coup de grâce to fair notice and due process, and a shining example of executive hubris masquerading as legislation, is contained in the final paragraph of this clause:

> This clause shall not apply to any material support the alien afforded to an organization or individual that has committed terrorist activity, if the Secretary of State, after consultation with the Attorney General, or the Attorney General, after consultation with the Secretary of State, concludes in his *sole unreviewable discretion*, that this clause should not apply. [emphasis added]

Granting the executive branch ultimate authority to determine who falls within and without the boundaries of engaging in terrorist activity is eerily reminiscent of a duo of U.S. legislative enactments passed during the latter part of the eighteenth century as the fledgling country stood on the precipice of war with France. The Alien Act of 1798 gave the president broad authority to deport those aliens deemed dangerous to the peace and safety of the United States or those suspected of treasonable or secret machinations against the government. Its partner statute, the Sedition Act of 1798, made it unlawful for any person to write, print, utter, or publish any false, scandalous, and malicious writings about the government with the intent to defame or bring the government into contempt or disrepute or to excite the hatred of the people against America. Ostensibly designed to protect American shores from enemy infiltration during a time of heightened national security concern, these acts were eventually used to suppress the largely Democratic-Republican immigrant vote and to quell domestic political dissent, particularly viewpoints that attacked the Federalist Party agenda. Fifteen people were indicted under the Sedition Act, resulting in ten convictions; all of them were Democratic-Republicans, who were assessed heavy fines and imprisoned. While no aliens were deported or taken into custody under these statutes, immigrants fled American shores in large numbers, fearing eventual arrest, detainment, and deportation. Subsequent public backlash against the Federalist Party for its role in creating such repressive legislation spelled the end of that party and heralded the emergence of the Democratic-Republicans, the nation's first opposition party.

Since 9/11, the executive branch has adopted a decidedly ahistorical approach to addressing the undeclared war on terrorism, ignoring, in practically every instance, lessons from the past that dictate caution over excess in times of crisis. Although unsuccessful in his effort to defeat the Alien and Sedition Acts over two centuries ago, Senator Edward Livingston nevertheless exposed the insidious contradiction that necessarily obtains when a nation purportedly committed to the highest principles of democracy takes a repressive stance toward its own people under the guise of protecting national security:

> Do not let us be told that we are to excite a fervor against a foreign aggression to establish a tyranny at home; that like the arch traitor we cry "Hail Columbia" at the moment we are betraying her to destruction; that we sing "Happy Land," when we are plunging it in ruin and disgrace; and that we are absurd enough to call ourselves free and enlightened while we advocate principles that would have disgraced the age of Gothic barbarity.[36]

Section 412 authorizes the attorney general to detain alien terrorist suspects for up to seven days upon certification that reasonable grounds exist to believe that they are engaged in conduct that threatens the national security of the United States or are inadmissible or deportable for other terrorist-related reasons. Within this seven-day window, the attorney general must formally commence proceedings against the detainee designed to effectuate removal from the country or initiation of a criminal prosecution. Failure to comply with the Patriot Act's version of the "speedy trial rule" will result in the detainee's release from custody. However, an alien who has not been removed from the country, and whose removal is unlikely in the foreseeable future, "may be detained for additional periods of up to six months . . . if the release of the alien will threaten the national security of the United States or the safety of the community or any person." If the detainee is held for longer periods of time, the attorney general is required to review the certification every six months, and "if the Attorney General determines, *in the Attorney General's discretion,* that the certification should be revoked, the alien may be released on such conditions as the Attorney General deems appropriate, unless such release is otherwise prohibited by law" (emphasis added). The alien may also request a reconsideration of the certification every six months and may submit documents or other evidence in support of the request. The attorney general's determinations are subject to review only under federal writs of habeas corpus, with a limited right of appeal to the United States Court of Appeals for the District of Columbia. As a paean to congressional oversight, the attorney general must file a biannual report to the Committee on the Judiciary in both the Senate and House of Representatives.

This section of the Patriot Act is in apparent conflict with the military order issued by President Bush on November 13, 2001, which, by its terms, applies to the same category of noncitizens as contemplated by Section 412. Such an obvious conflict is highly indicative of the haste with which Congress enacted this legislation, failing at the most basic level to determine whether other standards were being contemplated to address the conduct described in Section 412. The military order, entitled "Detention, Treatment, and Trial of Certain Non-Citizens in the War Against Terrorism," states in pertinent part that

the term "individual subject to this order" shall mean any individual who is not a United States citizen with respect to whom [the President determines] from time to time in writing that:

(1) there is reason to believe that such individual, at the relevant times,

    (i)   is or was a member of the organization known as al Qaeda;

    (ii) has engaged in, aided or abetted, or conspired to commit, acts of international terrorism, or acts in preparation therefor, that have caused, threaten to cause, or have as their aim to cause, injury to or adverse effects on the United States, its citizens, national security, foreign policy, or economy; or

    (iii) has knowingly harbored one or more individuals described in subparagraphs (i) or (ii) of subsection 2(a)(1) of this order; and

(2) it is in the interest of the United States that such individual be subject to this order.

According to the order, individuals subject to its provisions may be detained at an appropriate location designated by the secretary of defense outside or within the United States; treated humanely; afforded adequate food, shelter, clothing, and medical treatment; and allowed to practice their religion. When tried for their alleged crimes, military tribunals

shall have exclusive jurisdiction with respect to offenses by the individual; and . . . the individual shall not be privileged to seek any remedy or maintain any proceeding, directly or indirectly, or to have any such remedy or proceeding sought on the individual's behalf, in . . . any court of the United States, or any State thereof, any court of any foreign nation, or any international tribunal.

There is an apparent definitional overlap between Section 412 and the military order concerning the categories of individuals who might fall within the jurisdiction of each. Specifically, "aliens who endanger national security" under Section 412 may also be "those engaged in, assisting or conspiring to commit acts of international

TABLE 2. Key Differences between Section 412 of the USA Patriot Act and the President's Military Order

	Individuals Covered	Length of Detention	Decision Making	Forum	Appellate Review
USA Patriot Act, Section 412	Aliens who endanger national security or are inadmissible or deportable for other terrorist-related reasons	Not longer than seven days without proceedings; if can't be removed from country and will be a threat to national security, then may be detained for up to six months	Attorney general certifies based on "reasonable grounds"; may delegate power to deputy attorney general	U.S. federal courts	Habeas corpus proceeding, which may only be appealed to U.S. Court of Appeals for District of Columbia
Military Order	Current or former al-Qaeda members; those engaged in, assisting with, or conspiring to commit acts of international terrorism against the U.S.; those knowingly harboring terrorists	Indefinite	President determines based on "reason to believe"	Military commissions	Three-member review panel appointed by secretary of defense; president makes final decision

terrorism" under the military order. Uncertainty as to which mandate is applicable in any given situation gives the government wide latitude to impose dramatically different punishments on similarly situated individuals. That is, under Section 412, a semblance of due process prevails. The government must comply with time limitations or risk release, a detainee is entitled to access the federal court system, and the government is required to justify its detainment on a biannual basis. In sharp contrast, detainment under the military order as currently implemented condemns a detainee indefinitely to Guantanamo Bay, Cuba, a "permanent penal colony for the human detritus of the campaign against terrorism."[37]

Although noncitizens have been detained under both standards, it is nevertheless unclear whether these interrelated mandates will operate exclusively or in tandem. One could well imagine that, in our current environment, where lengthy detainments of noncitizens on sparse evidence are apparently symbolic of fighting the war on terrorism, it would not be beyond the pale for the government to strategically use both provisions to justify political objectives.

Challenges Ahead

We were warned thirty years ago about the vicissitudes and inherent dangers of unfettered governmental authority wielded indiscriminately against innocent citizens in the name of national security. After the September 11 tragedy, the DOJ, in a blatant attempt to seize power in a moment of national crisis, struck swiftly and decisively, giving Congress a wish list of proposed legislation calling for unprecedented governmental intervention into the lives of citizens and noncitizens alike. Congress, still deciphering the impact of the 9/11 attacks and feeling pressure from constituents to "do something," blindly caved in to the wishes of the executive branch, ceding nearly all of its oversight authority, lest its members appear unpatriotic at a time when patriotism is seemingly defined by one's ability to submit without question to governmental authority for the sake of national cohesiveness. The USA Patriot Act was the legislative result, and, while its impact is still largely unknown, initial assessments do not bode well.[38] There are some, however, who believe that Patriot Act naysayers are alarmists and are making much ado about nothing. Yet, in 2002, the previously silent FISA court spoke publicly for the first time, revealing that it is not so dismissive of these concerns.

Consistent with his interpretation of the broad grant of authority in the Patriot Act, in March 2002 the attorney general filed a motion with the FISA court requesting that the court now grant orders for electronic surveillance and physical searches if the investigation is "primarily for a law enforcement purpose, so long as a significant foreign intelligence purpose remains."[39] In response, the court first noted that its duty in reviewing FISA surveillance requests is to "ensure that the intrusiveness of foreign intelligence surveillances and searches on the privacy of U.S. persons is 'consistent' with the need of the United States to collect foreign intelligence information from foreign powers and their agents."[40] Explaining how this function is accomplished, the court observed that, "[i]n order to preserve both the appearance and the fact that FISA surveillance and searches were not being used *sub rosa* for criminal investigations, the Court routinely approve[s] the use of information screening 'walls,'"[41] which restrict the flow of information between foreign intelligence agents and criminal investigators.[42]

Against this backdrop, the court examined the attorney general's motion for expanded exchange of information, concluding that, according to the attorney general's interpretation, "criminal prosecutors are to have a significant role *directing* FISA surveillances and searches from start to finish in counterintelligence cases having overlapping intelligence and criminal investigations or interests, guiding them to criminal prosecution."[43] The court opined that this may be "because the government is unable to meet the substantive requirements of these law enforcement tools, or because their administrative burdens are too onerous," but stressed that the court was not persuaded by such justifications.[44] In denying the government's request for unrestricted sharing of information, the court ordered that

law enforcement officials shall not make recommendations to intelligence officials concerning the initiation, operation, continuation or expansion of FISA searches or surveillance. Additionally, the FBI and the Criminal Division shall ensure that law enforcement officials do not direct or control the use of the

FISA procedures to enhance criminal prosecution, and that advice intended to preserve the option of a criminal prosecution does not inadvertently result in the Criminal Division's directing or controlling the investigation using FISA searches and surveillances toward law enforcement objectives.[45]

After the ruling, Senator Patrick Leahy lauded the decision, observing that this "ray of sunshine from the judicial branch is a remarkable step forward for constructive oversight . . . and [provides] a window on the process that will help us better understand how the laws are being implemented and how well they are working." As to its long-term impact, Leahy predicted that the FISA court ruling might "save the Justice Department from overstepping constitutional bounds in ways that could have dire consequences in our most serious national security cases."[46]

Despite Senator Leahy's guarded optimism, at this writing, the Center for Public Integrity, a nonpartisan organization dedicated to "public service journalism," has disclosed to the media a document that outlines a new DOJ wish list, apparently designed to expand upon the powers already granted in the Patriot Act. Ominously labeled "Patriot II," the document proposes, among other things, the expansion of power to wiretap American citizens, easier governmental access to credit reports and financial information, and the voluntary loss of American citizenship for anyone found to have materially supported a hostile terrorist organization. Although none of these provisions has been formally proposed to Congress, they, like the abandoned TIPS program, are indicative of the current executive branch ethos that cavalierly abandons civil liberties in the name of national security. When asked about the leaked Patriot II document, Attorney General Ashcroft responded, "Percolating ideas into the system is very important."[47]

As the Patriot Act nears its two-year anniversary, there is little cause for celebration as individuals and organizations spanning the political spectrum are mounting numerous challenges to the act's expansive provisions across the country. This escalating backlash includes nearly 150 state and local governments that have each passed legislation condemning the act and, in some instances, have refused to enforce its provisions. In July 2003 the American Civil Liberties Union (ACLU) filed a lawsuit in the U.S. district court in

Michigan alleging that Section 215 of the Patriot Act, which authorizes searches of business, library, and bookstore records, is unconstitutional and being used primarily to target individuals based upon ethnicity, religion, and political associations.

There is also growing resistance in Congress, as the House recently voted 309 to 118 to discontinue funding for governmental activities that facilitate the sneak and peek warrant provision of the act. In addition, a more sweeping revision of the act is currently being proposed as Congress attempts to rein in some of its more constitutionally questionable provisions. Senator Lisa Murkowski introduced legislation in August 2003 designed to provide greater definition for the expanded powers in the act and to ensure that the law is working as intended. Among other things, Senator Murkowski's bill seeks to

- Ensure that only an individual who has violated one of the federal crimes of terrorism while operating within the jurisdiction of the United States could be designated as a domestic terrorist
- Permit intelligence agencies to seek warrants for a broad range of evidence, but require a showing of "reasonable cause" that the individual to whom the records pertain is a foreign power or an agent of a foreign power
- Raise the standard for the government to look at medical records, library records or records involving the purchase or rental of books, videos and music by requiring the government to show "probable cause" to gain such search powers
- Ensure that libraries will not be required to turn over Internet usage information about their patrons, unless the government meets the standards required by the Foreign Intelligence Surveillance Act
- Require a court order approving an electronic surveillance to specify either the identity of the target or the location of the facility where the surveillance will occur
- Add judicial review for "pen registers" and "trap and trace" device requests by requiring that the government show specific facts that indicate that a crime has been, is, or will be committed

- Define the types of Internet usage and email information that can be obtained
- Require greater public reporting on activities conducted under the Foreign Intelligence Surveillance Act (FISA)
- Apply discovery procedures already in place under the Classified Information Procedures Act (CIPA) to other court proceedings that will use evidence collected under FISA
- Restore the former requirement that the "primary purpose" for electronic surveillance and physical searches under the Foreign Intelligence Surveillance Act is to obtain foreign intelligence
- Provide for greater judicial review of government requests for educational records by requiring the government to set forth specific facts indicating the education records are relevant to an investigation.[48]

Despite the intensifying challenges, Attorney General Ashcroft and FBI director Mueller continue to vigorously support the act as a critical tool in the war against terrorism, albeit with persistent reluctance to submit their activities to congressional scrutiny. In May 2003, under pressure from Congress, the DOJ revealed that, under the Patriot Act provisions, it had detained fewer than fifty people as material witnesses without charging them and had received only forty-seven delayed notification search warrants. However, the report also indicated that the act's provisions were being used for nonterrorism-related cases including securing the forfeiture of assets from a lawyer who absconded with client funds. The report, however, did not provide specific information on the number of libraries that had been approached for patron records.

A later report released in July 2003 by the DOJ's inspector general's office revealed that 1,073 new complaints of civil rights and civil liberties violations have arisen under the Patriot Act, 34 of which were deemed "credible." According to the report, these abuses range from abusive treatment by prison officials to unlawful searches of prison cells and private residences.[49] In an effort to quell resistance, the DOJ is currently planning what amounts to a USA Patriot Act public relations tour purportedly to set the record straight as to how the act's provisions are being used to effectively wage the war against terrorism. However, this effort may be too little too late. As widespread resistance to the Patriot Act's more egregious provisions increases, it is perhaps inevitable that Americans through their democratic institutions will restore the balance between national security and civil liberties and return the reason, sense of fair play, freedom, and respect for others that served as the impetus for founding a great nation more than two centuries ago.

5 Other Post-9/11 Legal Responses

Although the USA Patriot Act was the federal government's major, and potentially most far-reaching, legal response to the September 11 terrorist attacks, other significant legal responses should not be overlooked. These have come not only from the legislature but also from the executive and judicial branches of government. This chapter examines those legal responses in turn.

Subsequent Legislative Responses

There have been a number of legislative responses from Congress since the September 11 terrorist attacks. Among them are the Aviation and Transportation Security Act, establishing the TSA; the Enhanced Border Security and Visa Entry Reform Act, designed to reinforce border security; and the Public Health Security and Bioterrorism Preparedness and Response Act. While these are individually important legislative responses to the emerging terrorist threat, they are not as significant as the legislative responses authorizing President Bush to use military force in pursuit of al Qaeda and the initiative to create a new cabinet-level office for homeland security. Consequently, those latter two pieces of legislation are the focus of the following discussion.

Joint Resolution Authorizing Use of Force

On September 14, 2001, Congress passed a joint resolution authorizing the president to use force "against those responsible for the recent attacks launched against the United States." The modus operandi conforms generally to that used by Congress since the passage of the War Powers Resolution in 1973, whereby the latitude conferred on the executive by the legislature is broad enough to accomplish the task at hand with military operations but outside parameters are set beyond that which the executive theoretically cannot maneuver absent an invasion that he is required to repulse.

The language proposed by the administration was extremely broad:

That the President is authorized to use all necessary and appropriate force against those nations, organizations, or persons he determines planned, authorized, harbored, committed, or aided in the planning or commission of the attacks against the United States that occurred on September 11, 2001, and to deter and pre-empt any future acts of terrorism or aggression against the United States.[1]

According to the chief minority counsel for the House International Relations Committee, who helped negotiate the language on behalf of Congress, reaction to this wording

was immediately negative. . . . [H]ad this authority become law, it would have authorized the President to use force not only against the perpetrators of the September 11th attacks, but also against anyone who might be considering future acts of terrorism, as well as against any nation that was planning "aggression" against the United States. Given the breadth of activities potentially encompassed by the term "aggression," the President might never again have had to seek congressional authorization for the use of force.[2]

As promulgated, the final language of Section 2 provides the specific authorization as well as the specific limitations in scope and purpose:

[T]he President is authorized to use all necessary and appropriate force against those nations, organizations, or persons he determines planned, authorized, committed, or aided the terrorist attacks that occurred on September 11, 2001, or harbored such organizations or persons, in order to prevent any future acts of international terrorism against the United States by such nations, organizations or persons.[3]

Clearly, the purpose of President Bush's use of military force is constrained to preventing future attacks against the United States. Thus, under the terms of this resolution, our forces could not be used to prevent al Qaeda attacks against Israel or Britain or Japan, although such force might still be used pursuant to some other applicable treaty or security arrangement. Moreover, because the purpose is specifically preventative against future acts, not retributive for past acts, the president must establish a threshold in his determination for when action must be ordered to prevent further attacks. Of course, such threshold will likely be low and definitely preemptive in nature.

The purpose for employment of military force is further limited to acts of "international" terrorism. Consequently, military force is not authorized under this grant of authority for "internal" acts of terrorism by al Qaeda. While the decision by Congress to allow military operations outside the United States but not inside reflects its historic institutional caution about unleashing the armed forces domestically, this characterization of international versus internal acts of terrorism is interesting in that all four of the flights that were hijacked and converted to guided missiles on September 11 originated within the United States. Presumably, these would be considered internal acts of terrorism and, therefore, would not be covered by the terms of Section 2.

Perhaps a case could be made that the attacks were somehow "international" because the actors were foreign and were backed by a foreign-based terrorist network. But this line of reasoning fails when we are confronted with al Qaeda members launching attacks from within the United States who happen to be American citizens, like Jose Padilla. Perhaps domestic police power is sufficient, but the resolution would not cover this situation if Padilla had proceeded to target an area after landing at O'Hare Airport on May 8, 2002, and succeeded in constructing a dirty bomb.

The scope of executive authority is also limited. The president may use military force against those "nations, organizations, or persons he determines planned, authorized, committed or aided" the September 11 attacks or countries that "harbored" those who carried out the attacks. This language confines the president's range of targets to those who are, even tenuously, linked to the hijackings. On a primary level, this includes the al Qaeda organization and its operatives as individuals, as well as the Taliban government in Afghanistan.

On a secondary level, assuming "harbor" is interpreted loosely, this includes countries that may have provided support for al Qaeda or the Taliban—like Pakistan or perhaps even Saudi Arabia, with its demonstrated financial support. However, such friendly countries are unlikely to find themselves on the receiving end of U.S. military force. Because the resolution was written so soon after the attacks, it is more likely that legislative leeway was provided in the event that it could be shown that unfriendly countries like Iraq, Iran, Libya, or Syria were involved. Such evidence has thus far been lacking.

On a tertiary level, this allows the president to exercise military force in pursuit of anyone or any group associated with the al Qaeda network prior to September 11. Consequently, while U.S. troops can participate in flushing out Abu Sayef rebels on the southern islands of the Philippines because of their prior association with al Qaeda, American forces cannot be employed under the terms of Section 2 against Lebanon's anti-Israeli terrorist group Hizbollah— which decided to associate itself with the remnants of al Qaeda in June 2002.

Senator Joseph Biden (D-Delaware), chair of the Senate Foreign Relations Committee, summed up the sense of Congress in crafting the language that simultaneously empowers and limits the president in his military response on behalf of America:

In all our anger, all our frustration, all our feelings, very bluntly, of hatred that exists now for those who perpetrated the act against us, we did not pell-mell just say: Go do anything, anytime, anyplace, Mr. President; you have to just go. We operated as our Founders, who were not naive people, intended us to operate. We operated under the rule of law.

We went to our civil bible, the Constitution, and we said: What does it call for here? What it calls for is the U.S. Congress to meet its constitutional responsibility, to say: Mr. President, we authorize you, in the name of the American people, to take action, and we define the action in generic terms which you can take.

We gave the President today . . . all the authority he needs to prosecute war against the individuals or countries responsible, without yielding our constitutional right to retain the judgment in the future as to whether or not force against others could, should, or would be used. . . . In short, the President is authorized to go after those responsible for the barbaric acts of September 11, 2001 *to ensure that those same actors do not engage in additional acts of international terrorism* against the United States.[4]

Finally, there is no ticking clock other than the periodic reporting requirement (at least once every six months) contained in the War Powers Resolution—which all presidents since 1973 have regarded as an unconstitutional limit on their authority. The September 14 resolution contains no time limit constraining the president in his prosecution of this "war on terrorism," nor does it contain any reporting provisions. Apparently, the legislature determined that the timing mechanisms in the War Powers Resolution were sufficient.[5]

The second part of Section 2 states, "consistent with section 8(a)(1) of the War Powers Resolution, the Congress declares that this section is intended to constitute specific statutory authorization within the meaning of section 5(b) of the War Powers Resolution. Nothing in this resolution supercedes any requirement of the War Powers Resolution." Thus, the legislature clearly considers the controversial 1973 delineation of war powers applicable, operative, and incorporated by reference in the current situation.

All presidents since Nixon, whose veto of the War Powers Resolution was overridden, have complied at some point with its reporting requirements, except President Carter, who encountered no similar military engagements during his term beyond the failed hostage rescue mission to Iran.[6] President Bush, like his predecessors, considers the War Powers Resolution unconstitutional; however, if history is an indicator, he will likely comply with applicable reporting or consulting provisions ostensibly as a courtesy but realistically to avoid a judicial crisis that may result in a formal loss of power by the executive branch. As Columbia Law School's Lori Fisler Damrosch notes:

No President explicitly conceded that Congress has a constitutional entitlement to share in the decision to introduce troops into hostilities; no president conceded that Congress could constitutionally control the Commander-in-Chief in the exercise of his Article II powers; yet patterns of compliance with the War Powers Resolution did emerge that are suggestive of an unwillingness to force differences of principle to a concrete confrontation.[7]

Thus, the War Powers Resolution, designed to reinforce the framers' constitutional determination that the power to initiate war lay with Congress while the power to repel sudden attacks lay with the president,[8] operates in the context of this administration's war on terrorism as a gap filler. Indeed, by its own terms, Section 2(c) recognizes the president's Article II authority to respond militarily to "a national emergency created by attack upon the United States, its territories or possessions, or its armed forces."[9] So, where the president introduces military force beyond the scope of the September 14 joint resolution (such as in Iraq absent evidence of linkage to al Qaeda) and not in response to a direct attack on the United States as conceived under Article II of the Constitution, he does so under the War Powers Resolution.

This means that such operations would be subject to much stricter reporting and consultation requirements. Specifically, President Bush would have sixty days after the submission of his first report to Congress, or after which it is supposed to have been submitted, to complete his use of military force. After that period, if Congress has not declared war, has not extended the sixty-day period, or is unable to meet due to an armed attack on the United States, the president must withdraw the troops. He has a thirty-day grace period to effectuate this withdrawal if doing so immediately would precipitate a military catastrophe and he certifies such executive decision to Congress in writing. Congress also has the power to demand removal of troops from foreign operations sooner if it so directs by concurrent resolution.[10] A glance around the Eastern

Hemisphere reveals where the United States is currently pursuing, and might likely expand, its military operations in its widening war on terrorism.[11]

Philippines

While the Filipino constitution prohibits military operations by foreign forces within their country, U.S. armed forces have provided logistical support for Manila's campaign against the Abu Sayyaf, a militant Muslim group believed to have links with Osama bin Laden dating back to the early 1990s. Around six hundred American troops have been deployed to assist in the hunt for these rebels, who operate in the south of the country. Filipino officials believe that the Abu Sayyaf has received arms, training, and other logistical support from al Qaeda and that the rebel group's methods of kidnapping and hostage taking are indicative of al Qaeda methods.

Malaysia

There has been a series of arrests since September 11 of Islamic militants suspected of having links to Osama bin Laden's al Qaeda network. Intelligence and law enforcement agencies in the region now say al Qaeda's roots in Southeast Asia are stronger than was first suspected. Two of the alleged hijackers who took part in the September 11 attacks on the United States, Khaled al-Midhar and Nawaq al-Hamzi, were filmed at a meeting in Kuala Lumpur with other known al Qaeda operatives. Another indication of linkage to al Qaeda is the time spent in Afghanistan by members of the rebel Malaysian Mujahideen Group (KMM), perhaps at terrorist training camps.

Indonesia

America could target parts of Indonesia, where Islamic militants have gained a strong foothold. The Bush administration is frustrated by the Indonesian government's unwillingness or inability to target or rein in these groups. Indonesia is the world's largest Islamic country, with a population of 400 million. The head of the country's National Intelligence Agency, Lieutenant General Hendropriyono, recently confirmed that al Qaeda members have been fighting on the island of Sulawesi. Local militant groups, like the Laskar Jihad, which has trained thousands to fight against Christians, are believed to have links with al Qaeda.

There is also an al Qaeda–type pan-Islamic terrorist network operating throughout the archipelago, albeit on a regional rather than a global basis. Jemaah Islamiyah, headed by Abu Bakar Baaysir, has divided the country into three geographic areas, known as *mantiqi*, each with its own terrorist coordinator and each carrying out coordinated but independent missions. This group has worked with al Qaeda in the past but is not reliant on it for logistics, training, money, or direction. The fear is that a network like Jemaah Islamiyah could evolve to fill the void left by al Qaeda when it is finally destroyed. Jemaah Islamiyah was responsible for the 2002 bombing of a Western nightclub in Bali that killed over 200 people and crippled the country's tourist industry and is believed responsible for the August 2003 bombing of the Jakarta Marriott Hotel that claimed 14 lives and injured 148.

U.S. authorities are considering the familial linkage of Indonesian would-be terrorists. Bashir, the head of Jemaah Islamiyah, Jafar Umar Thalib, the head of Laskar Jihad, and Habib Husein Habsy, the head of Indonesian Muslim Brotherhood, are all Indonesian born, but each is Hadrami—a clan whose roots are not in Indonesia but in southern Yemen. Drawing deeper connections such as this may assist in the hardening of further American targets for military action.

Sudan

In 1998 Sudan was the target of American missile strikes, after the Clinton administration accused it of ties with al Qaeda, which the United States blamed for blowing up its embassies in Kenya and Tanzania earlier that year. There have been reports of an American contingency plan to attack targets in Sudan, where Osama bin Laden was based before moving to Afghanistan. However, since

September 11 the Sudanese government has stepped up its efforts to arrest and hand over terrorist suspects.

Yemen

Yemen is Osama bin Laden's ancestral home, and the United States suspects that his men were behind the attack on the USS *Cole* in the Port of Aden that killed seventeen American sailors in 2000. In December 2001 Yemeni security forces—with the help of U.S. intelligence—attacked mountain villages suspected of harboring members of bin Laden's al Qaeda network. It was the first time since the September 11 attacks on the United States that an Arab government used military force to confront suspected members of al Qaeda.

A year later, in November 2002, U.S. military unmanned aircraft (operated by the CIA) confirmed satellite identification of six al Qaeda operatives driving in the remote northern region of Yemen and fired missiles at the target, killing all on board. One of those assassinated was Qaed Salim Sinan al-Harethi, al Qaeda's chief operative in Yemen—and the man believed responsible for coordinating the attack on the USS *Cole*.

Somalia

American intelligence has determined that al Qaeda does have bases in Somalia, and the U.S. Navy has begun patrolling the sea lanes leading to that nation's coastline. The mostly Muslim country has no effective central government, and much of the country is divided into fiefdoms presided over by competing warlords. Somalia's interim prime minister, Hassan Abshir Farah, has strongly rejected American charges, but he has also indicated he would welcome the deployment of U.S. military teams in Somalia to investigate the possible presence of al Qaeda members.

Tajikistan

American and European military forces have been operating in Tajikistan, Afghanistan's immediate neighbor to the north. Prior to the September 11 attacks on the United States, al Qaeda trained and backed fundamentalist Islamic rebels fighting the Tajik government. In the past, Tajikistan has been accused by surrounding states—specifically China, which is attempting to suppress its own Islamic rebellion in the far western region of Xinjiang Province—of tolerating the presence of training camps for Islamist rebels on its territory. Tajikistan strongly denies this assertion.

Uzbekistan

The United States has used the airspace and airports in Uzbekistan, with Russian consent, during the war in Afghanistan. The Uzbek government has its own problems with Islamic militants, and few believe Tashkent's cooperation has come without a price. Washington says the Islamic Movement of Uzbekistan (IMU) has ties to al Qaeda and poses a regional threat that must be rooted out. Many believe that the United States might help Uzbekistan do that, while turning a blind eye to government crackdowns on opposition groups.

The "Axis of Evil"

Iran

Iran was singled out by President Bush as a dangerous regime in his January 2002 State of the Union speech. He said that North Korea, Iraq, and their "terrorist allies," along with Tehran, constitute an "axis of evil." There is no evidence linking Iran to al Qaeda, the Taliban, or the September 11 attacks on the United States. In fact, Iran agreed to offer sanctuary to any American pilots shot down over its territory during the American-led military campaign in neighboring Afghanistan. Nonetheless, Iran was accused of aggressively pursuing WMD and exporting terror. While President Bush said such activities could not be tolerated, he left it vague as to what action the United States would take.

This impasse, however, could be approaching a critical brink—and pushing Iran further away from cooperation with the West. Iran's nuclear capabilities became more alarming when an unknown plutonium plant was discovered in 2003, complementing the already known uranium plant. A French report on Iran's progress termed it "surprisingly close" to achieving a weapon. Moreover, Tehran recently disclosed that it is holding several senior al Qaeda members in captivity but has refused to hand them over to the United States. The geostrategic position of Iran is also increasingly precarious, with U.S. military forces directly to the east in Afghanistan, to the south in the Persian Gulf, to the west in Iraq, and around air bases in neighboring Pakistan and Turkmenistan.

North Korea

There is no evidence linking North Korea to the September 11 attacks, but President Bush has warned the communist government of Kim Il Sung in Pyongyang that it could soon become a target in the war on terror. In his State of the Union address, the president put North Korea among a small group of the world's most dangerous regimes. He accused it of arming itself with missiles and WMD that could be used in turn to arm international terrorists. In describing North Korea as part of "an axis of evil," he left his warning vague without mentioning specific actions that could be taken but hinted that he would move to use full military force if necessary.

However, North Korea's huge conventional armed forces clearly mitigate against a military solution to the crisis provoked by its recent emergence as a nascent nuclear power (plus the implied ability to take out Tokyo with a single nuclear-tipped Nodong missile). Consequently, despite a hard political line, the administration remains committed, for now, to seeking a diplomatic solution through multilateral talks that include Russia, China, South Korea, and Japan—to which North Korea has finally agreed after much effort seeking bilateral talks with the United States.

Iraq

Despite no clear evidence linking Iraq to the September 11 attacks, that country was invaded by U.S. military forces on the president's order in May 2003 and remains an occupied country. Justification for action prior to the attack rested primarily on security grounds (possible links to terrorists, possible development of nuclear arms, etc.) but shifted after the war to encompass the removal of despots and the encouragement of democracy and freedom generally. The forcible removal of Saddam Hussein from power occurred in the absence of UN Security Council authorization but with domestic congressional authority in support. Broad public support was encouraged by the administration's persistent efforts to blend any action against Iraq into a wider, more amorphous war on terrorism.

That domestic support, however, was by no means unanimous. Without a substantial link between Saddam Hussein's regime and al Qaeda, many—such as Brent Scowcroft, national security advisor in the first Bush administration—believed that attacking Iraq would detract from the war on terrorism proper. As former secretary of state Madeleine Albright noted:

> As evil as Mr. Hussein is, he is not the reason antiaircraft guns ring the capital, civil liberties are being compromised, a Department of Homeland Defense is being created and the Gettysburg Address again seems directly relevant to our lives. In the aftermath of tragedy a year ago, the chief executive told our nation that fighting terrorism would be "the focus of my presidency." That—not Iraq—remains the right focus.[12]

Nevertheless, approximately 150,000 American forces remain in occupation of Iraq for the foreseeable future. Construction of new military bases are also envisioned there—partly to better stabilize the region and police Iraq's redevelopment and partly to offset the loss of American base use in Saudi Arabia as that country gradually extricates itself from such a visible alliance with the United States, bowing to domestic opposition in the process. It is hoped that, in the long term, the founding and survival of a successful democracy in Iraq will spread the yearning for similar freedoms to other parts of the Middle East, now ruled in large part by autocratic regimes.

Legal Basis for Future Military Action

Besides the fact that each of the countries included in President Bush's "axis of evil" despises the United States for different reasons, another common factor shared by them is the lack of evidence tying them to al Qaeda. Without such linkage, Congress's Joint Resolution on the Use of Force would not cover any military action President Bush might undertake against them. This is why the president secured separate congressional authorization for the Iraq war in October 2002.

In the absence of such legislative authorization, he would have to act on his own authority under Article II of the Constitution to repel an imminent attack. Attorneys from the administration's DOJ and Homeland Security Office have argued that this includes the possibility of America conducting a preemptive strike against a foreign country or a group within a country harboring them. They also argue that such a move is supported by the language of the September 14 resolution and that no other congressional articulation on the matter is needed.[13]

However, under international law, the existence of an imminent threat must be shown prior to undertaking such a move (which is ostensibly illegal under the UN charter).[14] So, absent such evidence of an imminent threat, the president would still be bound by the War Powers Resolution regarding the introduction of troops into hostilities. But in either case, he would remain bound by that law's reporting provisions.

Creation of Homeland Security Department

Legislation creating a new Department of Homeland Security was not requested immediately after the September 11 attacks. It was not until several months later that critical defects in federal agency information sharing, threat analysis, and processing capability— which led to the greatest intelligence failure in American history— came to light. The government's responses prior to its decision to create such a unified department in the summer of 2002 were instead focused on establishing an office within the White House to advise the president on homeland security and efforts to internally reform the existing agencies that had failed so spectacularly in their mission to protect the United States.

On October 8, 2001, President Bush issued an executive order establishing the Office of Homeland Security. The office's mission was to "develop and coordinate the implementation of a comprehensive national strategy to secure the United States from terrorist threats or attacks." It had the following functions: national strategy, detection, preparedness, prevention, protection, response and recovery, incident management, continuity of government, public affairs, cooperation with state and local governments and private entities, review of legal authorities and development of legislative proposals, and budget review.

However, as noted in chapter 3, this office was widely regarded inadequate to the task in terms of power and budget to achieve its goals. The only major initiative generated was the color-coded public warning system for terrorism alerts. While seemingly innocuous, there is growing concern that this system not only alerts the public to the appropriate level of awareness they should undertake, but also can be interpreted by local and state law enforcement officials as telegraphing permission to infringe greater levels of civil liberty as they seek to provide greater levels of security and "watchfulness."

Under this theory, it was no coincidence that, after America went to a heightened level of orange alert on September 10, 2002, Florida law enforcement officers overreacted to a tip from a woman who overheard three Middle Eastern medical students talking about the 9/11 anniversary in a Shoney's Restaurant. The officers tracked and stopped their cars, closed down Interstate 75 between Miami and Ft. Meyers, and detained them for questioning without reasonable suspicion or probable cause.

Beyond establishing the advisor's position in the White House, the executive order also established the Homeland Security Council. This group comprises the director of the Federal Emergency Management Agency (FEMA), the director of the FBI, and the director of the CIA. The order stated that it did not alter the existing authorities of the U.S. government departments and agencies but that they were ordered to assist the council and the assistant to the president for homeland security in carrying out the order's purposes.[15]

Simultaneously, in an effort to get the key agencies in its administration to form an alliance and to increase their communication and effectiveness, the White House used the tools provided it by the USA Patriot Act to make changes within the FBI and the CIA, including the shift within the FBI from solving crimes to gathering domestic intelligence and giving the CIA the authority to influence FBI surveillance operations within the United States, plus the ability to obtain evidence from the FBI gathered by grand juries and wiretaps. This shift within the FBI meant that the agency's primary focus turned to counterterrorism.[16]

Then the attorney general announced a "wartime reorganization and mobilization" of the DOJ that included the abandonment or reduction of manpower working current responsibilities (running the gamut from civil rights enforcement to environmental pollution prosecution to local investigations such as undercover drug operations). Ashcroft said that they "must focus on our core mission and responsibilities, understanding that the department will not be all things to all people." Ten percent of DOJ, FBI, and other agency employees would be transferred to field offices around the country as part of a five-year restructuring plan. Reforms planned for the FBI and the INS proceeded and emphasized counterterrorism.[17]

The effort to internally reform agencies and make them work together more efficiently continued into the new year. In January 2002, James Ziglar, head of the INS, stated that his agency would work more closely with the FBI and CIA to share information and screen visitors before they arrive. During the prior month, he had announced that the names of 314,000 foreign nationals who remained in the United States despite deportation orders would be entered into the FBI national database.[18]

In May FBI director Mueller proposed creating a new "super squad"—headquartered in Washington—to conduct all major international terrorism investigations. The proposal would employ hundreds of agents and analysts and would involve creating an Office of Intelligence (the director would be a former CIA official); the Office of Intelligence would become a national clearinghouse for classified terrorism information. Nonterrorism investigations would continue to be pursued, but not at the same level. The Office of Intelligence would be used to analyze information. The next day, INS officials announced that the backlog of immigration applications was growing rapidly due to the inability in some offices to access a new security database (Interagency Border Inspection System) and the lack of training to use the database.[19]

By the end of that month, Mueller had announced the FBI's plan for reorganization (discussed in chapter 3), putting twenty-six thousand agents on permanent counterterrorism duty and attempting to hire nine hundred linguists, computer experts, engineers, and scientists—all in an effort to improve both the gathering and analysis of information. In addition, fifty CIA employees were put on Joint Terrorism Task Forces in field offices, while another twenty-five CIA employees were transferred to the FBI as counterterrorism analysts. Ashcroft also rewrote department guidelines to give field agents more authority to open terrorism investigations, to conduct preliminary inquiries for a full year without being based on leads or probable cause, and to open undercover probes without having to seek clearance from FBI headquarters.[20]

Nonetheless, it had become apparent by the end of spring that agency reform efforts would not alone suffice to meet the country's enhanced security needs. Thus, President Bush decided to move ahead with the internally debated action of requesting legislation to create a new cabinet-level Department of Homeland Security in June 2002 that would unite several agencies, including the Coast Guard, Border Patrol, Customs Service, TSA, and FEMA. The department would have four tasks: controlling borders; working with state and local authorities to respond quickly to emergencies; developing technologies that detect biological, chemical, and nuclear weapons while working on vaccines and treatments for increased protection; and reviewing intelligence and law enforcement information. Most employees would be drawn from the combined agencies in order to avoid duplication and overlap.[21]

One of the divisions, Information Analysis and Infrastructure Protection, would analyze almost all of the information gathered by the FBI, CIA, and other agencies. Then the department would develop strategies for response. The FBI would no longer issue terrorist-related warnings to local law enforcement but would cede that responsibility to the department. Eighty percent of the Information Analysis and Infrastructure Protection data would be pulled from the FBI's National Infrastructure Protection Center. The CIA and FBI would continue to run their operations and analyze their data but would be expected to turn over most of the intelligence gathered.[22] Both the FBI and CIA directors testified in support of the legislation, referring to the new department as a "customer" for their respective intelligence-gathering and analytical capabilities.

In support of the initiative, and to further clarify its vision for the new bureaucracy, the White House unveiled the National Strategy for Homeland Security with the creation of the new department as its centerpiece. It identifies three objectives: preventing terrorist attacks in the United States; reducing America's vulnerability to terrorism; and, in the event of attacks, accelerating recovery while making damage as minimal as possible.[23]

Two of the more ominous notes struck by the National Strategy for Homeland Security concerned information control and use of the military. The "law" portion of the plan called for tightening up public disclosure of information related to the war on terror and the government's efforts to further it. This, of course, would hamper the public's ability to monitor whether the executive's actions remain within the realm of the law. Review of the *posse comitatus* doctrine was also suggested. Under this doctrine, the U.S. military services are prohibited from enforcing law within the United States absent authorization to do so by Congress. Giving the military a free hand within our borders would be a massive increase in power to the executive branch. No legislation has been requested on these points yet.[24]

Congress responded to the president's request by passing the Homeland Security Act, creating the new Department of Homeland Security, and confirming Tom Ridge as its first secretary. After its creation, many federal agencies were transferred to Homeland Security, such as FEMA, the DOJ's INS, the Department of Transportation's Coast Guard and TSA, the Department of Treasury's Secret Service and Customs Service, and the Department of Energy's Nuclear Incident Response Team.

As the new cabinet-level entity comes on-line, the executive Office of Homeland Security is likely to be marginalized and could eventually fade from the scene, while its limited initiatives, such as the creation of the color-coded federal alert mechanism, are likely to be incorporated into the department's threat analysis and public information systems.

Despite worries in Congress, the new department is not likely to get into the raw intelligence collection business, relying on the FBI and CIA instead. However, the degree to which overlap in analytical functions exists could open the FBI to charges that agents assigned to redundant terrorism analysis tasks come at the expense of nonterrorism criminal investigations. Knowing this, any increase in organized crime, white-collar crime, drug-related activity, or Racketeer Influenced and Corrupt Organizations (RICO) infractions can be used to demonstrate that intelligence sharing and analysis arrangements must be reorchestrated.

Perhaps more so than the other two, more deliberative branches, the executive branch is expected by the public it serves to respond quickly, directly, and decisively when tragedies on the scale of the September 11 terrorist attacks unfold. When the Japanese Empire attacked Pearl Harbor in 1941, President Roosevelt mobilized our forces and publicly requested a declaration of war from Congress the next day. When the Cuban missile crisis erupted into a cold war showdown in 1962, President Kennedy circled the wagons and announced not only to America but to the world that we were ready and practically willing to engage in a nuclear exchange with Kruschev's Soviet Union. Immediate threats to our country do not go unchallenged, and it is incumbent upon any president to present a strong and confrontational figure in such situations.

Not surprisingly, President Bush's response to al Qaeda's coordinated attacks on Manhattan and Washington, D.C., comported exactly with these expectations. Indeed, he cut a particularly strong and resolute figure when he addressed a joint session of Congress five days after the disaster. Although he did not request Congress to invoke its Article I war power, he did insist that a state of war existed between the civilized world and the forces of terror, formally linked those forces to existing states that offer them aid and sanctuary, issued threatening demands on the Taliban government of Afghanistan, and announced the creation of a new cabinet-level office dedicated to ensuring homeland security.

All parties agreed that the president emerged that day as a changed figure on the national scene. Gone were the unsure glances skyward, the bottom-lip-chewing boyish face of indecision, and the stuttering, broken syntax so characteristic of his father. Indeed, George Walker Bush became a walking example of the moment defining the man. He grew into his job that week, projecting a persona of confidence and direction and the single-minded determination of a man who suddenly understands the significance of his chief mission. The president's cabinet reflected his aura as well—some, such as Attorney General Ashcroft, to the unfortunate extent that they characterized anyone who questioned the administration's policy initiatives as unpatriotic supporters of terrorism.

So it was that the president's legal responses directly following the attacks were understandably laced with emotion of the moment and promulgated perhaps too quickly for adequate consideration of consequences under the considerable public pressure that any president faces in like circumstances. Nonetheless, after several months' reflection, policy flaws can, and do, emerge that must be responsibly addressed. The challenge to those who suggest such modifications (such as the authors of this book) is to do so without questioning the integrity of the officials who formulated the response. Equally, the challenge to officials tasked with implementation is to accept such analysis in the vein of bettering the policies, to engage in the dialogue of democracy, and to unwed themselves from a personal stake in that part of our government's response to terrorism that they are charged with undertaking.

However, the cavalier attitude of this administration in conducting the war on terrorism has drawn criticism from the press already. Hearst Newspaper columnist Helen Thomas, former White House correspondent for United Press International since the Kennedy administration and keen observer of every administration since, was provoked to pen these words:

> The imperial presidency has arrived. On the domestic front President Bush has found that in many ways he can govern by executive order. In foreign affairs he has the nerve to tell other people that they should get rid of their current leaders. Amazingly, with Americans turning into a new silent majority and Congress into a bunch of obeisant lawmakers, he is getting away with such acts. The lawmakers are worried that Bush will play the "patriot card" in the November elections to attack dissenters and opponents. The Democratic leaders have already rolled over. They have given him a blank check by passing the USA Patriot Act, which permits outrageous invasions of privacy, and by seconding Bush's foreign policy with a weak "me too."
>
> Whatever happened to congressional oversight? I remember all too well the senators who gave President Lyndon B. Johnson a free hand to do whatever he believed was necessary in Southeast Asia. They lived to regret it. The result was the Vietnam War that ripped our country apart. The list of the president's self-empowerment moves grows almost daily and will continue unless the Supreme Court calls his hand. Did I

say Supreme Court? Forget it. Not with this court. It handed him the 2000 election, and it would probably cite some World War II decisions that allowed the government to violate citizens' civil rights, especially those of Japanese Americans, in the name of national security.

Civil rights are now clearly being ignored by government agents in the war on terrorism who want to make the vulnerable detainees talk. The agents' methods of extracting information are not disclosed. And the imprisoned suspects and material witnesses cannot get in touch with lawyers or their families. I'm not talking about Russia's infamous gulags. I am talking about us. The president made the arbitrary decision to designate as a foreign "enemy combatant" the Brooklyn-born Jose Padilla, who is suspected of being an al-Qaeda scout seeking to locate targets for a "dirty bomb" attack. He is being held incommunicado in a military brig without due process of law and without being charged.

Where are the great constitutional law experts who might protest such treatment? It appears they have bowed to the exigencies of our time and are accepting Bush's end-runs around the law involving some 2,400 detainees, who are reportedly being held indefinitely by U.S. authorities. Can Americans really tolerate the denial of rights to these people?

Overseeing much of the chipping away at our privacy and other civil liberties is Attorney General John Ashcroft. He is enthusiastically using the patriot law to let federal agents wiretap and access the e-mail of untold numbers of citizens and to listen in on conversations between lawyers and clients. Now FBI agents are checking lists of readers at libraries and book stores. Is book burning in our future?

Ashcroft also sent a memo to federal agencies promising that the Justice Department will back them up anytime they want to deny freedom of information requests from scholars and journalists. Here, he is protecting Bush from criticism over the administration's clamp-down on government information. Rest assured he could not do this without the imprimatur of the White House.

We should not forget that Bush, early in his tenure, blocked the implementation of the release of President Reagan's White House papers. Under the Presidential Records Act of 1978, his official documents were to be available to the public 12 years after he left office. So they were due for release last year, but Bush simply overrode that law. Was he trying to protect Reagan from the probing of historians and the media? Or was he really trying to protect his father, George H. W. Bush, who was Reagan's vice president and who succeeded him as president? White House aides issued a flimsy excuse—that the order was designed to institute an orderly release of the papers. But my guess is that No. 43, as W calls himself, was trying to protect No. 41.

Equally blatant examples of Bush's arrogance of power are in his foreign policy. What right does he have to tell Yasser Arafat that he has to go or to tell the Palestinians they cannot vote for Arafat in coming elections? Bush's speech could have been written by Israeli Prime Minister Ariel Sharon. Although he speaks of his compassion for the suffering Palestinians under Israel's military occupation, Bush is tightening the screws by making it clear he will deny them any aid unless Arafat is deposed. Plans to topple Iraq's Saddam Hussein have also been on the president's radar screen since he took office. When did the United States get the right to tell other countries and people who should lead them?

The president has been flexing America's military muscles and threatening pre-emptive first strikes against nations suspected—suspected!—of wanting to harm the United States. That also is a break with our past traditions. Bush is due for a reality check. We need allies whenever we contemplate such drastic actions, and our allies are worried about his constant saber rattling. Some day he is going to try to give a war and nobody is going to come.[25]

The legislature's capitulation to the executive branch in passing the USA Patriot Act served as a de facto and de jure green light for the administration to move ahead with accretion of power to itself on other fronts. Shortly thereafter, the president announced the creation of military tribunals to try suspected terrorists outside the jurisdiction of federal courts. Then the attorney general issued new directives within the DOJ expanding his power to detain immigrants indefinitely, increasing the use of secret deportation hearings, contracting the information available to the public under the Freedom of Information Act, and waiving the attorney-client privilege for terrorist suspects in custody by executive fiat.

In the still vacuum of legislative and judicial silence, FBI investigation and surveillance rules were rewritten—allowing agents to enter houses of worship and to monitor civilians and noncivilians without any indicia of illegal activity, not even reasonable suspicion, let alone probable cause. Sensing no groundswell of opposition, the administration took its next step—indefinite detention of American citizens within the United States without access to counsel, without charges being filed, without trial by jury, and held incommunicado while in solitary confinement. This last act touched a nerve in the American psyche, causing both conservative and liberal political and libertarian groups to rouse themselves in suspicion of the executive's motives.

But the increased power had already settled into the minds of administration officials, apparently convincing them that they held a monopoly on truth; thus, their actions in the best interest of the country were beyond reproach. Consequently, the DOJ, fearful that they could lose custody of their terrorist suspects who were American citizens, labeled them "enemy combatants" and handed them over to the DOD—which promptly threw them into military brigs for interrogation without counsel. They continue to languish there today. The remaining sections of the chapter explore some of these administration initiatives in greater depth.

Presidential Military Order

One month after the administration had secured passage of the USA Patriot Act and detected no strong opposition, the president issued a military order establishing military commissions to try terrorists captured in America's new war on terrorism. According to the terms of the order, its provisions do not apply to U.S. citizens, this prohibition having been established during the Civil War by the Supreme Court's opinion in *Ex Parte Milligan*.[26] Therefore, only aliens can be tried by such military tribunals, but how wide is this jurisdictional net cast?

Three types of aliens, detained either here or abroad, are subject to this order. First is any former or current member of al Qaeda. Second is anyone who has "engaged in, aided or abetted, or conspired to commit, acts of international terrorism, or acts in preparation therefor" directed at the United States or its interests or citizens—in other words, any nondomestic terrorist threatening America. Third is anyone who "knowingly harbors" a person that falls into the definition laid out in the prior two categories.[27]

Upon promulgation, Harvard constitutional law scholar Laurence Tribe pronounced the order "rife with constitutional problems and riddled with flaws," noting that its language allowed the government to capture and arrest not only terrorists abroad but resident aliens at home who might once have had contact with a terrorist a decade ago. According to Tribe, the undefined terms "knowingly harbored," "aided and abetted," and "international terrorism" give the order an elasticity that makes it almost impossible to limit.[28] Moreover, the absence of a temporal limit on activities for which people could be apprehended raises ex post facto issues.

The order also suspends the writ of habeas corpus. Section 7 states that defendants tried by military commission "shall not be privileged to seek any remedy or maintain any proceeding . . . in any [U.S.] court."[29] Other departures from normal criminal process by the order include a much lowered standard of admissible evidence ("probative value to a reasonable person"), which can include hearsay, the defendant's right to counsel, right to appeal, right to confront witnesses against him, right to trial by jury, right to examine evidence against him, and right against indefinite detention.

Most of these rights that flow from our Constitution do not necessarily attach to the detainees while they are outside of the United States. However, the Third Geneva Convention protecting the rights of prisoners of war guarantees many of them.[30] Thus, if the Geneva Convention, a treaty to which both the United States and Afghanistan belong, is found to apply to the detainees held at Guantanamo Bay, Cuba, then those parts of the president's military order that violate the treaty's provisions are illegal and will fail. This is because, under Article VI of the Constitution, treaties and federal statutes are coequal as supreme law of the land and therefore override contrary executive orders and Supreme Court opinions. Treaties such as the Geneva Convention cannot be overridden by subsequent presidential orders.[31]

In order for the Third Geneva Convention protections to apply,

two criteria must be met. America must be at war, and those captured by us must be enemy combatants. According to our government, we are at war and have been since September 11, 2001. In his
address to a joint session of Congress five days after the attacks,
President Bush announced that America was at war with terror, and
again he said this in his State of the Union message in January
2002—a point he reiterated in his speeches commemorating the
one-year anniversary of the catastrophe.[32] Indeed, Congress passed
a joint resolution authorizing the use of American military forces to
prosecute the war. Although this measure was not a formal declaration of war, the chairman of the Senate Foreign Relations Committee referred to it as the constitutional equivalent.[33] Thus, by all
accounts, the country is engaged in war, and the first criterion for
the Geneva Convention to apply is met.

The second criterion—whether those captured are enemy combatants—is more problematic. Naturally, the critique directed at
characterizing those captured in this war on terrorism as POWs,
and therefore entitled to Geneva Convention protections, is that
other non-Americans captured in other public policy "wars" like
the War on Drugs or the War on Poverty have not been treated as
POWs. However, such critique is easily dismissed. First, the war on
terrorism constitutes an armed conflict under international law,
whereas the other public policy wars do not. Second, the intent of
the actors is widely divergent. The intent of terrorists is typically to
kill in furtherance of a political objective. The intent of drug manu-
facturers and dealers in the War on Drugs is to widen addiction and
secure profit. The intent of slum lords preying on the poor in the
War on Poverty is also to maximize their profit with minimum
investment.

According to international law:

> Entitlement for prisoner of war status under the Geneva
> Conventions is restricted to those who can show that they fulfill
> the four conditions necessary to acquire the status of "combat-
> ants." The Geneva Convention extended privileged prisoner of
> war treatment to resistance movements operating in occupied
> territory. Another category, possibly not identical to the afore-
> mentioned group, but still qualifying for prisoner of war status,
> includes members of armed forces who profess allegiance to a
> government or an "authority" not recognized by the detaining

power. Such members would, in any event, fight "on behalf" of a party to the conflict. There is still some uncertainty as to what link is required between independent forces such as resistance movements and parties to the Convention.

By changing the required conditions for combatants, Protocol I of 1977 widens the protection of prisoners of war: since the conditions are reduced a person may now qualify as a prisoner of war although he would not have enjoyed protection under the Third Geneva Convention. This extension will prove to be more useful than the presumption clause in the Geneva Convention that protection of a prisoner of war will continue until any question concerning his status has been settled by a competent Tribunal.

In practice even persons who do not fulfill the conditions of combatancy have been given prisoner of war status. To encourage the surrender of guerillas and spies, commanders have sometimes asked the political organs of their home state for permission to treat unprivileged combatants as prisoners of war. Such practice developed, for example, in the Malaysian conflict to distinguish between "captured enemy personnel" (CEP) and "surrendered enemy personnel" (SEP), whereby the latter group would also be treated as prisoners of war. The all-important question for prisoner of war status is whether there is a war. If a State can argue that there is no such conflict it may also attempt to evade all obligations incumbent on it relating to the specific treatment of prisoners of war. It is clear that non-recognition of an entity as a State does not necessarily lead to non-combatant status of persons. China refused to admit that there was a war in Korea and denied United States pilots, for that reason, the status of prisoners of war. They were instead treated as "spies" captured overflying China's territory.[34]

President Bush's military order establishing secret military tribunals to try, convict, and sentence these suspects undermines such a process. It delineates a clear distinction between American citizens—who continue to enjoy access to open courts with strict evidentiary and procedural rules, trial by a jury of civilians, and conviction only upon unanimity—and noncitizens (probably Muslims), who will disappear into closed courts administered by neither the judiciary nor the DOJ but by the DOD, with relaxed evidentiary and procedural rules, and undergo trial by a panel of military officers who may convict on a two-thirds vote.[35]

The illegal nature of this order only serves to perpetuate a sense of unfairness. As written, this order does run afoul of the Third Geneva Convention. The Truman administration signed this treaty in 1949, and it was ratified under Eisenhower in 1956, fourteen years after the last military commission in the United States, convened by Roosevelt, tried and convicted eight Nazi saboteurs.[36] This 1942 conviction is the precedent cited most often in defense of the president's order as applied within the United States. Military commissions were last used outside the United States by General MacArthur in Japan in 1945. Obviously, no more recent cases can be cited because the rules changed in 1956 with the entry into force of the treaty— which extinguished prior law or court opinions that were in conflict. Thus, the government's reliance on prior case law is faulty.

Assuming noncitizens suspected of terrorism who are captured in this conflict are considered prisoners of war, not a far leap of logic since the government insists that "we are at war,"[37] such people are guaranteed certain procedural safeguards by the Geneva Convention. Specifically, they are granted the right to be tried by an independent and impartial court, freedom from coerced confession, the right to counsel with private conferral, the right to a speedy trial (no longer than three months in prior detention), use of the Uniform Code of Military Justice (UCMJ) in sentencing, and the right of appeal. The president's military order guarantees some Geneva Convention protections, such as humane treatment, adequate sustenance, free exercise of religion during detention, and the right to counsel during trial.

However, it breaches other protections by eliminating the right to appeal, by not ensuring an independent and impartial court, and by not providing for private conferral with counsel. Moreover, the possibility of receiving the death sentence "upon the concurrence of two-thirds of the members of the commission present" does not track the unanimity requirement in the UCMJ[38] as it must according to the treaty. Incongruencies between the president's order and the treaty make the order legally untenable. The military order of November 13 cannot modify provisions of the Third Geneva Convention; it must comply with them. Only a subsequent statute or treaty, both requiring congressional action, can modify those terms.

The administration's response to this legal problem has been to studiously ignore it. They have labeled those captured on the battlefield in Afghanistan and brought to Camp X-Ray "unlawful combatants" instead of enemy combatants to avoid calling the detainees POWs—which would mean providing them their treaty rights. According to the administration's view, articulated more clearly by Yale University's Professor Wedgwood, while POWs would normally be tried by military courts under the UCMJ, non-POWs receive no such privilege:

> A privileged prisoner of war is sometimes tried in the same mode as his adversary's soldiers. But al-Qaeda members have not fulfilled the prerequisite conditions of the Third Geneva Convention of 1949—failing to observe the laws of war, or to wear identifying insignia, or to carry arms openly—and may thus fairly be considered as "unlawful combatants."[39]

The administration's sudden discovery of "unlawful combatant" status is certainly a clever way to dodge U.S. obligations under the Geneva Convention and to save the legality of the presidential order. However, designating these detainees as unqualified for POW status through executive political fiat is not allowed under the terms of the treaty. Article 5 requires a determination by a competent tribunal of a prisoner's status under the convention when that status is in doubt. For the administration to merely state that they have no doubt as to the detainees' status and to expect the world to believe they are complying with their treaty-bound duties is to deny the language of the treaty its ordinary meaning as required under international legal rules of treaty interpretation. Ironically, the Senate Foreign Relations Committee said in 1995, upon approving the Geneva Conventions:

> We should not be dissuaded by the possibility that at some later date a contracting party may invoke specious reasons to evade compliance with the obligations of decent treatment which it has freely assumed in these instruments. Its conduct can now be measured against their approved standards, and the weight of world opinion cannot but exercise a salutary restraint on otherwise unbridled actions.[40]

Nonetheless, Defense Secretary Rumsfeld had the power to save the president's order from manifest illegality. Sections 4 and 6 of the order required Rumsfeld to issue rules and procedures for the establishment and functioning of military commissions. By drafting these guidelines to closely mirror UCMJ safeguards protecting American military servicemen—such as the unanimity rule, right of appeal, establishment of guilt beyond a reasonable doubt, and strict rules of evidence—compliance with the treaty would have been implicit because the UCMJ itself complies with it.[41] Therefore, the order could have become legal.

However, the DOD failed to take advantage of that opportunity. The rules issued by the DOD under the military order in March 2002, while ameliorating some of the harsher aspects of the process, did not go far enough to save the tribunals from being illegal upon their creation. In fact, DOD officials announced on the day the rules were issued that detainees who are tried and acquitted can still remain in custody indefinitely as a threat to national security. Consequently, the tone was set for basic human rights—such as the right against indefinite detention without charges or counsel, guaranteed by customary international law and other multilateral treaties, to be violated even if the tribunals worked in the unlikely event to acquit anyone.[42]

Even if the protections of the Geneva Convention can be kept at arms length through definitional hijinks, customary international law and human rights norms require minimum procedural safeguards. The University of Houston's Professor Jordan Paust, a former military lawyer, identified these violations shortly after the implementation rules were disclosed:

> The President's . . . Military Order had set up several per se violations of international law. Instead of attempting to avoid them, the DOD Order . . . continued the violations . . . [which include] intentional and per se discrimination on the basis of national or social origin, intentional and per se denial of equal protection, and "denial of justice" to aliens in violation of various international laws. Nearly every impropriety concerning the Peruvian military commissions addressed by the Inter-American Court of Human Rights has been built into the Bush military commissions.[43]

In particular, under the DOD order, civilians may not be tried in civilian courts, the accused have been detained for months without charges, detainees do not enjoy the right to be brought promptly before a judge or to file habeas corpus petitions, defense attorneys will lack access to some witnesses, the accused will not be able to cross-examine all witnesses against them, portions of trials can be held in secret, and the accused lack the right of appeal to an independent and impartial tribunal. Furthermore, most of the customary minimum due process requirements reflected, for example, in Article 14 of the International Covenant on Civil and Political Rights, have been spurned.

In particular, there will be a denial of a "fair and public hearing by a competent, independent and impartial tribunal established by law"; detainees have not been "informed promptly and in detail . . . of the nature and cause" of any charges against them; an accused will not fully enjoy the right to "counsel of his choosing"; an accused will not fully enjoy the right "to be tried in his presence" or to "defend himself . . . through legal assistance of his own choosing"; an accused will not fully enjoy the right "to examine, or have examined, the witnesses against him"; and an accused will not enjoy "the right to his conviction and sentence being reviewed by a higher tribunal according to law."[44]

Yet another deficiency in the rules, according to Amnesty International, is the absence of any provision making evidence obtained through torture or coercion inadmissible.[45] In American civilian and military courts, such evidence is deemed untrustworthy, and therefore cannot be considered against the defendant. However, the lower bar to evidence under the DOD rules would allow in any evidence of "reasonable probative value" as determined by the presiding judge or a majority of the panel—which could be constituted of nonlawyer military officers (only the presiding judge must be a judge advocate general [JAG] officer).

Observance of laws, both domestic and international, is key to America's success. This is all the more important when the United States, as a free country, helps craft the laws in the treaties and agrees to be bound by them. What message does it send to the world when America acts to change the rules of the game in order to win? If our country is acting justly, with faith in its cause and truth on its side, then it will prevail. America doesn't need to change the rules. They are sufficient for their purpose and fairly crafted to ensure a legitimate outcome. Indeed, as defenders of human rights around the world for decades, it has been the United States that has criticized others for unfair use of secret military courts.

Condemning similar practices in Peru in 1999, the Department of State noted, "proceedings in these military courts—and those for terrorism in civilian courts—do not meet internationally accepted standards of openness, fairness, and due process." And addressing denials of fair public trials in Egyptian military courts, the United States found that

> the military courts do not ensure civilian defendants due process before an independent tribunal. . . . There is no appellate process for verdicts issued by military courts; instead, verdicts are subject to review by other military judges and confirmation by the President, who in practice usually delegates the review function to a senior military officer.[46]

Under President Bush's military order and the DOD rules, verdicts against the detainees are subject to review by other military judges and then the recommendation is sent to the president, who may delegate his final review function to the secretary of defense. Did the Bush administration actually adopt the very review process used by Egyptian military courts that America condemned as violative of human rights not three years earlier? The similarity, and hypocrisy, cannot be ignored.

True, establishment of such tribunals is rightly justified by prosecutors as more expeditious and less complicated due to the ability to use classified evidence without compromising national security.[47] But the inherent distinction based on nationality unwittingly feeds the mind-set of non-American Muslims as victimized and unworthy of treatment according to higher standards reserved for Americans. This, of course, does nothing to ameliorate the hatred simmering below the surface. Shortly after the catastrophe, former secretary of state Madeleine Albright reassured the world on television that America was "a nation of laws," and President Bush promised to bring those involved to "justice." Redefining the laws and redefining "justice" for non-Americans as somehow less than that accorded Americans actively works at cross-purposes with our mission to spread American democratic values.

Military Action in Conformity with International Law

The U.S. invasion of Afghanistan that toppled the Taliban government in early 2002 was undertaken in conformity with domestic law, under Congress's September 14 joint resolution, and sanctioned by international law. This is important if the response is to be viewed as legitimate by the world and especially by the Islamic world.[48]

First, under the UN charter, America has the right of self-defense. Article 51 allows us to exercise this individually or collectively in response to an armed attack and to continue its exercise "until the Security Council has taken the measures necessary to maintain international peace and security." Indeed, in resolutions issued the day after the attack and again on September 28, the UN Security Council defined the situation as an inherent threat to international peace and security and recognized the invocation of Article 51.[49] Given the gravity of the September 11 attacks and the tacit support of the most traditionally recalcitrant permanent members of the council, Russia and China, it is unlikely that the council would act to truncate the ongoing action in Afghanistan.

Second, under the North Atlantic Charter, America is backed in this action by its NATO allies. For the first time since its adoption in 1949, the charter's military response obligation in Article 5 has been triggered.[50] This key provision declares that

> an armed attack against one . . . of them . . . shall be considered an attack against them all and consequently they agree that, if such an armed attack occurs, each of them, in exercise of the right of individual or collective self-defence recognised by Article 51 of the Charter of the United Nations, will assist the Party or Parties so attacked by taking forthwith, individually and in concert with the other Parties, such action as . . . necessary, including the use of armed force.[51]

Thus, the forces deploying on the ground in Afghanistan for peacekeeping purposes are primarily NATO forces. The British will occupy the airbase at Bagram field north of Kabul, the French will occupy the airbase at Mazar-e Sharif, and the Turks will lead a multinational mostly Muslim force to police Kabul, "ensuring that no single Afghan militia is able to monopolize power in the capital."[52]

Third, under customary practice, because the attack came during peacetime and was in violation of international law, the president can invoke the old doctrine of reprisal against the offending state. Of course, the perpetrators were an organization, not a state; thus,

President Bush went out of his way to connect the terrorists to the state by linking them in a principal-agency relationship so this legal rationale can be utilized. The other elements of the doctrine require a request for redress, which Bush made in his address to Congress when he ticked off the list of demands for the Taliban,[53] followed by a denial, which the Taliban dutifully provided. The military response that flows from this doctrine of reprisal must then be proportional to the injury suffered.[54] Here, the toppling of the repressive Taliban, the pursuit of international terrorists, and the creation of conditions for a new coalition government in Afghanistan are certainly proportional to the massive loss of life in America coupled with the attending physical destruction of airliners, skyscrapers, government facilities, and collateral infrastructure damage.

Many international law scholars hold that armed reprisals became unlawful with the adoption of the UN charter in 1945. They argue that the charter preempts the field of states' prerogatives on international use of force and allows for only the self-defense exception contained in Article 51. They rely heavily on a combination of Resolution 188, where the UN Security Council, in response to Britain's attack on Yemen in 1964, condemned military reprisals as incompatible with the purpose of the UN, and a literal reading of Article 2(4), which provides:

All members shall refrain in their international relations from the threat of force against the territorial integrity or the political independence of any state, or in any other manner inconsistent with the Purposes of the United Nations.

However, an even closer reading of Article 2(4) by Ohio State University's Professor Gregory Travalio reveals that this prohibition is perhaps not the blanket prohibition that antireprisalists make it out to be. He argues that, in the context of using military force in response to terrorist attacks, "force to eliminate a terrorist threat does not violate the territorial integrity or political independence of the state in which the terrorists are being harbored, and is otherwise consistent with the U.N. Charter" due to the flood of pronouncements against terrorism in the last two decades.[55] Thus, from a purpose standpoint, what in effect are reprisals, such as America's launch of cruise missiles against Sudan and Afghanistan in 1998 in response to the attack on our embassies in Africa, were not precluded by Article 2(4)[56] and, therefore, did not need to be justified under Article 51.

Others take the view that the "inherent" clause of Article 51 preserves customary law as it was in 1945 to include both reprisal and preemptive strikes (or anticipatory self-defense) as legal possibilities. The academic debate on this point appears to be resolving in favor of defining both as illegal under Article 51, even as states such as the United States and Israel continue to invoke it as inclusive and condemnation of those actions on the ground remains far from universal.[57] Thus, the legal basis in the charter, aside from customary practice, may yet allow for reprisals to lurk in the passages of Articles 2(4) and 51.

Beyond legality, in the real world, some scholars recognize a potential deterrent value in the possibility of a military reprisal.[58] But this value remains distinct from its purpose. Unlike the self-defense mechanism allowed under Article 51, the purpose of which is to counter an immediate physical danger to the invoking state, the purpose of a reprisal is to "coerce another state to abide by international law."[59] Indeed, the U.S. Army Field Manual defines appropriate reprisals as

> [a]cts of retaliation in the form of conduct which would otherwise be unlawful, resorted to by one belligerent against enemy personnel or property for acts of warfare committed by the other belligerent in violation of the law of war, for the purpose of enforcing future compliance with the recognized rules of civilized warfare.[60]

Thus, revenge is rejected as a motivating factor,[61] even though that might be what the aggrieved public demands at the time. Catholic University's Professor Michael Noone predicted that, in response to the September 11 terrorist attacks, "U.S. authorities could respond to public demands for retaliation by saying that the customary international law of reprisal would permit attacks, targeting, and tactics that would otherwise be illegal, but the right to do so is limited to opposing belligerent forces, however ill-defined, and by the principle of proportionality."[62] This is what happened with the American invasion of Afghanistan and the coercion of that country to follow international law, which it now does (absent the Taliban regime and al Qaeda headquarters).

The political significance of legal changes since September 11 has altered the global dynamic such that support continues to coalesce around our efforts. Specifically, the broad coalition assembled by Secretary of State Colin Powell involved lifting sanctions against Pakistan[63] and India imposed after their nuclear tests several years ago. Further signals of support to the Islamic world include intervening to dismiss the civil damages case by former hostages against Iran in exchange for Tehran's acquiescence in the campaign and the agreement to help downed U.S. airmen on Iranian soil;[64] lifting sanctions against Sudan imposed after the American embassy bombings in Africa;[65] allowing Syria to accede to the UN Security Council despite past involvement in terrorist activities;[66] and restarting the Middle East peace process by resurrecting the dormant Mitchell Plan (although in the wake of Arafat's inability to control Palestinian suicide bombers, this effort has wilted).[67] Accordingly, legitimacy has been secured for America's action under international law and through international cooperation.

Prosecutorial Discretion

It is better that ten guilty persons escape than one innocent suffer.
—Sir William Blackstone, English jurist (1723–80),
Commentaries on the Laws of England

Prosecutorial discretion is an executive function carried out by thousands of prosecutors (local and federal) across the country thousands of times each week. It is nothing more than the judicious exercise of discretion as to whether the government will charge an individual with a particular crime and seek to try him for it. Many times, this decision rests on whether the state can effectively bring a winnable case before a jury in open court. Prosecutors, as elected or appointed officials, will usually seek to pursue as many winnable cases as possible so as to bolster their conviction record. The winnability of a case, in turn, depends on the quality of evidence available against the accused. So, in reality, the exercise of prosecutorial discretion is oftentimes a function of whether the prosecutor believes he or she can prevail in court, not whether the accused is innocent or guilty.

John Ashcroft's DOJ has been presented with many opportunities to exercise such prosecutorial discretion since 9/11. By most accounts, this discretion has been abused. Ashcroft has tried to manipulate federal statutes, such as the material witness law, to hold Americans in custody indefinitely without charging them; however, this move has met resistance in federal courts. Consequently, he has shifted such individuals over to the DOD after classifying them as "enemy combatants"—subjecting them to military jurisdiction; again no charges need be brought, access to counsel is denied, and the men are held incommunicado.

Immigrants, by virtue of their status as noncitizens rather than as human beings, are treated worse. Hundreds of Middle Eastern and South Asian men have been rounded up in a huge dragnet, held in secret for months, interrogated, subjected to secret immigration hearings, and then summarily deported. Thousands of others who could not be arrested on technical visa or traffic violations were "invited" to appear before the U.S. attorneys in their districts for questioning about any knowledge or involvement with al Qaeda, the Taliban, the September 11 attacks, or terrorism generally.

Indeed, not only has the administration been hijacked by a bunker mentality since 9/11 but the DOJ in particular has demonstrated its zealous intent to pursue those responsible for the attacks by altering constitutional and legal checks on its power where possible and violating other constraints where necessary. Such abuse of power has not gone unnoticed by the public. When asked in an Associated Press poll conducted in August 2002, "How concerned are you that new measures enacted to fight terrorism in this country could end up restricting our individual freedoms?" 63 percent replied that they were concerned or somewhat concerned and only 35 percent replied that they were either unconcerned (15 percent) or not too concerned (20 percent), while 2 percent replied that they "didn't know."[68]

The incongruent treatment accorded various prisoners based on their status should be troubling to the American judiciary. Status-based detentions are usually suspect as constitutionally violative. Table 3 demonstrates the seemingly arbitrary discrepancies.

TABLE 3. Incongruent Status/Treatment of Persons Detained/Prosecuted by Federal Government since 9/11

Person(s)	U.S. Citizen?	Legal Classification	Current Status
Jose Padilla (Abdullah al-Muhajir) (held in U.S.)	Yes • Born in Puerto Rico • Apprehended in Chicago	"Enemy combatant" Member of al Qaeda	Turned over to military, denied access to counsel, held indefinitely by DOD
John Walker Lindh (held in U.S.)	Yes • Born in Marin Co., CA • Apprehended in Afghanistan	"Enemy combatant" Member of Taliban	Indicted by federal grand jury and prosecuted by DOJ in U.S. federal district court—case settled
Yaser Esam Hamdi (held in U.S.)	Yes • Born in Louisiana • Apprehended in Afghanistan	"Enemy combatant" Member of al Qaeda	Turned over to military, denied access to counsel, held indefinitely by DOD
Zacarias Moussaoui (held in U.S.)	No • Born in France • Apprehended in Minneapolis	"Enemy combatant?" Member of al Qaeda	Indicted by federal grand jury and prosecuted by DOJ in U.S. federal district court—case in progress
DOD detainees (held in Cuba)	No • Various nationalities (e.g., Saudi, Egypt, France, UK, Pakistan) • Apprehended in Afghanistan	"Unlawful combatants" GC apparently doesn't apply and detainees are subject to MTs	Turned over to military, denied access to counsel, held indefinitely by DOD
DOJ (INS) detainees (held in U.S.)	No • Various nationalities (mostly Middle Eastern) • Apprehended in U.S.	Immigration violators, some designated as "material witnesses" and transferred to DOD	Denied access to counsel, deported or held indefinitely by DOJ or DOD

6 Judicial Reaction to the Post-9/11 Legal Responses

> I know of no duty of the Court which it is more important to observe, and no powers of the Court which it is more important to enforce, than its power of keeping public bodies within their rights. The moment public bodies exceed their rights they do so to the injury and oppression of private individuals.
>
> —Nathaniel Lindley, English jurist,
> *Robert v. Gwyrfai District Council* (1899)

> A court which yields to the popular will thereby license itself to practice despotism, for there can be no assurance that it will not on another occasion indulge its own will.
>
> —Justice Felix Frankfurter, U.S. Supreme Court,
> *American Federation of Labor v. American Sash and Door Co.* (1949)

In the aftermath of the September 11 terrorist attacks in the United States, federal authorities were quickly presented with the problem of how to legally handle the diverse group of individuals taken into custody—from American citizens fighting on foreign battlefields to Americans at home with allegiances to al Qaeda, from foreign nationals of Islamic faith inside the United States to foreign combatants caught during the invasion of Afghanistan. What happens to them? Are they all treated similarly? Do they all have the same basic set of legal rights? Should they be prosecuted, detained for questioning, deported, or held indefinitely during hostilities?

190

Initially, there was a determination that Americans captured at home or abroad on the wrong side of the government's war on terror would be tried in regular courts, as would foreign nationals captured inside the United States; however, foreign al Qaeda and Taliban members caught abroad would be detained as "unlawful combatants," and unsympathetic Islamic foreigners found in violation of INS regulations would simply be deported.

Thus, John Walker Lindh, the American Taliban, and Zacarias Moussaoui, a French national al Qaeda member caught in Minneapolis, were arraigned and charged in federal courts. However, as the cases against them began to simultaneously unfold, tapping more government resources and risking exposure of intelligence data, the administration decided to switch tracks and to begin shunting Americans into military imprisonment for indefinite detention without access to counsel instead of facing the specter of an unpredictable and time-consuming adversarial process. Consequently, Yaser Hamdi, another American Taliban, and Jose Padilla, an American al Qaeda member, subsequently found their way into naval brigs instead of courtrooms.[1]

So who's job is it to protect individual liberties from being trampled into the dust by the government in its zealous pursuit of bogeymen, be they communist sympathizers during the cold war or terrorist sympathizers during the war on terror? Since the days of John Marshall, the federal judiciary has recognized its constitutional responsibility to tell Congress and the president when they are stepping over the line delineating their respective powers and to order them to take a step back. Several initiatives have been undertaken in court both by and against the government in its war on terror. However, due to the reactive and deliberative nature of our judicial system, this branch of government necessarily responds more slowly to events than do the other two branches.

Thus, two years after the attacks, there has been no meaningful constitutional challenge to the USA Patriot Act or other legislative initiatives; the executive has not yet empanelled any military tribunals; most of the thousand INS detainees have been released or deported; the Lindh case has been settled; the Moussaoui case has been stayed; Hamdi and Padilla have been relegated to solitary confinement; and the attorney general's aggressive detention, surveillance, and deportation programs have enjoyed some judicial support and some sporadic judicial resistance—yielding decidedly mixed legal results.

Nonetheless, it remains useful to survey the current lay of the post-9/11 judicial landscape, if for no other purpose than to gauge the potential involvement of that branch and to get a sense of where litigation may ensue and what the outcome may be. An inseparable corollary to this challenge involves the timeliness of judicial reaction. Almost 140 years ago, the Supreme Court defended the continued application of constitutional protections during wartime in *Ex Parte Milligan:*

> The Constitution of the United States is a law for rulers and people, equally in war and in peace, and covers with the shield of its protection all classes of men, at all times, and under all circumstances. No doctrine, involving more pernicious consequences, was ever invented by the wit of man than that any of its provisions can be suspended during any of the great exigencies of government. Such a doctrine leads directly to anarchy or despotism, but the theory of necessity on which it is based is false.[2]

That seminal case is still cited today by constitutionalists but is sought to be avoided by the current administration in its conduct domestically of the war on terror. During the Civil War, one of the many powers President Lincoln accrued to the executive as a wartime exigency was the power to order summary military detention of civilians for the duration of hostilities and even trial by military tribunal. When this power was challenged as unconstitutional absent legislative assent by Chief Justice Taney in the 1861 *Ex Parte Merryman* decision, Lincoln ignored the opinion—but released Merryman anyway and later secured Congress's retroactive permission to suspend habeas corpus protections.[3]

In 1866, a year after the war had ended and Lincoln had died, the Supreme Court returned to the issue in the *Milligan* case, cognizant of the fact that such problems could be sorted out better in the absence of hostilities or immediate threats to the nation's survival:

> The importance of the main question presented by this record cannot be overstated; for it involves the very framework of the government and the fundamental principles of

American liberty. During the late wicked Rebellion, the temper of the times did not allow that calmness in deliberation and discussion so necessary to a correct conclusion of a purely judicial question. Then, considerations of safety were mingled with the exercise of power; and feelings and interests prevailed which are happily terminated. Now that the public safety is assured, this question, as well as all others, can be discussed and decided without passion or the admixture of any element not required to form a legal judgment.[4]

In their decision, the Court recognized the government's need to detain people who posed an immediate threat to the country but agreed with Taney's earlier assertion in *Merryman* that a national emergency, such as recent war, could not sanction the military detention and trial of a civilian not subject to military law or the laws of war when federal civil courts were open and functioning to hear criminal accusations. Milligan was a U.S. citizen who lived in Indiana for twenty years (not a zone of hostilities during the war) when he was arrested at his home in Indianapolis by the military in 1864, held in "close confinement," charged with treason, tried by military tribunal in 1865, and sentenced to hang.

This time the executive was acting pursuant to legislative authority by way of the 1863 Habeas Corpus Act. However, the Court found the law's provisions to have been misapplied by the government. Moreover, indefinite detention was not allowed: "it was not contemplated that such person should be detained in custody beyond a certain fixed period, unless certain judicial proceedings . . . were commenced against him."[5]

Specifically, the act directed the secretaries of state and war to furnish lists of persons who they thought should be held in custody to Article III judges in those jurisdictions where the persons were held. If a grand jury convened and adjourned without indicting, then the person was to be discharged. Moreover, the executive's refusal to issue the lists could not operate to the detriment of those detained and not indicted because the unindicted individuals were equally entitled to discharge twenty days after the time of their arrest and the termination of the grand jury session.[6]

The government tried to exclude Milligan from the terms of this act by characterizing him as a prisoner of war; however, the Court was not persuaded:

It is not easy to see how he can be treated as a prisoner of war.
. . . If in Indiana, he conspired with bad men to assist the
enemy, he is punishable for it in the courts of Indiana; but,
when tried for the offense, he cannot plead the rights of war;
for he was not engaged in legal acts of hostility against the
government, and only such persons, when captured, are prisoners of war. If he cannot enjoy the immunities attaching to
the character of a prisoner of war, how can he be subject to
their pains and penalties?[7]

However, the principle derived from *Milligan*—that Americans
cannot be detained by and subjected to military jurisdiction if they
are not prisoners of war when civilian courts are open to hear
charges against them—has been skirted thus far by the Bush administration. That principle was not overturned when the Supreme
Court heard a similar case in 1942 (*Ex Parte Quirin*), since the American Nazi in that matter was captured as a prisoner of war in uniform coming ashore to attack the United States. Perhaps propheti-
cally, the earlier *Milligan* Court noted:

This nation, as experience has proved, cannot always
remain at peace, and has no right to expect that it will always
have wise and humane rulers, sincerely attached to the principles of the Constitution. Wicked men, ambitious of power,
with hatred of liberty and contempt of law, may fill the place
once occupied by Washington and Lincoln; and if this right is
conceded, and the calamities of war again befall us, the dangers to human liberty are frightful to contemplate. If our
fathers had failed to provide for just such a contingency, they
would have been false to the trust reposed in them. They
knew—the history of the world told them—the nation they
were founding, be its existence short or long, would be
involved in war; how often or how long continued, human
foresight could not tell; and that unlimited power, wherever
lodged at such a time, was especially hazardous to freemen.
For this, and other equally weighty reasons, they secured the
inheritance they had fought to maintain, by incorporating in a
written constitution the safeguards which time had proved
were essential to its preservation.[8]

Two years have passed since the terrible events of September 11, 2001. American federal courts must rouse themselves to the task of checking the executive's power grab ostensibly justified in terms of national security. They need not wait for the end to the war on terror, as the Supreme Court waited until after the Civil War, to return balance to the Constitution. It must be returned now.

Article III Federal Courts

Long ago, the U.S. Supreme Court declared, "ours is the accusatorial as opposed to the inquisitorial system. Such has been the characteristic of Anglo-American criminal justice since it freed itself from practices borrowed by the Star Chamber from the Continent whereby an accused was interrogated in secret for hours on end."[9] In practice, this premise is embodied in substantive and procedural mandates derived from our constitutional system of government and applicable to all criminal proceedings.

Article III federal courts are the bulwark of freedoms in our legal system, ensuring the basic canon of the Fourth, Fifth, and Sixth Amendments against illegal searches, seizures, and self-incrimination and guaranteeing a speedy trial, access to court, access to counsel, access to a jury, and the right to confront adverse witnesses and evidence. The panoply of protections emanating from these amendments breathes life and meaning into the fundamental notions of due process and equal justice and is applicable to all who come within the jurisdiction of American courts.

The challenge in the post-9/11 aggressive prosecutorial environment will be ensuring that two centuries of precedent interpreting constitutional protections and carving a delicate balance between truth seeking and equal justice in the criminal process are not vitiated in the name of expediency and scapegoating.

Fumbling into the Court System: The Lindh and Moussaoui Cases

The first case concerns John Walker Lindh, an American citizen and the son of a wealthy San Francisco area family.[10] He was captured in Afghanistan fighting for the Taliban. A convert to Islam after reading the autobiography of Malcolm X, Lindh moved to Yemen, enrolled in a *madrasah*, and later answered the call to jihad—fighting with Islamic fundamentalist groups in Kashmir and Kunduz.[11] After his capture, Lindh was held for about a month in Camp Rhino outside Kabul and then transported back to the United States to face criminal charges for his actions on behalf of the Taliban, namely, conspiracy to kill U.S. nationals outside the United States, providing material support to a foreign terrorist organization, and engaging in prohibited transactions.[12] He was indicted in Virginia federal district court on February 5, 2002.[13]

Because Lindh was processed through the U.S. criminal justice system, he was entitled to the same constitutional protections afforded every U.S. citizen, including the right to counsel and the right to be fully advised of the charges against him.[14] Represented by competent criminal defense counsel, one of the first constitutional challenges to Lindh's detainment and prosecution alleged that the criminal charges were vague, ambiguous, and not sufficiently stated so as to provide fair notice of the charges against him. Consequently, Lindh's attorneys filed a motion for a bill of particulars requesting that the government identify the:

- nationals and military personnel he is alleged to have conspired to kill
- date, time, and place where he agreed to join the illegal conspiracy
- exact nature of the material support and resources he is alleged to have provided to the conspiratorial enterprise
- specific illegal activity he was alleged to have advanced by his support or services

Essentially, Lindh sought to compel the government to state its charges with more specificity to ensure the indictment alleged criminal conduct and was not simply a vehicle to prosecute him for mere association with an unpopular group.[15] The judge, however, rejected the defense motion.[16]

Lindh also attacked the government's use of incriminating statements allegedly made while he was a captive in Afghanistan.[17] The legal basis for these arguments was the fifty-five-day delay between Lindh's capture and his arrival in the United States, where he was finally allowed access to legal counsel. Lindh alleged that he was subject to coercive interrogation tactics at Camp Rhino and held incommunicado for fifty-five days. Lindh further contended that, because there was no justifiable reason for the delay in presenting him for arraignment in U.S. court (even though the government had begun preparing its case against him), any statements made during that period of unlawful confinement should be inadmissible.

The case continued for five months with the government struggling to refine and present its case against Lindh while also maintaining the secrecy of classified information. Finally, on July 15, 2002, in a move that surprised most observers, a plea agreement between the government and Lindh was announced. Under the agreement Lindh pleaded guilty to two counts in the indictment (supplying services to the Taliban and carrying explosives in the commission of a felony) in exchange for serving two consecutive ten-year sentences and fully cooperating with the government in its investigation of al Qaeda. While prosecutors hailed the accord as eminently fair and a "victory in the war on terrorism," it did not escape notice that the government's willingness to bargain coincidentally escalated as constitutional infirmities in its case were gradually revealed.[18]

The second case concerns Zacarias Moussaoui, the suspected twentieth hijacker who failed to follow through on his part of the 9/11 terrorist attacks. Moussaoui, a thirty-five-year-old French national of Moroccan descent, was a member of al Qaeda and an alleged coconspirator of the nineteen Islamic hijackers who carried out the attacks that destroyed the WTC and damaged the Pentagon. In February 2001, Moussaoui entered the United States and enrolled in flight school in Norman, Oklahoma. However, he failed his training program and subsequently reenrolled at another flight school in Minnesota. While at the Minnesota school, Moussaoui expressed an unusual interest in learning to fly larger aircraft, constantly peppering his instructors with questions about specifications and technical operations. Eventually, Moussaoui's detailed questions relating to complex aircraft systems aroused suspicion, and those misgivings were relayed to the FBI. In August 2001, Moussaoui was arrested on visa and immigration violations.[19]

As evidence of his involvement in the 9/11 attacks mounted, Moussaoui was transferred to the federal prison in Alexandria, Virginia, where, on January 3, 2002, he was arraigned on six counts of conspiracy to commit murder and terrorism in connection with the terrorist attacks. Perhaps foreshadowing the bizarre twists and turns the case would eventually take, when apprised of the charges against him and asked how he would plead, Moussaoui refused "in the name of Allah" to enter a plea, prompting the judge to enter a not guilty plea on his behalf.[20]

In the ensuing months Moussaoui has flooded the court with handwritten motions impugning the motives and competency of his attorneys and making derogatory remarks about the trial judge in his case. Indeed, his invective against his court-appointed attorneys was so offensive that the judge eventually permitted Moussaoui to represent himself on the condition that he have an attorney act as his cocounsel.[21]

After a series of legal battles concerning whether Moussaoui's proceedings would be televised and whether he was competent to stand trial, Moussaoui shocked the court by electing to plead guilty to four of the charges against him, only to abruptly shift course when advised of the consequences of his guilty plea. Due to the wrangling over complex legal issues connected with the discovery phase of the case, Moussaoui's trial has been indefinitely delayed. However, in the ensuing months since Moussaoui's arrest and detention, the government's case against him has been plagued by a number of embarrassing missteps. For example, in an effort to comply with Moussaoui's right to receive certain information necessary to the preparation of his case, the government inadvertently left classified documents in his cell. Later, while retrieving those documents, federal marshals engaged in potentially incriminating conversations with Moussaoui without advising him of his right to remain silent.

At this writing, the parties appear to have reached a stalemate on the issue of access to material witnesses. Moussaoui is seeking to personally interview high-ranking al Qaeda member Ramzi Binalshibh, whose testimony Moussaoui claims will exonerate him of the charges against him. The government has refused such access on the grounds that national security interests might be jeopardized if the two men are permitted direct contact.[22] U.S. district judge Leonie Brinkema ruled that the testimony of the witness would be relevant and necessary to Moussaoui's defense and ordered the government to produce him for a deposition carried out under conditions set by the *government*. Dissatisfied with this outcome, the government appealed to the Fourth Circuit Court of Appeals, which ultimately determined that it does not have jurisdiction over the case until the government first refuses to comply with Judge Brinkema's order and she imposes penalties for their noncompliance. Judge Brinkema is currently considering penalties that could range from complete dismissal of the case to informing future jurors of the government's failure to comply with the court's order.

Implicit in the government's obstinancy is the looming threat that Moussaoui's case might be removed altogether from the civilian court and transferred into a military court, where presumably the pathway to execution will be paved with fewer obstacles. The prospect of removing Moussaoui's case to the military courts to avoid compliance with a district court order raises fundamental questions concerning the American criminal justice system's ability to handle terrorism cases, particularly those in which the defense might legitimately hinge on access to sensitive national security information. Indeed, as the Fourth Circuit succinctly observed,

> This appeal is one of extraordinary importance, presenting a direct conflict between a criminal defendant's right "to have compulsory process for obtaining witnesses in his favor," U.S. Const. amend VI, and the Government's essential duty to preserve the security of this nation and its citizens.[23]

As many courts have done in the past, Judge Brinkema's order adroitly strikes a balance between the competing concerns of due process and national security, yet the government steadfastly refuses to comply.

But, perhaps more importantly, the prosecution's noncompromising approach to the Moussaoui case brings into sharp focus America's commitment to equal justice under the law within its criminal justice system. To examine this issue, consider the likelihood that Moussaoui will receive a plea deal similar to John Walker Lindh's. After all, comparing the facts of the cases, Lindh was on the battlefields of Afghanistan, bearing arms, face to face with American soldiers, prepared to fight and presumably kill on behalf of his radical beliefs. By contrast, Moussaoui was, at best, a religious zealot whose own ineptitude exposed him as a "suspicious" individual, leading to his arrest and, thereby, rendering him useless to the 9/11 plot. Indeed, his handwritten diatribes fashioned as court pleadings and his bitter outbursts in court have led many to question his mental competency.[24] Lindh's guilty conduct was witnessed firsthand by soldiers who captured him in Afghanistan, while Moussaoui's alleged guilt is contained in reams of documents yet to be presented at trial, and the government is seeking the death penalty against him.[25]

Both men are alleged to have known about the September 11 plot. Why then does it appear that the government is taking a hard-line aggressive prosecutorial stance in Moussaoui's case? Could it be that Moussaoui is not only the alleged twentieth hijacker but ultimately symbolic of all the other 9/11 hijackers as well? America needs a 9/11 defendant, a physical being in the defendant's chair representing those who callously inflicted pain and anguish on innocent victims through heinous acts of terrorism. With his foreign status, physical appearance, demeanor, and resolute adherence to radical Islamic beliefs, Moussaoui fits the bill quite nicely. He is one of them, he knew them, he conspired with them, and for that he may pay with his life—through a military justice process if not though civil justice.

Americans as "Enemy Combatants": The Hamdi and Padilla Cases

The power of citizenship as a shield against oppression was widely known from the example of Paul's Roman citizenship, which sent the centurion scurrying to his higher-ups with the message: "Take heed what thou doest—for this man is a Roman."

—Robert H. Jackson, U.S. Supreme Court
associate justice, *Edwards v. California* (1941)

It is psychologically troubling for Americans to learn that fellow Americans wish their country ill. It is more troubling to learn that these citizens would join organizations such as the Taliban and al Qaeda to carry their ill wishes into action. However, it is shocking to learn that our federal government is stripping U.S. citizens of their supposedly guaranteed due process rights under the banner of national security. Yet that is exactly what is happening to Jose

Padilla and Yaser Hamdi—leading to what may become a split in the federal circuit courts over whether the executive branch is acting beyond its power by affixing labels to citizens that effectively suspend their constitutional rights.

Jose Padilla, a.k.a. Abdullah al-Muhajir, is of Hispanic origin. He is an American citizen, born in Brooklyn, who recently left the country and joined al Qaeda. He was apprehended in May 2002 reentering the country at Chicago with plans to allegedly detonate a "dirty" radiological bomb in furtherance of al Qaeda's unholy cause. Attorney General Ashcroft first labeled him a "material witness" as a pretext to hold him indefinitely without prosecuting; however, when a New York federal judge ruled such use of the material witness statute inappropriate, Padilla was redesignated an "enemy combatant" and turned over to the DOD. He has since been denied access to counsel and is undergoing interrogation in a South Carolina military prison.[26]

When he was taken into custody, Attorney General Ashcroft announced at a news conference in Moscow, where he was visiting, "We have captured a known terrorist . . . [and have] disrupted an unfolding terrorist plot to attack the United States by exploding a radioactive 'dirty bomb.'"[27] However, without access to a lawyer, without access to civil courts, without access to anyone beyond his military captors, Padilla has no method of challenging the attorney general's announcement. Thus, his indefinite detention (now going on two years) may amount to summary conviction by announcement.

Yaser Esam Hamdi is of Arabic origin, born in Louisiana when his father was employed there. He is an American citizen who left the country with his Saudi family as a child. It is unclear whether he ever returned. But he eventually joined al Qaeda and sought to do harm to fellow Americans. He was captured in Afghanistan, transferred to Guantanamo Bay, Cuba, and then shuttled to a military base in Virginia upon discovery of his citizenship. He too has been labeled an "enemy combatant," and a decision by a federal judge that he is entitled to a public defender is now being challenged by the DOD on appeal.[28] Meanwhile, he continues to linger in solitary confinement in a holding facility in South Carolina after being transferred from Virginia in July 2003.

What will become of the two Americans detained indefinitely, without access to counsel, incommunicado—in direct violation of their Fifth Amendment due process rights and Sixth Amendment rights to counsel? If they are not tried in federal courts like Lindh, where can they be prosecuted? President Bush's military order establishing tribunals in the DOD currently excludes the possibility of trying American citizens[29]—a political concession designed to tamp down on public resistance to the order. In hindsight, it works to block trial of either Padilla or Hamdi by military tribunal unless the order is revised, which may be politically impossible.

Consequently, by labeling them "enemy combatants," the government must try them, if it decides to do so, before regular military courts under the UCMJ. This is provided for in the Geneva Convention.[30] But to take this route opens the door to criticism that American citizens are accorded treaty rights while non-Americans receive second-rate justice—because both Americans and non-Americans were captured as enemy combatants.[31]

Alternatively, the government can just throw away the key and let them languish indefinitely. So far, the government's justification has been an undisguised effort to extract information from them. As the DOJ argued in its case to dismiss Padilla's habeas petition, "The detention of enemy combatants is critical to preventing additional attacks on the United States, aiding the military operations, and gathering intelligence in connection with the overall war effort."[32]

In the case of enemy combatant Hamdi, whose cause has gone further in the courts than that of Padilla, Judge Robert G. Doumar of the federal district court in Norfolk, Virginia, twice ordered the government to allow Hamdi access to a lawyer. The government refused to comply and appealed the orders to the Fourth Circuit Court—which stayed the orders and returned the case to Judge Doumar, who then asked the government to show him evidence that Hamdi qualified as an enemy combatant. Frustrated that they did not receive a rubber stamp, the government refused to do this as well, claiming the need to protect classified information, and appealed that order.[33]

The Fourth Circuit Court of Appeals ruled on January 8, 2003, that because Hamdi was captured overseas fighting for the Taliban he could be held indefinitely as an enemy combatant by the military, effectively without access to an attorney, based solely on the government's assertion that he is one—and this cannot be challenged by him or anyone else acting in representative capacity.[34]

While acknowledging the continued right of judicial review even in wartime, the court essentially noted that this had little meaning given the sweeping deference due the president under the Constitution:[35]

> The constitutional allocation of war powers affords the president extraordinarily broad authority as commander in chief and compels courts to assume a deferential posture in reviewing exercises of this authority. . . . The safeguards that all Americans have come to expect in criminal prosecutions do not translate neatly to the arena of armed conflict. In fact if deference is not exercised with respect to military judgments in the field, it is difficult to see where deference would ever obtain.[36]

Hamdi retains his habeas rights as an American citizen, but any inquiry into his detention must remain "extremely limited."[37] Indeed, the court denied Hamdi the right to challenge any facts presented by the government against him supporting his designation as an enemy combatant subject to indefinite detention. Moreover, the court held that Geneva Convention protections guaranteeing combatants the right to have their status reviewed by a competent tribunal were unavailable to Hamdi because those treaty provisions are not self-executing and, therefore, give no rise to individually assertable rights, only state and government rights.[38]

The Second Circuit Court of Appeals is considering similar arguments on Padilla's fate. Because he was being held in New York as a material witness before he was reclassified as an enemy combatant, that jurisdiction has remained seized of his case despite the government's attempts to transfer the case, as it has the prisoner, to South Carolina.[39] Directly contrary to the Fourth Circuit's decision in *Hamdi*, the lower court in Padilla's case found that he "has the right to present facts" refuting the government's assertions that he is an enemy combatant; thus he must have access to counsel for this purpose.[40]

However, if the Second Circuit rules similarly on appeal to the Fourth Circuit in *Hamdi*, those decisions could constitute a green light from the judicial branch for the administration to move ahead with creation of its proposed enemy combatant designation committee, first reported in 2002. For Americans suspected of false allegiance, the attorney general, secretary of defense, and CIA director will decide whether a suspect is to be relegated to indefinite detention in military custody as an enemy combatant. If the suspect is a foreigner, the national security advisor will join this new Ashcroft-Rumsfeld-Tenet triumvirate in its decision.[41]

So how does the government decide who is an enemy combatant? What are the criteria? That is for the administration to know and for Americans not to ask about. Solicitor General Ted Olsen, whose wife was killed in the 9/11 terrorist attacks, defends the decision to keep the criteria a secret: "There will be judgments and instincts and evaluations and implementations that have to be made by the executive that are probably going to be different from day to day, depending on the circumstances."[42]

Secret criteria, based on instinct, that change day to day? That sounds suspiciously like the secret and ever-changing criteria determined by congressional cabals led by Senator McCarthy a half-century ago to determine who was a communist sympathizer and then to publicly destroy them. Indeed, history should make us wary whenever a self-anointed portion of the government presumes to define "un-American" and then hold citizens accountable for activities that fall under such a designation.

Significantly, the only authority the government can show to support its retrograde detention policy is the sixty-year-old Supreme Court opinion in *Ex Parte Quirin.* There, the Court decided that Americans working in collusion with German Nazi saboteurs seeking to destroy industrial targets in the United States could be tried by military commissions instead of civilian courts.[43] Widely criticized, *Quirin* had rested on the trash heap of other infamous and unjust decisions like *Plessy v. Ferguson, (Dred) Scott v. Sanford,* and *Korematsu v. United States,* until it was resurrected by the attorney general in his desperate attempt to justify the detention policies of his department in the absence of any other authority.[44]

Politically, however, the legal position of indefinite detention is untenable in the long term. Nevertheless, it is the likely outcome for two of these U.S. citizens. The compelling question generated by this action concerns why indefinite detention of Americans by the military inside the United States is necessary. The only reason identified beyond the government's national security rationale deduced by legal scholars is one of judicial efficiency—they simply can not or will not undertake the tremendous effort to mount full-scale prosecutions and discovery efforts in each of these cases and the many more that are likely to occur.[45] In effect, they may as well have shrugged and suggested that perhaps during "wartime" anything is possible—even in America.

It was wrong in the 1940s to inter 120,000 Japanese Americans without charges, evidence, trials, or the ability to demonstrate their allegiance to America. It was wrong in the 1950s to arrest, harass, and destroy the reputations of American "communists" without evidence of traitorous intent or false allegiance. It is wrong today to snatch Americans off the street, designate them as "enemies," and throw them into military brigs without access to counsel, courts, the evidence against them, or the opportunity to refute the designation, be they Taliban, communists, or Japanese.

But perhaps the most psychologically sinister aspect of how America is treating its own in this regard involves the debilitating degree of isolation visited upon them. Indefinite detention in military prison not only means that enemy combatants have no access to counsel—it means they have no access to the outside world whatsoever. Padilla's and Hamdi's respective families have had no contact with them since their confinement. This raises serious international human rights issues, ironically the very same issues raised by the United States on countless occasions against other countries.

So long as Padilla and Hamdi are considered viable intelligence sources and demonstrable threats to the country in its war on terror (according to the low threshold the government must meet), they amount to no more than isolated canaries in a cage with the drape pulled down. Having secured limited judicial acceptance of this practice, the Bush administration is now in the process of extending this treatment to foreign nationals within the United States.

Ali Saleh Kahlah al-Marri, a Qatari student pursuing a master's degree at Bradley University in Peoria, Illinois, was arrested by the FBI and charged in federal court with lying about his travels shortly after September 11, 2001, and with credit card fraud. But on June 23, 2003, the president issued an order declaring him an enemy combatant with alleged ties to al Qaeda and transferred him out of the civilian court system into military imprisonment on a navy brig in South Carolina.[46] Al-Marri's lawyers from his criminal case in Illinois (suddenly without their client) have undertaken arguments in federal court there against the president's power to summarily pull defendants from the civilian criminal court system and transfer them to the military.

Consequently, the Seventh Circuit may emerge as a new judicial battleground in this ongoing battle the government is undertaking to secure favorable judicial opinions supporting its conduct. In an apparent decision to limit the possibility of more negative judicial reaction, however, the DOJ has requested transfer of the al-Marri case out of Illinois to the federal court in South Carolina—the current physical location of the defendant and, coincidentally, a jurisdiction that has already ruled favorably on the detention of Hamdi.[47]

Other Federal Court Rulings

Federal courts have begun ruling in cases beyond the headliners of Lindh, Moussaoui, and the enemy combatants. Several members of what the DOJ styles "al Qaeda sleeper cells" within the United States have been arrested and indicted in Oregon and New York.[48] District courts have also taken up cases involving the status of immigrants and closed deportation hearings within the INS system, as well as cases involving the ability of captured foreign detainees at Guantanamo Bay, Cuba, to petition for release.

Domestic Terrorist Cells: The Buffalo and Oregon Cases

On September 14, 2002, three days after the first anniversary of the devastating 9/11 terrorist attacks, federal law enforcement agents arrested six Arab American men in Lackawanna, New York, a Buffalo suburb. All of the suspects, who are American born and of Yemeni descent, were charged with operating a terrorist cell in western New York and knowingly and unlawfully providing material support to al Qaeda by attending a terrorist training camp in Afghanistan, where Osama bin Laden allegedly lectured the men about the alliance of the Islamic jihad and al Qaeda.[49]

Coincidentally, the Buffalo suspects are alleged to have attended the same terrorist training camp as John Walker Lindh, who, as part of his plea arrangement with the government, agreed to cooperate fully with authorities investigating terrorism at home and abroad. It is not known what role Lindh might have played in leading the government to its investigations in Buffalo. Pleas of not guilty have been entered for all of the men, and their cases are currently pending in the federal criminal court system.[50]

A month later, four more Americans were arrested in Portland, Oregon, and indicted in federal court along with two others (one citizen extradited back to the United States from Malaysia and another noncitizen still at large) for plotting to join al Qaeda and Taliban fighters in their jihad against America.[51] The six individuals allegedly developed a plan to go to Afghanistan and take up arms against coalition forces, having trained with Chinese rifles in Oregon to prepare for the trip, but the plan never came to fruition.[52]

According to the FBI, there was no indication that the alleged members of the Portland cell sought to attack targets within the United States: "They had not gotten to a point where they were identifying targets or anything like that." The tip that led to these arrests came from a Hamas sympathizer of Palestinian origin who is serving thirty months in prison on weapons and fraud charges.[53]

Why weren't the alleged members of the Buffalo and Portland cells tagged with the label "enemy combatant" and transferred to the DOD? That is an open question. However, three possible reasons present themselves. First, there was clearly much more FBI surveillance undertaken in these cases, several months' worth actually, to build up a strong evidentiary case against them. In contrast, there was little evidence compiled against Hamdi and Padilla—certainly not enough to withstand the scrutiny of an Article III federal court.

Second, when the alleged terrorist cells in Buffalo and Portland were broken up and their cadre arrested, the courts hearing challenges in the Hamdi and Padilla cases had not spoken on the extent of the executive's power to do what it had done with those two citizens. Consequently, the cautious approach was to proceed along the path of charging these new defendants with multiple violations of Title 18 Section 2339 prohibiting support of a terrorist organization. But if the Second Circuit follows the lead of the Fourth Circuit and extends judicial approval of the government's enemy combatant designation and detention policy to citizens captured in the homeland, it would be no surprise if the attorney general directs agents to detain and then turn over future terrorist-supporting suspects to the military.

Third, the secret criteria for designating enemy combatants may require positive action in furtherance of an attack. Hamdi was captured abroad with a weapon fighting against coalition forces, Padilla was captured in Chicago seeking targets for a radiological bomb plot, and al-Marri's alleged conduct is classified.[54] Conversely, there is no indication that any of the suspects apprehended in either Buffalo or Portland were physically participating in a terrorist action against the United States. Of course, this is mere guesswork since the criteria for deciding who falls into enemy combatant status are unknown to the public and could change on a daily basis according to Solicitor General Olsen.[55]

Nonetheless, the chief law that these and future defendants not designated as enemy combatants will face as they are prosecuted by assistant U.S. attorneys is a constitutionally problematic one. The Antiterrorism and Effective Death Penalty Act of 1996 criminalized providing "material support" to any group designated by the government as a terrorist group.[56] Material support is statutorily defined as providing to the illegal organization any of the following:

> [C]urrency or monetary instruments or financial securities, financial services, lodging, training, expert advice or assistance, safehouses, false documentation or identification, communications equipment, facilities, weapons, lethal substances, explosives, personnel, transportation, and other physical assets, except medicine or religious materials.[57]

According to David Cole of the Georgetown University Law Center, this statute is unconstitutionally overbroad—effectively chilling protected activities.[58] Moreover, he argues, the lack of any intent element in the crime itself unfairly relieves the prosecution of proving in court that defendants actually meant to do the country harm through their perhaps misguided actions:

> It allows the government to obtain convictions for so-called terrorist crimes without proving any intent to engage in or

further terrorism. The government need only show that the individual provided a proscribed group with some "material support," which . . . can be mere attendance at a training camp. The law is written so broadly that it would make it a crime to write a column or to file a lawsuit on behalf of a proscribed organization, or even to send a book on Gandhi's theory of non-violence to the leader of a terrorist group in an attempt to persuade him to forego violence.[59]

At least two federal district courts in California have ruled this part of the statute unconstitutional. Prior to the war on terror, in 1998, the court for the Central District of California held that the portion of the statute's material support definition in section (b) that prohibits providing personnel and training to terrorist organizations was impermissibly vague and thus stricken from the statute.[60] In that case, several American groups were "supporting" two foreign groups listed as terrorist organizations—the Kurdistan Worker's Party (PKK), an ethnically distinct secessionist group in southeast Turkey, and the Liberation Tigers of Tamil Eelam (LTTE) in Sri Lanka.[61]

The court's reasoning for finding the act vague was that the statute did "not . . . appear to allow persons of ordinary intelligence to determine what type of training or provision of personnel is prohibited. Rather, [it] appears to prohibit activity protected by the First Amendment—distributing literature and information and training others to engage in advocacy."[62]

Four years later, in June 2002, the federal district court in Los Angeles dismissed the DOJ's case based on the same statute against seven individuals accused of diverting charitable donations to the People's Mujahedeen[63]—a group implicated in the takeover of the U.S. embassy in Iran in 1979 that is still listed as a terrorist organization even though it opposes the current regime in Teheran.[64] The basis for the judge's determination that the statute was unconstitutional rested on the inability of such groups designated as "terrorist" to contest that designation:

[T]he law gives these groups "no notice and no opportunity" to context their designation as a terrorist organization, a violation of due process, Judge Takasugi ruled. "I will not abdicate my responsibilities as a district judge and turn a blind eye to the constitutional infirmities" of the law. . . . Because the government made its list of terrorist organizations in secret, without giving foreign groups a chance to defend themselves, the defendants "are deprived of their liberty based on an unconstitutional designation that they could never challenge," he said.[65]

It is unclear whether the government will appeal this case, but it is clear that the administration cannot continue to rely principally on a flawed statute without risking the loss of significant convictions. Consequently, it would not be surprising to find this case taken up by the Ninth Circuit Court of Appeals—the first step in making its way to the Supreme Court; nor would it be surprising to hear Attorney General Ashcroft proposing some amendments to the existing law or new antiterrorism laws altogether in the next legislative session.

Immigrant Status: The Haddad and North Jersey Media Cases

And if a stranger sojourn with thee in your land, ye shall not do him wrong. The stranger that dwelleth with you shall be unto you as one born among you, and thou shalt love him as thyself.
—Leviticus 19:33

Attorney General Ashcroft, a devoutly religious man, turned this biblical guidance on its head when he said at a November 2001 DOJ press conference that "foreign terrorists who commit war crimes against the United States, in my judgment, are not entitled to and do not deserve the protections of the American Constitution."[66] Although defending the president's decision to keep noncitizen terrorist suspects captured abroad offshore and subject to an executive-controlled judicial system, the statement is indicative of the adminstration's mind-set in this regard.

During the months immediately following 9/11, the federal government dispersed its agents throughout the country to implement the largest single dragnet in American history. It succeeded in rounding up approximately twelve hundred men of mostly Arabic and South Asian origin, whom it then detained for questioning. Many of these individuals were arrested for technical violations of their immigration status. No names were released of those detained, and all hearings on their immigration status and requests for deportation were held in secret.[67]

By November 2001, a federal gag order had been issued prohibiting officials from discussing the detainees and even forbidding defense attorneys from taking documents out of the courtroom. Due to the secrecy of the process, no government oversight or review of the actions occurred. There was no possibility of appeal from the hearings. Immigration courts, as executive branch bodies that are part of the DOJ—not part of the Article III federal judiciary—had no choice but to comply with the department's directives.

Several court challenges were mounted against the government's detention policies—specifically attacking the decision not to release the names of individuals held, the secrecy of the immigration hearings, and the misuse of the material witness statute to hold individuals indefinitely without filing charges against them and allowing them access to counsel. The results have been decidedly mixed, as the courts continue to wrestle with the proper balance between equal justice and national security. Consequently, a split in the circuits has occurred that can only be resolved with a Supreme Court ruling.

At the end of October 2001, the ACLU filed a request for information under the Freedom of Information Act (FOIA) concerning the identity of the individuals. The executive branch remained nonresponsive. In December the group filed suit in federal district court, seeking to compel the government's compliance with FOIA. To justify its secrecy, the DOJ argued that the nature of its actions was necessary for national security reasons—that identifying the detainees would alert terrorists as to how the investigation was proceeding and could aid in future terrorist plots. The decision by Judge Gladys Kessler came down in August 2002 against the DOJ, holding that the government had to release the names of the detained individuals. However, she stayed her order pending appeal.[68]

She noted that "secret arrests are a concept odious to a democratic society."[69] Judge Kessler's rationale rested on the importance of verification that the government was operating within the bounds of the law, and it was her sworn duty as a member of the judicial branch to make sure that the executive branch acted appropriately:

> The court fully understands and appreciates that the first priority of the executive branch in a time of crisis is to ensure the physical security of its citizens. . . . [But] the first priority of the judicial branch must be to ensure that our government always operates within the statutory and constitutional constraints which distinguish our democracy from a dictatorship.[70]

On behalf of Ashcroft's DOJ, an assistant attorney general chastised the judge for her ruling in a remarkably strong-worded statement that not only questioned the judge's patriotism but also accused her of helping terrorists succeed in their mission:

> The Department of Justice believes today's ruling impedes one of the most important federal law enforcement investigations in history, harms our efforts to bring to justice those responsible for the heinous attacks of September 11 and increases the risk of future terrorist threats to our nation.[71]

By the time of Judge Kessler's ruling, all but 74 of the detainees had been deported or released. Most, like the 131 Pakistanis who were secretly spirited back to their homeland on a chartered Portuguese jet, left the United States quietly, without fanfare and without a public hearing of their cases.[72] Later that month, the American Bar Association voted to oppose the secret detention of foreign nationals within the United States. Unfortunately, neither of these actions came in time to help the other 1,000 nameless individuals who were held, interrogated, and disposed of by the government without judicial or public scrutiny.[73]

Five months after the ACLU action was filed, the *Detroit Free Press* together with the *Detroit News* and Congressman John Conyers from Michigan commenced an action in Detroit's federal district court to open up the secret immigration hearings against Ann Arbor resident Rabih Haddad—a native of Lebanon who had overstayed his tourist visa. In April Judge Nancy G. Edmunds ruled in favor of the newspapers to open the hearings. In so doing, she relied on both history and practice in the absence of law to the contrary:

> The statutory and regulatory history of immigration law demonstrates a tradition of public and press accessibility to removal proceedings. From the start of the federal government's regulation of immigration in the last quarter of the nineteenth century, the governing statutes and regulations have expressly closed exclusion hearings (i.e. hearings to determine whether an alien may enter the United States), but have *never* closed deportation hearings (i.e. hearings to determine whether an alien already within the country may remain).[74]

On appeal, the Sixth Circuit agreed with Judge Edmunds. The decision, handed down at the end of August, found that the modicum of enhanced national security argued by the government as a basis to continue deportation hearings in secrecy was vastly outweighed by society's interest in public and press oversight of how the government wields its delegated power. Indeed, Judge Damon J. Keith scolded the DOJ, stating that "democracies die behind closed doors."[75] He specifically emphasized the rationale of this important concept in his opinion:

> Since the end of the 19th Century, our government has enacted immigration laws banishing, or deporting, non-citizens because of their race and their beliefs. While the Bill of Rights jealously protects citizens from such laws, it has never protected non-citizens facing deportation in the same way. In our democracy, based on checks and balances, neither the Bill of Rights nor the judiciary can second-guess government's choices. The only safeguard on this extraordinary governmental power is the public, deputizing the press as the guardians of their liberty.
>
> Today, the Executive Branch seeks to take this safeguard away from the public by placing its actions beyond public scrutiny. Against non-citizens, it seeks the power to secretly deport a class if it unilaterally calls them "special interest" cases. The Executive Branch seeks to uproot people's lives,

outside the public eye, and behind a closed door. . . . The First Amendment, through a free press, protects the people's right to know that their government acts fairly, lawfully, and accurately in deportation proceedings.

When government begins closing doors, it selectively controls information rightfully belonging to the people. Selective information is misinformation. The Framers of the First Amendment "did not trust any government to separate the true from the false for us" [citing prior Supreme Court opinions]. They protected the people against secret government.[76]

New Jersey's federal district court judge John Bissell essentially agreed with Judge Kessler's determination to open government immigration hearings when he ruled in May 2002 that the government could only close such hearings on a case-by-case basis, not under a blanket secrecy order.[77] In the case of *North Jersey Media Group v. Ashcroft,* several media outlets and the ACLU sued to open the hearings on the basis of due process violations and the public's right to monitor the actions of government officials.[78]

The government appealed the decision to the Third Circuit Court of Appeals and sought a stay during appeal. A three-judge panel from the Third Circuit denied the government's motion,[79] but the DOJ appealed this to the Supreme Court, arguing in its brief that "This is an extraordinary case, touching on the nation's very ability to defend itself against the continuing threat of hostile attack from myriad and unknown sources"—referring to the value that releasing the names of those detained could have for terrorist cells.[80] The justices eventually granted the stay to keep the hearings secret during appeal. No opinion accompanied the Supreme Court's order.[81]

Three months later, the Third Circuit ruled in Philadelphia that the INS blanket secrecy order was appropriate,[82] given the deference due to the executive branch—reversing Judge Bissell's decision to open the hearings on a vote of two to one.[83] Chief Judge Edward Becker, writing for the court, noted:

We are keenly aware of the dangers presented by deference to the executive branch when constitutional liberties are at stake, especially in times of national crisis. On balance, however, we are unable to conclude that openness plays a positive role in special-interest deportation hearings at a time when our nation is faced with threats of such profound and unknown dimension.[84]

The plaintiff's attorney criticized the court for accepting the government's "parade of horribles," and Hofstra University law professor Eric Freedman added that "Closed proceedings are always more convenient to the executive branch. . . . The real scandal here is that history, law, policy and the precedents of the Supreme Court, to say nothing of the Constitution, require the opposite result." Most of the 752 people specifically detained on immigration violations have been deported or released—only 81 remain in custody.[85]

In the spring of 2003, the DOJ's own inspector general issued a report sharply criticizing the FBI and INS for the detention of so many aliens in unnecessarily harsh conditions for unnecessarily long periods of time—blaming in particular the DOJ's blanket "hold until cleared" policy, which amounted to a guilt before innocence standard. "The clearance process took an average of 80 days, primarily because it was understaffed and not given sufficient priority by the F.B.I. . . . Even in the chaotic aftermath of the Sept. 11 attacks, we believe the F.B.I. should have taken more care to distinguish between aliens who it actually suspected of having a connection to terrorism from those aliens who, while possibly guilty of violating federal immigration law, had no connection to terrorism."[86]

Attorney General Ashcroft's response to the House Judiciary Committee on this matter was unapologetic. He specifically defended the manner in which the detentions were carried out, promised to look into allegations of abuse while refusing to appoint a special counsel, and noted his hope that things would go better next time: "[I]f we ever have to do this again, we hope that we can clear people more quickly."[87]

The Material Witness Dilemma

The government's alternate policy of indefinitely detaining people in secrecy as material witnesses when there are no immigration violations to hold them on was also questioned by a New York federal district court in May 2003. Judge Shira A. Scheindlin ruled that the

DOJ overreached its power in detaining a Jordanian man, Osama Awadallah—a student in California with a green card—as a material witness who authorities believe might have information for grand juries investigating terrorism. The judge determined that a person may only be held with probable cause under the material witness statute—which the judge ruled had not been applied correctly. Moreover, Judge Scheindlin ruled that such "witnesses" could only be detained after an indictment was returned.

The material witness statute was designed to allow for detention of an individual who had information critical to a criminal proceeding that was in progress if that individual could not be compelled to testify in any other way. The judge wrote, "Since 1789, no Congress has granted the government the authority to imprison an innocent person in order to guarantee that he will testify before a grand jury conducting a criminal investigation." She relied on a prior statement by Attorney General Ashcroft that he would utilize this rarely invoked law aggressively to prevent, disrupt, and delay new terrorist attacks to support her conclusion that this misuse was improper: "*Relying on the material witness statute* to detain people who are presumed innocent under our Constitution *in order to prevent potential crimes* is an illegitimate use of the statute." Ashcroft rejected the decision as an anomaly.[88]

Two months later, while the government was appealing Scheindlin's decision to the Second Circuit Court of Appeals, Judge Michael B. Mukasey, also of the New York federal district court, ruled in favor of the administration—characterizing the previous ruling by Scheindlin as an incorrect interpretation of the statute. According to Mukasey's decision, the government could proceed to use the statute to indefinitely detain individuals in secrecy in pursuit of its war on terror. With such conflicting decisions at the district level, it will be up to the Second Circuit to clarify whether the law is being manipulated or followed appropriately.[89]

Nonetheless, public opinion is steadily coalescing against Ashcroft's legal initiatives to detain noncitizens. Professor David Cole summed it up this way: "It's really unprecedented that we have locked up several hundred individuals in secret. It's as close to 'disappearing' individuals (like in South American dictatorships) as we in this country have ever come. They don't want us to know how much they're just shooting in the dark on this investigation."[90] And editorials, such as this one from the *St. Louis Post-Dispatch*, have begun to pepper newspapers across the country since litigation against secret detentions by the government has ensued:

In this country, we don't imprison people unless there is evidence they committed a crime. We don't hold detention hearings behind closed doors. We don't imprison people for crimes they might commit in the future. All these things are fundamental. Yet since Sept. 11, Attorney General John D. Ashcroft has used the federal material witness law in exactly those ways, locking up two dozen people. Last week, a federal judge in New York called Mr. Ashcroft's tactics "illegitimate."

A material witness is not a crime suspect, but has information that is important to a prosecution. If the witness might flee, prosecutors can lock him up to get a sworn statement. But Mr. Ashcroft has used the law more broadly, imprisoning people he thinks might commit a crime. Last week's ruling freed Osama Awadallah, a Jordanian with a legal resident alien's green card who attended college in California.

The FBI found his first name and old telephone number in a car used by one of the Sept. 11 hijackers. The government says he lied when asked during a polygraph exam if he had advance knowledge of the Sept. 11 attacks. A judge held him as a material witness. For 20 days, Mr. Awadallah was shuttled among four prisons, held in solitary confinement, shackled, strip-searched and held incommunicado.

On Oct. 10, while handcuffed to a chair, he testified before a grand jury he had met two of the hijackers, but could remember the name of only one, Nawaf Al-Hazmi. He denied knowing another hijacker, Khalid Al-Mihdar, even after the government produced a college examination book in which Mr. Awadallah had written "Khalid." He was charged with perjury. Last week, U.S. District Judge Shira A. Scheindlin ruled the detention illegal. She said the material witness law only applied after a criminal case starts—not to the grand jury investigation before it starts. Holding an innocent person during a grand jury investigation might violate the Fourth Amendment's requirement that an arrest be based on evidence of a crime, she said.

Mr. Ashcroft is appealing. He notes that many other judges have approved the use of the material witness law during grand juries. He says that locking up material witnesses is essential to disrupting new terrorist attacks. But even if Mr. Ashcroft's use of the law was justified in the first confusing days after Sept. 11, it certainly has been abused since.

Consider the case of Abdallah Higazy, an Egyptian-born student who was arrested as a material witness on Dec. 17 when he returned to a hotel near the World Trade Center to retrieve possessions left behind on Sept. 11. The FBI confronted him with a ground-to-air radio found at the hotel. After three weeks of detention, Mr. Higazy seemed to confess and was charged with interfering with an investigation. But a few days later, another hotel guest claimed the radio. The government released Mr. Higazy in prison garb and with a $3 subway fare.

Compounding these abuses is the secrecy that has shrouded the use of the law. The Justice Department won't say how many people have been held as material witnesses. Nor are the court proceedings involving material witnesses open to the public. We all want to be safe, but in this country, we hold certain values fundamental. The Justice Department's tactics are fundamentally wrong.[91]

As of November 2002, the government had jailed forty-four people as material witnesses—holding them indefinitely without access to counsel or under indictment by a grand jury. Nine of these are still known to be in custody, twenty-nine have since been released, and it is unclear what happened to the other six. The DOJ has no comment on the matter.[92]

Battlefield Detainees: The Guantanamo Bay Cases

Camp Delta, a prison camp at the U.S. Naval Base in Guantanamo Bay, Cuba, is home to 620 detainees captured largely during the American-led invasion of Afghanistan in 2001. The newly constructed Camp Delta is a more permanent facility than Camp X-Ray, the makeshift maze of cages that served as the original detention center. The detainees are either members of al Qaeda or Taliban fighters—most are Saudi Arabian, but there are at least forty-three nationalities represented. None has appeared before any sort of tribunal to have his status determined as combatant, none has access to counsel or home government, and none has been accorded legal rights guaranteed under international law—although all have been treated humanely and are kept in good physical condition.[93]

The basic rule is that both citizens and noncitizens who are arrested as suspects in criminal activity in the United States are arraigned and processed through Article III civilian courts. Both are usually accorded habeas corpus relief. Outside the United States, the rules change. In wartime, noncitizen prisoners of the enemy's forces who are captured in battle and detained abroad are processed for any criminal activity according to the terms of the UCMJ—which is brought into application through the terms of the Third Geneva Convention on Treatment of Prisoners of War.[94]

Because the Bush administration did not want its detainees accorded POW status, even though they were captured as byproducts of America's war on terrorism, the invasion of a foreign country, and the occupation of that country,[95] the DOD labeled them "unlawful combatants" and argued that the treaty protections do not apply[96] so therefore the UCMJ process does not apply. Consequently, the administration believes it can run them through military commissions to be established under the president's November 13 military order,[97] where they will enjoy fewer rights as defendants than in front of a regular court martial or Article III federal court.

The administration's definition and use of the legal status "unlawful combatant" are broad. Apparently, Taliban detainees (whom the government now recognizes as covered by the Geneva Convention as the de facto army of Afghanistan but not as POWs) and al Qaeda detainees (who the government says are not covered by the treaty) are both unlawful combatants because they failed to follow the rules of warfare, such as wearing identifiable insignia, uniforms, and so forth.[98] If they are not POWs, then by implication they are not recognized as members of the armed forces—which would make them civilians.

As civilians, their status would be covered by the Fourth Geneva Convention protecting civilians during armed conflict.[99] These treaty terms would accord them rights to be tried, if they are to be tried, by regularly constituted civilian courts (Article III federal courts). The administration has not specifically addressed this argument but is likely to broaden its definition of "unlawful combatant" even further—analogizing the detainees to spies and mercenaries who could traditionally be summarily executed under historical practice in warfare. What does this process do to American justice? What does it do to how America is perceived by other people around the world?

Many countries, including America's allies, have criticized the administration's mass detention policies for captives of the Afghan campaign and the intentional blurring of their legal status as prisoners at Camp Delta. Such unnecessary discord and antagonism undermine the support willingly pledged by foreign governments to the United States in its war on terror after September 11, 2001.

Summary

While these examples present a mere sampling of the post-9/11 cases winding their way through the U.S. court system, definite patterns are emerging. The overwhelming majority of cases involve challenges to the detainment of men of Middle Eastern descent, whether on American or foreign soil and regardless of citizenship. These cases tell a tale of a justice system, although grounded in principles of equal justice, nevertheless being skewed to meet the demands of vengeance. In the process, our constitutional system is also distorted, shifting the judicial focus away from protecting the individual to blindly implementing executive mandates. The courts must not capitulate, as they are the last bastion of equal justice at a time when constitutional ideals are being shunted aside in the name of national security. In a different era, speaking on the role of courts in our constitutional system, Justice Hugo Black wrote:

> Today, as in ages past, we are not without tragic proof that the exalted power of some governments to punish manufactured crime dictatorially is the handmaid of tyranny. Under our constitutional system, courts stand against any winds that blow as havens of refuge for those who might otherwise suffer because they are helpless, weak, outnumbered, or because they are non-conforming victims of prejudice and public excitement. Due process of law, preserved for all by our Constitution, commands that no such practice . . . shall send any

TABLE 4. Legal Bases of Post-9/11 INS Detention, with Detainees by Nationality

Section 237 (8 USC 1227) General Classes of Deportable Aliens	Section 241 (8 USC 1231) Detention and Removal of Aliens Ordered Removed	Section 212 (8 USC 1182) General Classes of Aliens Ineligible to Receive Visas and Ineligible for Admission
65 Pakistan	2 Lebanon	71 Pakistan
59 Egypt	2 Yemen	10 Egypt
31 Yemen	2 Syria	9 Yemen
23 Turkey	1 Bangladesh	9 Jordan
21 Israel	1 Trinidad	9 India
20 Jordan	1 Kenya	5 Turkey
19 Saudi Arabia	1 India	4 Syria
15 Morocco		4 Morocco
13 India	**18 USC 1001** Fraud and False Statements	3 Guyana
11 Tunisia		2 Tunisia
6 Syria	1 Yemen	2 Senegal
5 Sri Lanka		2 Mexico
5 Lebanon	**Section 217 (8 USC 1187)** Visa Waiver Program for Certain Visitors	2 Israel
4 Palestine		2 Iran
4 Albania	3 Germany	2 Brazil
3 Iran	2 France	2 Afghanistan
3 France	2 Spain	1 Russia
2 Spain		1 Libya
2 South Africa	**Section 252 (8 USC 1282)** Conditional Permits to Land Temporarily	1 Cyprus
2 Senegal		1 Bangladesh
2 Russia	3 Pakistan	
2 Nepal	2 Saudi Arabia	**Section 235 (8 USC 1225)** Inspection by Immigration Officers; Expedited Removal
2 Mauritania		
2 Kuwait		1 Jordan
2 Austria		
2 Arab Emirates		
1 Zaire		
1 Trinidad		
1 Tanzania		
1 Czech Republic		
1 Afghanistan		

Note: Several detainees were held on multiple bases.

accused to his death. No higher duty, no more solemn responsibility, rests upon this Court, than that of translating into living law and maintaining this constitutional shield deliberately planned and inscribed for the benefit of every human being subject to our Constitution—of whatever race, creed or persuasion.[100]

The rights against executive abuse, lodged in our Constitution from the beginning and given life by succeeding generations of jurists, must be guarded jealously. Otherwise, the balance of power among the branches may shift—potentially harming the individual in his or her exercise of civil liberty. Constitutional protections are there for a reason. For example, the Fourth Amendment defines areas of privacy immune from governmental search or seizure in the absence of minimum levels of suspicion. The remedy for government misconduct is exclusion of the unlawfully obtained evidence from the criminal trial, which, in some instances, may be case dispositive. According to the U.S. Supreme Court in the seminal case establishing the applicability of the exclusionary rule to the states,

> If letters and private documents can thus be seized and held and used in evidence against a citizen accused of an offense, the protection of the Fourth Amendment declaring his right to be secure against such searches and seizures is of no value, and, so far as those thus placed are concerned, might as well be stricken from the Constitution. The efforts of the courts and their officials to bring the guilty to punishment, praiseworthy as they are, are not to be aided by the sacrifice of those great principles established by years of endeavor and suffering which have resulted in their embodiment in the fundamental law of the land.[101]

The Court concluded that an exclusionary rule prohibiting the introduction of illegally obtained evidence was "logically and constitutionally necessary" and, therefore, must be insisted upon as an essential ingredient to the right to be free from unreasonable searches and seizures.

In a similar vein of protecting individuals suspected of criminal conduct, the Fifth Amendment insulates the accused from compelled self-incrimination in an interrogation setting. In the oft-cited U.S. Supreme Court opinion in *Miranda v. Arizona*, the Court described the inherent compulsion of the interrogation room:

> It is obvious that such an interrogation environment is created for no purpose other than to subjugate the individual to the will of his examiner. This atmosphere carries its own badge of intimidation. To be sure, this is not physical intimidation, but it is equally destructive of human dignity. The current practice of incommunicado interrogation is at odds with one of our Nation's most cherished principles—that the individual may not be compelled to incriminate himself. Unless adequate protective devices are employed to dispel the compulsion inherent in custodial surroundings, no statement obtained from the defendant can truly be the product of his free choice.[102]

The prohibition against obtaining a confession of guilt through compulsory questioning reaffirms that, in the American criminal justice system, the government shoulders the burden of proving its case beyond a reasonable doubt. In fact, recognizing and acceding to a suspect's wish to remain silent are so vital to the American system of justice that law enforcement agents must affirmatively describe the applicable Fifth Amendments safeguards *and* confirm the suspect's understanding of the ramifications of waiving these protections *before* an interrogation proceeds. Hence, the evolution of *Miranda* warnings, which are so familiar to Americans that many can recite them from memory.[103]

Once a suspect has been arrested, the Sixth Amendment affords substantive and procedural protections designed to ensure that the accused is advised of the charges against him and that any subsequent trial proceedings are speedy, public, and impartial. Over the years, the U.S. Supreme Court has interpreted and expanded upon these constitutional safeguards. For example, explaining a criminal defendant's right to be apprised of the government's charges, the Court observed:

> The doctrine to be deduced from the American cases is that the constitutional right of the defendant to be informed of the

nature and cause of the accusation against him entitles him to insist, at the outset, by demurrer or by motion to quash, and, after verdict, by motion in arrest of judgment, that the indictment shall apprise him of the crime charged with such reasonable certainty that he can make his defence and protect himself after judgment against another prosecution for the same offence.[104]

Moreover, to ensure that lack of resources is not outcome determinative for the indigent, the Court has construed the Sixth Amendment as mandating a right to counsel for destitute defendants in criminal cases. As part of its reasoning the Court noted that state and federal governments routinely expend vast resources trying defendants accused of crimes and that lawyers for the government are considered instrumental to the process of protecting the public order; therefore,

[t]he [defendant's] right to be heard would be, in many cases, of little avail if it did not comprehend the right to be heard by counsel. Even the intelligent and educated layman has small and sometimes no skill in the science of law. If charged with crime, he is incapable, generally, of determining for himself whether the indictment is good or bad. He is unfamiliar with the rules of evidence. Left without the aid of counsel he may be put on trial without a proper charge, and convicted upon incompetent evidence, or evidence irrelevant to the issue or otherwise inadmissible. He lacks both the skill and knowledge adequately to prepare his defense, even though he have a perfect one. He requires the guiding hand of counsel at every step in the proceedings against him. Without it, though he be not guilty, he faces the danger of conviction because he does not know how to establish his innocence.[105]

Non-Article III Courts

Beyond the normal courts established by Congress under Article III of the Constitution, other judicial bodies either have already impacted the government's war on terror or may do so in the near future.

In May 2002, the Foreign Intelligence Surveillance Court, a statutorily created body pursuant to the FISA, handed down a shocking decision. Although the government was granted the eavesdropping authority it requested (no such requests have been turned down in the court's twenty-two-year history, including the 932 requests made last year),[106] the decision was surprising because it castigated the DOJ for breaching the wall separating intelligence gathered for criminal prosecution and that gathered for actual foreign intelligence purposes. It also chastised the FBI and DOJ for providing the court with false or erroneous information on which to base search warrants and wiretap authorizations on at least seventy-five occasions. The court rejected the attorney general's assertion that the new USA Patriot Act allowed the FBI much more leeway in its domestic surveillance capability.[107]

Judicial
Reaction

225

An appeal by the DOJ ensued. On November 18, 2002, the Foreign Intelligence Surveillance Court of Review emerged from nearly a quarter-century of silence. Perhaps itself impressed with the momentousness of that occasion, the court delivered a convoluted fifty-six-page opinion in which it

- chided the lower FISA court for adhering to minimization procedures governing the sharing of information developed by the DOJ and followed by the FBI and the DOJ in all physical searches of U.S. persons since their promulgation in 1995. ("The FISA court asserted authority to govern the internal organization and investigative procedures of the Department of Justice which are the province of the Executive Branch (Article II) and Congress (Article I).")[108]
- gratuitously insulted the amici curiae participants, whose contributions lent the process a scintilla of adversariness. ("The ACLU relies on Title III of the Omnibus Crime Control and Safe Streets Act of 1968, 18 U.S.C. §§ 2510–2522, to interpret FISA, passed 10 years later. That technique, to put it gently, is hardly an orthodox method of statutory interpretation.")[109]
- raised the question of whether FISA, as amended by the USA Patriot Act, is constitutional, concluding that the ques-

tion has no "definitive jurisprudential answer," further concluding that even if the standards do not comport with the Fourth Amendment, they "certainly come close," and finally concluding that "FISA as amended is constitutional because the surveillances it authorizes are reasonable."[110]

- repeatedly asserted that the lower FISA court's opinion "does not clearly set forth a basis for its decision," apparently ignoring the lower FISA court's statement that its analysis and findings are "based upon traditional statutory construction . . . [involving] straightforward application of the FISA as it pertains to minimization procedures, and . . . [raising] no constitutional questions that need to be decided."[111]

- rigidly relied upon legislative statements made during the hasty passage of the Patriot Act as conclusive proof of congressional intent, while blithely dismissing more recent statements concerning congressional intent, categorizing them as "legislative future" not entitled to authoritative weight.[112]

- described the government's efforts to challenge the long-standing dichotomy between foreign intelligence and law enforcement purposes as "heroic" even though the history of FISA, senatorial statements, a letter from the DOJ, and the Patriot Act clearly accept and legitimize such a dichotomy.[113]

- apparently accepted at face value the government's uncontested assertion that false, misleading, or inaccurate FBI affidavits in numerous FISA applications may have been a result of "confusion within the Department of Justice over implementation" of the wall procedures that the DOJ itself drafted and implemented.[114]

In addition, the court did not consider one crucial question, which, if carefully and objectively analyzed, would easily have laid bare the executive branch's thinly veiled quest for unconstrained authority to invade the privacy of U.S. citizens with minimal oversight. That is, why would the government need to alter procedures for obtaining FISA warrants when the lower FISA court had never rejected an application? Indeed, according to the lower FISA court opinion the court had "reviewed and approved several thousand FISA applications, including many hundreds of surveillances and searches of U.S. persons . . . [and had] long accepted and approved minimization procedures authorizing in-depth information sharing and coordination with criminal prosecutors." In fact, the language of the lower FISA court's opinion expressly provided that

> The FBI, the Criminal Division, and OIPR may consult with each other to coordinate their efforts to investigate or protect against foreign attack or other grave hostile acts, sabotage, international terrorism, or clandestine intelligence activities by foreign powers or their agents. Such consultations and coordination may address, among other things, *exchanging* information already acquired, identifying categories of information needed and being sought, preventing either investigation or interest from obstructing or hindering the other, compromise of either investigation, and long term objectives and overall strategy of both investigations in order to insure that the overlapping intelligence and criminal interests of the United States are both achieved. [emphasis added][115]

In light of the lower FISA court's holding regarding the exchange of information, can the government seriously contend that the minimization procedures that it drafted in 1995, which the lower FISA court dutifully adopted, were too restrictive, warranting a still more lenient approach?

Moreover, as recently revealed, even with the DOJ minimization procedures in place, the government on numerous occasions failed to strictly adhere to them as evidenced by the disturbing number of inaccurate FBI affidavits accompanying FISA applications in which the government's "misstatements and omissions involved information sharing and unauthorized disseminations to criminal investigators and prosecutors."[116]

The ruling is legally unsound. At various points throughout the opinion, the FISA review court conflates the ultimate use of criminal information gleaned from a legitimate FISA investigation with the methods used to obtain such information. The court relies upon several opinions in which the courts recognized that criminal investigation, arrest, and prosecution may be a part of FISA surveillance as long as foreign intelligence gathering remains the primary purpose. The FISA review court criticizes these opinions, however, for not linking the primary purpose test to actual statutory language and for interpreting foreign intelligence information to "exclude evidence of crimes."

Moreover, the FISA review court inexplicably treats these cases as if they somehow impeded full implementation of FISA surveillance, when, in fact, the opinions upheld the FISA warrants at issue, concluding that the primary purpose of each investigation was foreign intelligence gathering. Indeed, there is no evidence that those courts were interpreting "foreign intelligence information" to exclude evidence of crimes, and, in fact, they expressly acknowledged that criminal prosecutions may ensue in the wake of FISA investigations.

Curiously, the FISA review court also expends a great deal of energy demonstrating that the traditional dichotomy between foreign intelligence gathering and criminal investigations was "false," only to conclude that the Patriot Act now requires such a dichotomy. The court apparently assumes that, despite the Patriot Act's swift enactment and sparse legislative history, Congress actually took the time to construct this dichotomy out of whole cloth, rather than accepting the more logical conclusion that Congress simply modified the long-standing dichotomy that existed. Indeed, Senator Leahy noted at the time of the Patriot Act passage that "no matter what statutory change is made . . . the court may impose a constitutional requirement of 'primary purpose' based on the appellate court decisions upholding FISA against constitutional challenges over the past 20 years."[117]

As evidence of the need for expanded information exchange, the FISA review court points to recent testimony before the Joint Intelligence Committee that suggests "that the FISA court requirements . . . may well have contributed, whether correctly understood or not, to the FBI missing opportunities to anticipate the September 11th attacks."[118] What the court fails to point out, however, is that the Joint Committee also determined that, prior to September 11, "the intelligence community possessed no intelligence or law-enforcement information that would have linked 16 of the 19 hijackers to terrorism or terrorist groups."[119]

In addition, the Joint Committee concluded that, with respect to the three remaining hijackers, regardless of any information exchange hurdles, the "CIA should have acted to add these individuals to the State Department's watch list in March 2000 . . . [but failed to do so because] CIA personnel received no formal training on watch-listing . . . [and] learned about the watch-listing process through on-the-job training."[120]

By utilizing the failure to discover and prevent the September 11 hijackings as a basis for now permitting the unfettered exchange of information, the FISA review court minimized the ineptitude that apparently prevailed throughout various law enforcement agencies prior to September 11 and ignored the potential for self-serving after-the-fact rationalizations by the government designed to mask such incompetence and to shift responsibility for institutional mismanagement and chaos.

Ironically, the minimization procedures that the government now challenges as unduly burdensome would certainly not hinder its ability to investigate non-U.S. citizens entering the United States on multiple entry visas (as the hijackers did) because the lower FISA court makes clear that its "findings regarding minimization apply only to communications of or concerning U.S. persons . . . [meaning] U.S. citizens and permanent resident aliens . . . and does not apply to communications of foreign powers . . . [or] to non-U.S. persons."[121]

Essentially, the FISA review court's opinion would have the American public believe that the government has been obstructed at every twist and turn in its pursuit, investigation, and prosecution of terrorist activity, when, in fact, history reveals that just the opposite is true. The courts have been extraordinarily solicitous of the government's efforts, providing them with broad latitude to pursue counterterrorism objectives. It bears repeating that the lower FISA court has never denied a request for a FISA warrant. (The lower FISA court did not technically deny the request in the case at bar and instead issued the order with certain modifications.)

What the lower FISA court recognized and, indeed, what all Americans should legitimately fear is that the executive branch is disingenuously using its September 11 failures in conjunction with the hastily drafted and poorly crafted Patriot Act to "give the government a powerful engine for the collection of foreign intelligence information targeting U.S. persons."[122]

By adhering to the minimization procedures, the lower FISA court merely sought to assure that the balance between legitimate national security concerns and individual privacy was not disturbed by seemingly unconstrained executive power. Thus, rather than overstepping the bounds of an Article III court, the lower FISA court was, in fact, acting as Article III courts have throughout history, filling in the gaps when statutes, through their silence or ambiguity, threaten fundamental rights that inhere in a democratic society. One need only consider the U.S. Supreme Court's Fourth and Fifth Amendments jurisprudence to understand that Article III courts are not strangers to crafting and imposing standards necessary to animate the fundamental principles of a "constitutional democracy under the law."

There is no question that Congress bungled its legislative responsibility by hurriedly enacting a far-reaching statute without debate or analysis. There is also no question that the executive branch, which goaded Congress into its haste, now seeks to use this legislative failure as a means to specifically target U.S. citizens.

But perhaps most importantly, there is also no question that a secret FISA appellate court structure, with judges hand-selected by the chief justice of the U.S. Supreme Court, that hears only the government's evidence and grants only the government a right to appeal is a singularly inappropriate forum to resolve issues that threaten the fundamental rights and values of all U.S. citizens.

The only question that remains is how much further our justice system will be derailed in pursuit of the war on terrorism.

Executive Military Tribunals

As of 2003, the Bush administration has not impanelled any of the military commissions for which it has laid the legal groundwork by promulgating its military order[123] and the supporting DOD regulations.[124] Thus, it remains unclear how these courts will function in reality beyond the rules that establish them. However, it is becoming clear that Article III federal courts are reluctant to interfere in their jurisdiction or operation so long as the defendants remain outside the sovereignty of the United States.

At least two federal district court judges have determined that they have no jurisdiction to issue writs of habeas corpus in response to requests on behalf of detainees in Guantanamo Bay. A. Howard Metz of the federal bench for California's Central District Court ruled in February 2002 that neither he nor any other federal court judge could exercise his or her jurisdiction outside the sovereignty of the United States—which is where the naval base at Guantanamo Bay legally sits. He relied on prior decisions in the 1990s by the Eleventh Circuit Court of Appeals and the federal district court for Connecticut to determine that Guantanamo Bay, while under U.S. jurisdiction and control, remained under the sovereignty of Cuba according to the terms of the lease agreement between those two countries.[125]

Judge Colleen Kollar-Kotelly of the U.S. District Court for the District of Columbia agreed in July 2002, ruling that the Kuwaitis, Australians, and Britons seeking habeas relief for their relatives being detained in Cuba could not seek it in the federal courts for the same reasons articulated by Judge Metz. In dismissing their case, she suggested that international law might provide them some relief but that it would have to be worked out at the government-to-government level through their home countries.[126]

Given this ruling, it is apparent that the administration will not seek to impanel a military tribunal and begin a trial inside the United States or its territories, even though the president's military order allows it to do so. They simply would not want to risk interference from a federal court. Thus, when such tribunals appear, they will likely be "off-site" in Afghanistan, in another country, or in Camp Delta on Guantanamo Bay itself. An aircraft carrier or other warship would not likely suffice as a viable venue immune from the reach of federal district courts, as warships are commonly considered part of the territory of the sovereign to whom they belong.[127]

In the summer of 2003, the White House designated six Guantanamo Bay detainees as "eligible" for trial by military commission, comporting with a process laid out in DOD rules drafted to implement the president's military order providing for the establishment of the tribunals. Two of the six, Feroz Abbasi and Moazzam Begg, are British nationals. In response to domestic political pressure, Prime Minister Blair and Attorney General Goldsmith of Britain negotiated modifications to the treatment of these two from the process likely to be encountered by other detainees—exempting them from the death penalty, opening their trials to reporters, allowing for private consultations with defense counsel, and reserving the possibility of serving sentences at home in Britain if convicted.[128] Thus, staunch political allies in America's war on terror (and invasion of Iraq) may yet be able to secure tangible benefits from their continued support.

A National Security Court?

Harvey Rishikof, a law professor at Roger Williams University and former FBI counsel, has proposed the creation of a new national security court dedicated to handling the difficult issues that have confronted federal courts and embroiled the government in a nest of legal challenges over its actions since the September 11 attacks. The basis for his proposal is twofold: (1) the continuing war on terrorism is taking its toll on the federal court system, which is not designed to hold secret trials based on classified national security–related evidence; and (2) the alternative of trying terrorists in non-UCMJ tribunals only alienates our allies, who are vehemently against it, and creates a double-standard for non-Americans.[129]

While he concedes that federal courts functioned well in the Oklahoma City bombing case and in the first WTC attack, Rishikof argues that the system itself is unable to adapt in the long term to such a continuing terrorist conflict as we now find ourselves in: "The people we are fighting do not fit into our traditional legal classifications. We can continue to improvise our way through, compromising our federal criminal procedures and alienating our allies, or we can demonstrate our commitment to the rule of law by creating an institution that can handle new challenges without damaging our constitutional principles."[130]

As to structure, Rishikof suggests expanding the jurisdiction of the current Foreign Intelligence Surveillance Court, which is staffed by eleven federal judges on a rotation basis and approves secret search and seizure warrants based on classified intelligence, and providing for a route of appeal up to the Supreme Court. Moreover, a pool of specialized defense attorneys with prior clearances to participate could be drawn from to provide counsel. The advantages he cites that would stem from such a court include designation and fortification of an existing courthouse to hold terrorism trials—thus, streamlining physical security concerns—and the possibility of taking the court on the road to conduct hearings in remote locations, such as Camp Delta.[131]

While Professor Rishikof must be commended for the creativity of his suggestion, it must be noted that such a proposal runs directly counter to our American culture of open judicial proceedings, the fairness and legality of which are guaranteed by public scrutiny. This proposal, though well intended, likely raises more thorny constitutional and judicial process questions than it ultimately answers. Would there be a specialized pool of prescreened jurors who have special clearance? What would that do to the voir dire selection process?

Rishikof correctly points out that there are other specialized courts in the federal system for bankruptcy, tax, patents, international trade, and copyrights. However, these examples fail to support the creation of a secret tribunal because they do not operate outside public scrutiny. Allowing secret hearings for issuance of search and seizure warrants, as now happens with the FISA court, sets the outside limits of what our legal and political values permit. Allowing secret trials based on secret evidence with secret outcomes and no public scrutiny to ensure fairness breaches those limits.

A federal courthouse, designated and fortified, as Rishikof suggests, holding unidentified prisoners in cells belowground, sitting as a massive windowless concrete bunker to which access is restricted—be it in downtown Boston or rural Virginia—belongs more to the landscape of Soviet Russia or Communist China than to America. The Bush administration has, in its responses to 9/11, provided enough legal symbols of what the American legal system is *not* fundamentally about (the USA Patriot Act, the military tribunals, and the withdrawn TIPS program to enlist neighborhood informants). America does not need a lasting physical symbol such as this national security court to give it permanent form.

The U.S. Supreme Court: An Ultimate Destination

While cases challenging the government's authority to indefinitely detain individuals, to secretly surveil them, to hold them as material witnesses, or to summarily deport them are percolating in the lower federal courts, no case derived from America's post-9/11 war on terror has yet made its way to the Supreme Court. However, given the gravity of civil liberty abuse at stake, it is extremely likely that several soon will. Consequently, it is important to gauge the tenor of the current bench on such subjects. Since Chief Justice Rehnquist has given these issues considerable thought, albeit in historical context, his are the most significant writings to consider here.

In 1998, Rehnquist published a book entitled *All the Laws but One*, which discusses the place of civil liberties in wartime. He could not have known three years later how relevant that legal analysis would be. This book discusses civil liberties in wartime within the United States. Most of it covers the Civil War, with the remainder discussing World Wars I and II. Rehnquist's proposition is that one of war's necessities for a successful conclusion may be the temporary curtailment of civil liberties.[132]

This amounts to a sophisticated chicken and egg argument—if our country is not secure, then freedom does not matter because there is no country. In fact, the title of the book refers to a speech by Lincoln in which he asked the following rhetorical question when he was justifying the suspension of habeas corpus: "Are all the laws, but one, to go unexecuted, and the government itself to go to pieces, lest that one be violated?" Rehnquist allows for this silence of the laws in a time of war because it has always been balanced with responses by both the public and the legal community.

His whole argument, then, essentially rests on faith that this will always continue to be the case, handily disregarding Justice Brandeis's admonition, "Experience should teach us to be most on our guard to protect liberty when the Government's purposes are beneficent."[133] Shortly after his book's publication, Rehnquist noted in an address to the students at Drake University Law School:

> The courts, for their part, have largely reserved the decisions favoring civil liberties in wartime to be handed down after the war is over. Again, we see the truth in the maxim Inter Arma Silent Leges—in time of war the laws are silent. To lawyers and judges, this may seem a thoroughly undesirable state of affairs, but in the great scheme of things it may be best for all concerned.
>
> The fact that judges are loath to strike down wartime mea-

sures while the war is going on is demonstrated both by our experience in the Civil War and in World War II. This fact represents something more than some sort of patriotic hysteria that holds the judiciary in its grip; it has been felt and even embraced by members of the Supreme Court who have championed civil liberty in peacetime. Witness Justice Hugo Black: he wrote the opinion for the Court upholding the forced relocation of Japanese Americans in 1944, but he also wrote the Court's opinion striking down martial law in Hawaii two years later.

While we would not want to subscribe to the full sweep of the Latin maxim—Inter Arma Silent Leges . . . perhaps we can accept the proposition that though the laws are not silent in wartime, they speak with a muted voice.[134]

In a review of the book four years after its publication, *New York Times* reporter Adam Cohen noted, "[I]f Mr. Rehnquist the jurist sees the world as Mr. Rehnquist the historian does, there's cause for concern. . . . [The book's] central message is that in wartime, the balance between order and freedom tips toward order. In recounting the history, Justice Rehnquist gives all the arguments for order, and far too few for freedom. The people whose liberties are taken away are virtually invisible."[135]

As the U.S. Supreme Court begins to consider questions of equal justice and civil liberty as they are balanced against the executive's wartime administrative prerogatives, prior articulated opinions on the matter become increasingly important as a barometer of where the justices stand. Consequently, the chief justice's book, together with his public statements like those delivered at Drake and his court opinions on citizenship and its content like that given in the *Verdugo-Urquidez* case, corroborate one another as reflective of his mind regarding this critical balance.

In the 1990 case of *United States v. Verdugo-Urquidez*, the Supreme Court held that the Fourth Amendment did not apply to search and seizure by federal agents of property owned by a nonresident alien that was located in Mexico. Writing for the majority, Rehnquist concluded that the term "people" in the Fourth Amendment referred only to U.S. citizens—who were, therefore, the only individuals in whom Fourth Amendment rights could possibly be vested. Conversely, Fifth Amendment rights that vested in "persons" and Sixth

Amendment rights that vested in "the accused" could be relied on by citizens and noncitizens alike. This dichotomy together with the territorial limitation of constitutional rights mitigated against Verdugo-Urquidez being protected.[136]

This holding is consonant with his book's determination disapproving the Supreme Court's *Korematsu* line of cases in 1942–43 authorizing a curfew and detention of Japanese on the West Coast only because those cases lumped together Issei (Japanese immigrants) with Nisei (Japanese Americans). In his view, the government had much more leeway to deal with the prior class of individuals rather than the latter class based simply on their status.[137]

While the chief justice has not spoken on such issues definitively since 9/11, it may be assumed that he holds to the reasoning presented in his 1998 book and in his 1990 opinion in the *Verdugo-Urquidez* case. Although he is just one of nine justices who may decide how civil liberties are balanced against national security, or how equal justice is balanced against maintaining order, his persuasive effect on the conservative wing of the Supreme Court cannot be underestimated. Thus, it appears that defenders of the USA Patriot Act, and administration officials issuing orders and rules under it, will at least find a sympathetic ally in the chief justice should they find themselves in the Supreme Court while the war on terrorism is in progress.

7 Conclusion
Striking the Balance between Civil Liberties and Security

Equal and exact justice to all men, of whatever state or persuasion, religious or political; . . . freedom of religion; freedom of the press, and freedom of person under protection of habeas corpus, and trial by juries impartially selected. These principles form the bright constellation which has gone before us and guided our steps through an age of revolution and reformation.

The wisdom of our sages and blood of our heroes have been devoted to their attainment. They should be the creed of our political faith, the text of civic instruction, the touchstone by which to try the services of those we trust; and should we wander from them in moments of error or of alarm, let us hasten to retrace our steps to regain the road which alone leads to peace, liberty, and safety.

—Thomas Jefferson, first inaugural address, March 4, 1801

Pursuit of justice through repression of fundamental freedoms in the name of protecting a free society serves neither. The incongruity of this familiar trap is self-evident. Succeeding generations of Americans have wrestled with it: from the foundation of this fragile republic in the eighteenth century through the Civil War of the nineteenth to the communist scare of the McCarthy era in the twentieth. The events of September 11 have now thrust this dilemma on our generation in the twenty-first century. We must face it truthfully, with due regard to credible concerns on both sides of the argument. Balancing freedom and security in the scales of justice is no small task. But it perhaps becomes easier to comprehend when we step back and realize that justice is in the balance as well.

Both Presidents Lincoln and Wilson recognized the temptation to tip the balance between law and security in favor of security during wartime. Lincoln noted, after suspending habeas corpus and disregarding Chief Justice Taney's order to release a prisoner held by executive fiat in *Ex Parte Merryman*,[1] "The Constitution is different in its application in cases of Rebellion or Invasion, involving the Public Safety, from what it is in times of profound peace and public security."[2] And Wilson observed, "There is an old saying that the laws are silent in the presence of war. Alas, yes; not only the civil laws of individual nations but also apparently the law that governs the relation of nations with one another must at times fall silent and look on in dumb impotency."[3]

However, both presidents were faced with different kinds of wars than the threat posed by terrorists to our country. Congress had declared war in both instances when these executives decided to tip the balance toward security over justice. The nation was literally torn in half during the Civil War. And America, not yet a superpower, was embroiled in its first global conflict during World War I. Neither circumstance validates those actions but may explain them. In the war on terror, there is no visible enemy, no one country at which to direct our military might beyond Afghanistan, and no pronouncement of war from the people's representatives. Indeed, statements by congressmen admitting their irresponsible reaction to Attorney General Ashcroft's scare tactics indicate that Congress was coerced into passing the USA Patriot Act.

This book has analyzed the manifest possibilities for injustice that exist in that legislation. Some remain inchoate possibilities, others have risen to the level of probably, and still other injustices have been realized. The major thrust of the act—providing federal agencies with more surveillance options that are easier to activate while simultaneously decreasing judicial supervision of that process—has encouraged abuses that are just beginning to come to light. Given the increasing backlash to the act's provisions, the future portends much controversy, but the fallout may well be restoration of the delicate balance between the needs of national security and the demands of equal justice.

This book has also explored other legal responses to the September 11 attacks, from the joint resolution authorizing the use of force against al Qaeda and the creation of military tribunals to try those captured on the international side to the creation of a federal homeland security agency and the exercise of prosecutorial discretion on the domestic side. Judicial reaction, although only in its initial stage, has also been explored. Surveying this legal landscape, we have determined that the scales not only have shifted away from freedom and equal justice toward secrecy and national security in this war on terrorism but continue to shift in that direction today.

The executive branch's accrual of power to itself has not been checked by the legislature, which is paralyzed for fear of seeming unpatriotic, and the first decisions by the independent federal judiciary are just now beginning to come down—with mixed results and clearly not enough force to restore the balance as yet. The administration's entreaty to trust it not to abuse its increasing power has not been challenged by a cowed public; only the press has dared question it, as in this *New York Times* editorial of December 2001:

> The administration has argued that even if the powers it is seizing are broad, it will not use them abusively. This has been a constant theme of Mr. Ashcroft and the administration in general—that they are people who can be trusted to use these broad, repressive rules wisely. That is not the way the American system works. This is a nation built around the rule of law, not faith in the goodness of particular officials.[4]

Fundamental rights of American citizens have been curtailed without their knowledge. By rewriting FBI rules crafted to curb abuses of the J. Edgar Hoover era, the DOJ has given that agency the power to unleash its agents into the private lives of Americans without any indicia of illegal activity, let alone the former low-level presnooping requirements of reasonable suspicion or probable cause. Citizens can also now be detained as "material witnesses" indefinitely, without being charged, without access to counsel, incommunicado, and in solitary confinement.

Alternatively, when courts have challenged the use of that method, Attorney General Ashcroft has substituted in the label of "enemy combatant" to justify handing those Americans over to Secretary Rumsfeld's DOD—which threw them into military brigs and wrapped their detention in the shroud of secrecy. Does that mean that these Americans have been stripped of their citizenship? No. However, it does mean that the U.S. military is holding American civilians against their will.

Are they being interrogated? Are they being tortured? We don't know the answers to these questions. All we know is that they are Americans who have been summarily denied their rights as citizens. Based on the government's newfound power to use either of these labels, Americans can now be snatched off planes, off streets, and even out of their own homes, secretly "processed," and thrown into prison or a military jail indefinitely without a lawyer. Such tactics are the antithesis of due process and speak volumes about how far the American justice system has departed from its constitutional moorings.

Basic rights of noncitizen residents in the United States have also been infringed upon wholesale. Protection against preventive or indefinite detention, privacy of the attorney-client relationship, the right to a jury trial and to appeal, as well as the right to public hearings have all been swept aside by more Ashcroft initiatives implemented by the INS. The effect has been to construct an alternate justice system for noncitizens weighted in favor of the government to summarily deport people they deem undesirable.

Noncitizens outside the United States are not even accorded hearings guaranteed them under the Geneva Convention. Hundreds now languish below the tropical sun at Camp X-Ray in Guantanamo Bay, Cuba, undergoing military, FBI, and CIA interrogation without access to counsel. These detainees, known by the new sobriquet "unlawful combatants," could remain at this improvised but expanding prison forever—just beyond the territorial reach of American federal courts. They are victims of a legal status created by our government that refuses to acknowledge them as prisoners of war even though they were captured in the "war on terrorism," which Congress acknowledged through joint resolution as the constitutional equivalent of a declared war.

The government is also using its power to control information as a means of restricting public access to public records. Under new rules issued by Ashcroft to executive agencies directing them to read the parameters of the FOIA as narrowly as possible while the administration's war on terrorism continues, many formerly available documents are being reclassified and withheld from public scrutiny. As the following newspaper account shows, even mundane requests are increasingly denied:

> When United Nations analyst Ian Thomas contacted the National Archives in March to get some 30-year-old maps of Africa to plan a relief mission, he was told the government no longer makes them public. When John Coequyt, an environmentalist, tried to connect to an online database where the Environmental Protection Agency lists chemical plants that violate pollution laws, he was denied access. And when civil rights lawyer Kate Martin asked for a copy of a court order that has kept secret the names of some of the hundreds of foreigners jailed since Sept. 11, the Justice Department told her the order itself was secret. "They say, 'there's a secrecy order barring us from telling you this. But the language of the secrecy order is secret, so you'll just have to take our word for it,'" she says.[5]

Without access to basic information, the public, the press, nongovernmental organizations, and civil society itself cannot sufficiently assess the motives, actions, or justifications of our public officials. And if we cannot do that, then we cannot challenge those motives, actions, or justifications as illegal or otherwise unacceptable. Public debate in this free democracy is thereby reduced to charges and countercharges based on hearsay and speculation. When public discourse is reduced to such a level, paranoia flourishes and takes democracy as its primary hostage. Indeed, this is why individuals routinely avoid talking to Western reporters in closed societies.

All Americans, indeed most people around the world, understand that there is an inherent tension between the desire to have a free society and the desire to have a secure one. In a time of clear threat to our nation, there is a natural tendency to favor a secure one. However, if we compromise our most basic freedoms in order to have this "secure" society, are we truly any better off? Are we consciously trading one type of society for another? Did not the free societies emerge victorious over the closed societies in World War II? in the cold war? Is it not true now that how we as a society react to the threat we face will inevitably define us as a people?

> Freedom is not a luxury that we can indulge in when at last we have security and prosperity and enlightenment; it is, rather, antecedent to all of these, for without it we can have neither security nor prosperity nor enlightenment.
> —Henry Steele Commager, *Freedom, Loyalty, Dissent*
> (1954, during the height of McCarthyism)

Appendix A

The plea agreement between John Walker Lindh and the United States, resolving the first terrorism case linked to the events of September 11, 2001.

IN THE UNITED STATES DISTRICT COURT FOR THE
EASTERN DISTRICT OF VIRGINIA
Alexandria Division

UNITED STATES OF AMERICA,

v.

JOHN LINDH,
Defendant.)

CRIMINAL NO. 02–37A

PLEA AGREEMENT

Paul J. McNulty, United States Attorney for the Eastern District of Virginia, and Randy I. Bellows, David N. Kelley, and John S. Davis, Assistant United States Attorneys, and the defendant, John Lindh, and the defendant's counsel, James J. Brosnahan, George C. Harris, Tony West, Raj Chatterjee, and William B. Cummings, pursuant to Rule 11(e) of the Federal Rules of Criminal Procedure, have entered into an agreement, the terms and conditions of which are as follows:

GENERAL PROVISIONS

1. The defendant, John Lindh, pursuant to Rule 11(e)(1)(A), agrees to plead guilty to Count Nine of the Indictment and to a Criminal Information filed herewith. Count Nine charges the defendant with supplying services to the Taliban, in violation of Title 50, United States Code, Section 1705(b), Title 18, United States Code, Section 2, and Title 31, Code of Federal Regulations, Sections 545.204 and 545.206(a). The Criminal Information charges the defendant with carrying an explosive during the commission of a felony which may be prosecuted in a court of the United States, in violation of Title 18, United States Code, Section 844(h)(2). The maximum penalty for the violation of Count Nine is ten years' imprisonment; a fine of $250,000; three years of supervised release; and a $100 special assessment. The penalty for the offense charged in the Criminal Information is ten years' imprisonment, consecutive to any term of imprisonment imposed on Count Nine; a fine of $250,000; three years of supervised release; and a $100 special assessment. The defendant is aware that any term of supervised release is in addition to any prison term the defendant may receive, and that a violation of a term of supervised release could result in the defendant's being returned to prison for the full term of supervised release. The parties agree that if two terms of supervised release are imposed in this case, the terms are to be served concurrently. *See* 18 U.S.C. section 3624(e).

2. The defendant agrees that pending sentencing in this matter he will not seek release from detention.

3. Before sentencing in this case, the defendant agrees to pay a mandatory special assessment of one hundred dollars ($100.00) per count of conviction. Restitution is not applicable in this case.

4. At sentencing in this case, the Government will move to dismiss Counts 1 through 8, and Count 10.

SENTENCING MATTERS

5. Pursuant to Rule 11(e)(1)(B), the parties stipulate and agree that the correct application of the United States Sentencing Guidelines is as follows:

i. As to Count Nine, the most analogous offense guideline is section 2M5.2. The applicable base offense level is 26. A twelve-level upward adjustment is appropriate because the provisions of § 3A1.4 apply. The defendant's criminal history category, therefore, is Category VI. A three-level reduction is appropriate for Acceptance of Responsibility, pursuant to § 3E1.1(a) and (b), resulting in an Offense Level Total for Count Eight of 35. Accordingly, the Sentencing Guideline Range on Count Eight is 292–365 months, subject to the statutory maximum of ten years' imprisonment.

ii. As to the offense charged in the Criminal Information, the offense guideline is section 2K2.4, and the guideline sentence is ten years' imprisonment.

iii. Accordingly, the appropriate total sentence of imprisonment is twenty years. Neither party will seek an upward or downward departure from that sentence.

iv. As to both Count Nine and the offense charged in the Criminal Information, no fine is appropriate.

6. The defendant is aware that 18 U.S.C. Section 3742 affords a defendant the right to appeal the sentence imposed. Acknowledging all this, the defendant knowingly waives the right to appeal any sentence up to and including twenty years' imprisonment, or the manner in which that sentence was determined, on the grounds set forth in 18 U.S.C. Section 3742 or on any ground whatever, in exchange for the concessions made by the United States in this plea agreement. This agreement does not affect the rights or obligations of the United States to appeal as set forth in 18 U.S.C. Section 3742(b).

7. The United States will not further criminally prosecute the defendant for the specific conduct described in the Indictment, the Criminal Information, or the Statement of Facts.

WAIVER OF RIGHTS

8. The defendant represents to the Court that the defendant is satisfied that his attorneys have rendered effective assistance. The defendant understands that by entering into this agreement, the defendant surrenders certain rights as provided in this agree-

ment. The defendant understands that the rights of criminal defendants include the following:

a. If the defendant persisted in a plea of not guilty to the charges, the defendant would have the right to a speedy jury trial with the assistance of counsel. The trial may be conducted by a judge sitting without a jury if the defendant, the United States, and the judge all agree.

b. If a jury trial is conducted, the jury would be composed of twelve laypersons selected at random. The defendant and the defendant's attorney would assist in selecting the jurors by removing prospective jurors for cause where actual bias or other disqualification is shown, or by removing prospective jurors without cause by exercising peremptory challenges. The jury would have to agree unanimously before it could return a verdict of either guilty or not guilty. The jury would be instructed that the defendant is presumed innocent, that it could not convict the defendant unless, after hearing all the evidence, it was persuaded of the defendant's guilt beyond a reasonable doubt, and that it was to consider each charge separately.

c. If a trial is held by the judge without a jury, the judge would find the facts and, after hearing all the evidence and considering each count separately, determine whether or not the evidence established the defendant's guilt beyond a reasonable doubt.

d. At a trial, the United States would be required to present its witnesses and other evidence against the defendant. The defendant would be able to confront those witnesses and the defendant's attorney would be able to cross-examine them. In turn, the defendant could present witnesses and other evidence in the defendant's own behalf. If the witnesses for the defendant would not appear voluntarily, the defendant could require their attendance through the subpoena power of the Court.

e. At a trial, the defendant could rely on a privilege against self-incrimination to decline to testify, and no inference of guilt could be drawn from the refusal of the defendant to testify. If the defendant desired to do so, the defendant could testify in the defendant's own behalf.

9. The defendant agrees to cooperate fully, truthfully and completely with the United States, and provide all information known to the defendant. A failure to cooperate fully, truthfully and completely is a breach of this plea agreement, as determined by the Court. The defendant acknowledges that he has been advised that the United States will not seek a downward departure from the applicable sentencing guidelines, or from the sentence imposed, pursuant to Section 5K of the Sentencing Guidelines, Title 18 U.S.C. Section 3553(e), or Rule 35(b) of the Federal Rules of Criminal Procedure, in respect to the defendant's cooperation. In regard to that cooperation:

   a. The defendant agrees to testify fully, truthfully and completely at any grand juries, trials or other proceedings, including military tribunals.
   b. As required by the United States, the defendant agrees to be available for debriefing by law enforcement and intelligence officers and for pre-trial conferences with prosecutive authorities. The timing and location of such debriefings and meetings shall be determined by the United States. Should defense counsel wish to attend particular debriefings, the Government will seek to schedule such debriefings consistent with the schedule of defendant's counsel, who shall make themselves reasonably available.
   c. The defendant agrees to provide all documents, records, writings, or materials, objects or things of any kind in the defendant's possession or under the defendant's care, custody, or control relating directly or indirectly to all areas of inquiry and investigation, excepting documents privileged under the attorney-client privilege.
   d. The defendant agrees that, upon request of the United States, the defendant will voluntarily submit to polygraph examinations to be conducted by a polygraph examiner of the United States' choice. The defendant stipulates to the admissibility of the results of this polygraph examination if later offered in a proceeding to determine the defendant's compliance with this plea agreement; however, the defendant reserves the right to challenge the weight that should be attributed to such polygraphs by contesting the accuracy of such polygraphs.

e. The defendant agrees that the accompanying Statement of Facts is limited to information to support the plea. The defendant will provide more detailed facts relating to this case during ensuing debriefings.

f. The defendant is hereby on notice that he may not violate any federal, state, or local criminal law while cooperating with the government.

ADDITIONAL GENERAL PROVISIONS

10. The United States agrees not to use any truthful information provided pursuant to this agreement against the defendant in any other criminal prosecution against the defendant. Regardless of any other provision of this agreement, however, the United States may use any statement made by the defendant, whether in the form of the Statement of Facts accompanying this plea agreement or in the debriefing of the defendant or in some other form, against the defendant in any prosecution of the defendant resulting from the defendant's breach of the plea agreement, whether such breach is caused by the defendant's providing false information, failing to provide full and complete cooperation, or for any other valid reason. Such a prosecution includes, but is not limited to, a prosecution for perjury or false statements.

11. This plea agreement does not restrict the Court's or Probation Office's access to information and records in the possession of the United States.

12. This plea agreement is not conditioned upon charges being brought against any other individual. This plea agreement is not conditioned upon any outcome in any pending investigation. This plea agreement is not conditioned upon any result in any future prosecution which may occur because of the defendant's cooperation. This plea agreement is not conditioned upon any result in any future grand jury presentation or trial involving charges resulting from this investigation. This plea agreement is conditioned upon the defendant's providing full, complete and truthful cooperation.

13. The accompanying Statement of Facts signed by the defendant is hereby incorporated into this Plea Agreement. Defendant

adopts the Statement of Facts and agrees that the facts therein are accurate in every respect and that had the matter proceeded to trial, the United States would have proved those facts beyond a reasonable doubt.

ASSIGNMENT OF ANY PROFITS OR PROCEEDS FROM PUBLICITY

14. The defendant hereby assigns to the United States any profits or proceeds which he may be entitled to receive in connection with any publication or dissemination of information relating to illegal conduct alleged in the Indictment. This assignment shall include all profits and proceeds for the benefit of the defendant, regardless of whether such profits and proceeds are payable to himself or to others, directly or indirectly, for his benefit or for the benefit of the defendant's associates or a current or future member of the defendant's family. The defendant shall not circumvent this assignment by assigning the rights to his story to an associate or to a current or future member of the defendant's family, or to another person or entity who would provide some financial benefit to the defendant, to the defendant's associates, or to a current or future member of the defendant's family. Moreover, the defendant shall not circumvent this assignment by communicating with an associate or a family member for the purpose of assisting or facilitating their profiting from a public dissemination, whether or not such an associate or other family member is personally or directly involved in such dissemination.

SPECIAL ADMINISTRATIVE MEASURES

15. The defendant is aware of the provisions of 28 C.F.R. Section 501.2 governing conditions of incarceration in national security cases. If a determination is made that such special administrative measures are applicable, the government will endeavor nonetheless to treat the defendant in a manner comparable to the treatment of other federal inmates at the same security classification level, regarding such matters as access to educational opportunities, prison library privileges, books, magazines,

newspapers, radio and television, visitation, and religious observances. The government also will endeavor to modify the currently existing special administrative measures to effect the same result.

SUPERVISED RELEASE

16. During the period of supervised release, the defendant may in appropriate circumstances apply to the Court and his probation officer for permission to travel out of his district of supervision, including out of the country. *See* U.S.S.G. section 5D1.3(c)(1).

BREACH OF THE PLEA AGREEMENT

17. Any alleged breach of this agreement by either party shall be determined by the Court in an appropriate proceeding at which the defendant's disclosures and documentary evidence shall be admissible and at which the moving party shall be required to establish a breach of the plea agreement by a preponderance of the evidence.

18. If the defendant fails in any way to fulfill completely all of the obligations under this plea agreement, including but not limited to his candid, forthright, truthful and complete cooperation, the United States may seek release from any or all its obligations under this plea agreement. If released from its obligations under this plea agreement, the United States may prosecute the defendant to the full extent of the law. The defendant agrees that any prosecution and sentencing subsequent to a breach of this plea agreement is not barred by the Double Jeopardy Clause of the Constitution or any other Constitutional provision or law or rule and that such rights as he might otherwise have enjoyed under these provisions are hereby waived, except that the defendant may raise any defense or make any claim that he could have raised prior to the entry of the Plea Agreement.

19. If the defendant fails to fulfill his obligations under this plea agreement, and the matter proceeds to trial, the defendant understands and agrees that any statements he makes pursuant

to or associated with this plea agreement, including but not limited to the Statement of Facts submitted in connection with this plea agreement and such statements as the defendant makes during the debriefing process, are admissible if offered by the Government at pre-trial proceedings and/or at trial and may be used for any purpose. Defendant shall assert no claim under the United States Constitution, any statute, Rule 410 of the Federal Rules of Evidence, Rule 11(e)(6) of the Federal Rules of Criminal Procedure, or any other federal rule, that defendant's statements pursuant to this agreement should be suppressed or are inadmissible, except on relevancy grounds.

DESIGNATION

20. The Government agrees not to object to the defendant's request to the Court for a recommendation that he be assigned to a suitable Bureau of Prisons facility near his parents' homes. The Government further agrees to communicate to the Bureau of Prison, at the defendant's request, factors potentially relevant to the secure incarceration of the defendant during his term of imprisonment, and to make appropriate recommendations as to those factors, including recommendations related to personal safety. The parties recognize that it is solely within the discretion of the Bureau of Prisons to determine where and in what manner the defendant is actually incarcerated, and this plea agreement in no way limits the exercise of that discretion.

UNLAWFUL ENEMY COMBATANT STATUS

21. With the following exception, the United States agrees to forego any right it has to treat the defendant as an unlawful enemy combatant based on the conduct alleged in the Indictment. The exception is as follows: For the rest of the defendant's natural life, should the Government determine that the defendant has engaged in conduct proscribed by the offenses now listed at 18 U.S.C. § 2332b(g)(5)(B), or conduct now proscribed under 50 U.S.C. § 1705, the agreement contained in this paragraph shall be null and void, and the United States may immediately

invoke any right it has at that time to capture and detain the defendant as an unlawful enemy combatant based on the conduct alleged in the Indictment.

REPRESENTATIONS BY THE DEFENDANT

22. The defendant agrees that this agreement puts to rest his claims of mistreatment by the United States military, and all claims of mistreatment are withdrawn. The defendant acknowledges that he was not intentionally mistreated by the U.S. military.

CREDIT FOR TIME SERVED

23. The United States recommends that the defendant be given credit by the Bureau of Prisons for such time as he has been in custody of the United States, including the time period between December 1, 2001 and January 22, 2002, while the defendant was in the custody of the United States military. The parties recognize and acknowledge that the Bureau of Prisons will determine the computation of credit for time served.

CONCLUDING REPRESENTATIONS

24. This written agreement constitutes the complete plea agreement between the United States, the defendant, and the defendant's counsel. The United States has made no promises or representations except as set forth in writing in this plea agreement.

25. The defendant acknowledges that no threats have been made against the defendant and that the defendant is pleading guilty freely and voluntarily because the defendant is guilty. Any modification of this plea agreement shall be valid only as set forth in writing in a supplemental or revised plea agreement signed by all parties.

26. *Defendant's Signature:* I hereby agree that I have consulted with my attorney and fully understand all rights with respect to the indictment. Further, I fully understand all rights with respect to the provisions of the *Sentencing Guidelines and Policy Statements* which may apply in my case. I have read this plea agreement

and carefully reviewed every part of it with my attorney. I understand this agreement and I voluntarily agree to it.

Date: _____

John Lindh
Defendant

27. *Defense Counsel Signature:* We are counsel for the defendant in this case. We have fully explained to the defendant the defendant's rights with respect to the pending indictment. Further, we have reviewed the provisions of the *Sentencing Guidelines and Policy Statements* and we have fully explained to the defendant the provisions of those Guidelines which may apply in this case. We have carefully reviewed every part of this plea agreement with the defendant.

To our knowledge, the defendant's decision to enter into this agreement is an informed and voluntary one.

Date: _____

James J. Brosnahan, Esq.
George C. Harris, Esq.
Tony West, Esq.
Raj Chatterjee, Esq.
William B. Cummings, Esq.

Respectfully submitted,
PAUL J. McNULTY
UNITED STATES ATTORNEY
By:
Randy I. Bellows
David N. Kelley
John S. Davis
Assistant United States Attorneys
APPROVED: _____

Date:

Appendix B

The White House
President George W. Bush
For Immediate Release
Office of the Press Secretary

November 13, 2001

President Issues Military Order

Detention, Treatment, and Trial of Certain Non-Citizens in the
War Against Terrorism

By the authority vested in me as President and as Commander in
Chief of the Armed Forces of the United States by the Constitution
and the laws of the United States of America, including the Authorization for Use of Military Force Joint Resolution (Public Law
107–40, 115 Stat. 224) and sections 821 and 836 of title 10, United
States Code, it is hereby ordered as follows:

Section 1. Findings.

(a) International terrorists, including members of al Qaida, have
    carried out attacks on United States diplomatic and military
    personnel and facilities abroad and on citizens and property
    within the United States on a scale that has created a state of
    armed conflict that requires the use of the United States Armed
    Forces.

(b) In light of grave acts of terrorism and threats of terrorism, including the terrorist attacks on September 11, 2001, on the headquarters of the United States Department of Defense in the national capital region, on the World Trade Center in New York, and on civilian aircraft such as in Pennsylvania, I proclaimed a national emergency on September 14, 2001 (Proc. 7463, Declaration of National Emergency by Reason of Certain Terrorist Attacks).

(c) Individuals acting alone and in concert involved in international terrorism possess both the capability and the intention to undertake further terrorist attacks against the United States that, if not detected and prevented, will cause mass deaths, mass injuries, and massive destruction of property, and may place at risk the continuity of the operations of the United States Government.

(d) The ability of the United States to protect the United States and its citizens, and to help its allies and other cooperating nations protect their nations and their citizens, from such further terrorist attacks depends in significant part upon using the United States Armed Forces to identify terrorists and those who support them, to disrupt their activities, and to eliminate their ability to conduct or support such attacks.

(e) To protect the United States and its citizens, and for the effective conduct of military operations and prevention of terrorist attacks, it is necessary for individuals subject to this order pursuant to section 2 hereof to be detained, and, when tried, to be tried for violations of the laws of war and other applicable laws by military tribunals.

(f) Given the danger to the safety of the United States and the nature of international terrorism, and to the extent provided by and under this order, I find consistent with section 836 of title 10, United States Code, that it is not practicable to apply in military commissions under this order the principles of law and the rules of evidence generally recognized in the trial of criminal cases in the United States district courts.

(g) Having fully considered the magnitude of the potential deaths, injuries, and property destruction that would result from potential acts of terrorism against the United States, and the probability that such acts will occur, I have determined that an extraordinary emergency exists for national defense purposes, that this emergency constitutes an urgent and compelling government interest, and that issuance of this order is necessary to meet the emergency.

Sec. 2. Definition and Policy.

(a) The term "individual subject to this order" shall mean any individual who is not a United States citizen with respect to whom I determine from time to time in writing that:
  (1) there is reason to believe that such individual, at the relevant times,
      (i) is or was a member of the organization known as al Qaida;
      (ii) has engaged in, aided or abetted, or conspired to commit, acts of international terrorism, or acts in preparation therefor, that have caused, threaten to cause, or have as their aim to cause, injury to or adverse effects on the United States, its citizens, national security, foreign policy, or economy; or
      (iii) has knowingly harbored one or more individuals described in subparagraphs (i) or (ii) of subsection 2(a)(1) of this order; and
  (2) it is in the interest of the United States that such individual be subject to this order.
(b) It is the policy of the United States that the Secretary of Defense shall take all necessary measures to ensure that any individual subject to this order is detained in accordance with section 3, and, if the individual is to be tried, that such individual is tried only in accordance with section 4.
(c) It is further the policy of the United States that any individual subject to this order who is not already under the control of the Secretary of Defense but who is under the control of any other officer or agent of the United States or any State shall, upon delivery of a copy of such written determination to such officer or agent, forthwith be placed under the control of the Secretary of Defense.

Sec. 3. Detention Authority of the Secretary of Defense. Any individual subject to this order shall be—

(a) detained at an appropriate location designated by the Secretary of Defense outside or within the United States;

(b) treated humanely, without any adverse distinction based on race, color, religion, gender, birth, wealth, or any similar criteria;

(c) afforded adequate food, drinking water, shelter, clothing, and medical treatment;

(d) allowed the free exercise of religion consistent with the requirements of such detention; and

(e) detained in accordance with such other conditions as the Secretary of Defense may prescribe.

Sec. 4. Authority of the Secretary of Defense Regarding Trials of Individuals Subject to this Order.

(a) Any individual subject to this order shall, when tried, be tried by military commission for any and all offenses triable by military commission that such individual is alleged to have committed, and may be punished in accordance with the penalties provided under applicable law, including life imprisonment or death.

(b) As a military function and in light of the findings in section 1, including subsection (f) thereof, the Secretary of Defense shall issue such orders and regulations, including orders for the appointment of one or more military commissions, as may be necessary to carry out subsection (a) of this section.

(c) Orders and regulations issued under subsection (b) of this section shall include, but not be limited to, rules for the conduct of the proceedings of military commissions, including pretrial, trial, and post-trial procedures, modes of proof, issuance of process, and qualifications of attorneys, which shall at a minimum provide for—

(1) military commissions to sit at any time and any place, consistent with such guidance regarding time and place as the Secretary of Defense may provide;

(2) a full and fair trial, with the military commission sitting as the triers of both fact and law;

(3) admission of such evidence as would, in the opinion of the presiding officer of the military commission (or instead, if

any other member of the commission so requests at the time the presiding officer renders that opinion, the opinion of the commission rendered at that time by a majority of the commission), have probative value to a reasonable person;

(4) in a manner consistent with the protection of information classified or classifiable under Executive Order 12958 of April 17, 1995, as amended, or any successor Executive Order, protected by statute or rule from unauthorized disclosure, or otherwise protected by law, (A) the handling of, admission into evidence of, and access to materials and information, and (B) the conduct, closure of, and access to proceedings;

(5) conduct of the prosecution by one or more attorneys designated by the Secretary of Defense and conduct of the defense by attorneys for the individual subject to this order;

(6) conviction only upon the concurrence of two-thirds of the members of the commission present at the time of the vote, a majority being present;

(7) sentencing only upon the concurrence of two-thirds of the members of the commission present at the time of the vote, a majority being present; and

(8) submission of the record of the trial, including any conviction or sentence, for review and final decision by me or by the Secretary of Defense if so designated by me for that purpose.

Sec. 5. Obligation of Other Agencies to Assist the Secretary of Defense.

Departments, agencies, entities, and officers of the United States shall, to the maximum extent permitted by law, provide to the Secretary of Defense such assistance as he may request to implement this order.

Sec. 6. Additional Authorities of the Secretary of Defense.

(a) As a military function and in light of the findings in section 1, the Secretary of Defense shall issue such orders and regulations as may be necessary to carry out any of the provisions of this order.

(b) The Secretary of Defense may perform any of his functions or duties, and may exercise any of the powers provided to him under this order (other than under section 4(c)(8) hereof) in accordance with section 113(d) of title 10, United States Code.

Sec. 7. Relationship to Other Law and Forums.

(a) Nothing in this order shall be construed to—

   (1) authorize the disclosure of state secrets to any person not otherwise authorized to have access to them;

   (2) limit the authority of the President as Commander in Chief of the Armed Forces or the power of the President to grant reprieves and pardons; or

   (3) limit the lawful authority of the Secretary of Defense, any military commander, or any other officer or agent of the United States or of any State to detain or try any person who is not an individual subject to this order.

(b) With respect to any individual subject to this order—

   (1) military tribunals shall have exclusive jurisdiction with respect to offenses by the individual; and

   (2) the individual shall not be privileged to seek any remedy or maintain any proceeding, directly or indirectly, or to have any such remedy or proceeding sought on the individual's behalf, in (i) any court of the United States, or any State thereof, (ii) any court of any foreign nation, or (iii) any international tribunal.

(c) This order is not intended to and does not create any right, benefit, or privilege, substantive or procedural, enforceable at law or equity by any party, against the United States, its departments, agencies, or other entities, its officers or employees, or any other person.

(d) For purposes of this order, the term "State" includes any State, district, territory, or possession of the United States.

(e) I reserve the authority to direct the Secretary of Defense, at any time hereafter, to transfer to a governmental authority control of any individual subject to this order. Nothing in this order shall be construed to limit the authority of any such governmental authority to prosecute any individual for whom control is transferred.

Sec. 8. Publication.

This order shall be published in the Federal Register.

GEORGE W. BUSH
THE WHITE HOUSE,

November 13, 2001.

Notes

Preface

1. Dan Eggen, *Ashcroft Defends Anti-Terror Steps*, WASHINGTON POST, Dec. 7, 2001, at A1.

2. Editorial, *Ashcroft's Contempt*, ST. PETERSBURG TIMES, Dec. 10, 2001, at 14A.

3. Editorial, *Justice and the Attorney General*, BUFFALO NEWS, Dec. 10, 2001, at B4.

4. Theodore Roosevelt, Editorial, KANSAS CITY STAR, May 7, 1918, at 14.

Chapter 1

1. For example, the sweeping legislation and "alphabet soup" programs of President Franklin D. Roosevelt's New Deal appeared, at the time, the optimal solution to reinvigorate an economy in the grips of the Great Depression. In retrospect, however, this unprecedented governmental intervention was much more than a temporary economic palliative, for it signaled a drastic and, in some respects, enduring change in the government's relationship to the governed.

2. M. Cherif Bassiouni, *Legal Control of International Terrorism: A Policy-Oriented Assessment*, 43 HARV. INT'L L. J. 83, 84 (winter 2002).

3. *Id.* at 86.

4. Alex P. Schmid, *The Response Problem as a Definition Problem*, in WESTERN RESPONSES TO TERRORISM 7, 8 (Alex P. Schmid and Ronald P. Crelinsten eds., 1993).

5. The U.S. government has employed this definition of terrorism for statistical and analytical purposes since 1983.

6. Michael J. Jordan, *Terrorism's Slippery Definition Eludes UN Diplomats*, CHRISTIAN SCIENCE MONITOR, Feb. 4, 2002, at 7.

7. Alex P. Schmid, *United Nations Office for the Prevention of International Terrorism* (1992).

8. CALEB CARR, THE LESSONS OF TERROR 6 (2002).

9. WALTER REICH, *Understanding Terrorist Behavior: The Limits and*

Opportunities of Psychological Inquiry, in THE ORIGINS OF TERRORISM: PSY-CHOLOGIES, IDEOLOGIES, THEOLOGIES, STATES OF MIND 272 (1998).

10. *Id.* at 274.

11. Martha Crenshaw, *The Logic of Terrorism: Terrorist Behavior as a Product of Strategic Choice, in* THE ORIGINS OF TERRORISM 8 (Walter Reich ed., 1998).

12. Among the costs of terrorism, Crenshaw includes punitive government reaction, loss of popular support, and the risk that terrorist activities may be perceived as elitist because they are often carried out without the participation of the masses. However, the advantages include getting the attention of the public and relevant government organizations, setting the stage for revolt by undermining government authority, and potentially provoking repressive governmental responses that increase popular support for the terrorists' goals. *Id.* at 16–20.

13. *Id.* at 24.

14. *The Economic Consequences of 11 September and the Economic Dimension of Anti-Terrorism*, Draft General Report, NATO Parliamentary Assembly, Economics and Security Committee (2002).

15. According to Greek mythology, Dike was the daughter of Themis and Zeus and is known as the goddess of justice (in contrast to her mother, who was given the title of goddess of divine justice).

16. THOMAS AQUINAS, SUMMA THEOLOGAIE, II-II, Q. 58, art. 1 (Benziger Brothers, ed., and Fathers of the English Dominican Province, trans., 1947).

17. WILLIAM GALSTON, JUSTICE AND THE HUMAN GOOD 282 (1980).

18. LEONARD W. LEVY, ORIGINAL INTENT AND THE FRAMERS' CONSTITUTION 277 (1988).

19. *See, e.g.,* United States v. Armstrong, 208 U.S. 481 (1908); Caldwell v. Texas, 137 U.S. 692 (1891); Nobles v. Georgia, 168 U.S. 398 (1897); Howard v. Fleming, 191 U.S. 126 (1903).

20. Cooper v. Aaron, 358 U.S. 1, 17 (1958).

21. JOYCELYN M. POLLOCK, ETHICS IN CRIME AND JUSTICE: DILEMMAS AND DECISIONS 101 (1998) (quoting Norval Morris).

22. *Id.*

23. *Id.* at 103.

24. LEVY, *supra* note 18, at 259.

25. Shaughnessy v. Mezei, 345 U.S. 206, 212 (1953); Wong Wing v. United States, 163 U.S. 228, 238 (1896); Yick Wo v. Hopkins, 118 U.S. 356, 369 (1886).

26. Korematsu v. United States, 323 U.S. 214 (1944). Although Korematsu's case focuses on the internment of Japanese American citizens during World War II, there is incontrovertible evidence that both German Americans and Italian Americans endured similar harassment and restrictions on their freedom based solely on their nationalities.

27. This order was issued after the United States was at war with Japan and was apparently designed to protect against espionage and sabotage of national security and defense initiatives.

28. *See* http://www.jainternment.org/camps/detention.html. This

Web site, maintained by the National Asian American Telecommunications Association, documents the Japanese internment experience through historical documents, video clips, and photos.

29. There was no evidence to suggest that Korematsu was in any way disloyal to the United States or involved in espionage or sabotage activities.

30. *Korematsu*, 323 U.S. at 223.

31. *Id.* at 242.

32. *Id.* at 245–46.

33. A writ of *coram nobis* is a remedy by which a court can correct errors in criminal convictions where other remedies are not available. In Korematsu's case, since the Supreme Court had finally confirmed his conviction, he faced a tremendous uphill battle of proving that there had been outrageous and obvious governmental misconduct.

34. Such evidence included U.S. government intelligence reports that concluded that mass internment of Japanese Americans would serve no useful military or nonmilitary purpose.

35. Korematsu v. U.S., 584 F. Supp. 1406, 1420 (N. D. Cal. 1984).

Chapter 2

1. David C. Rapoport, *Fear and Trembling: Terrorism in Three Religious Traditions*, 78 AM. POL. SCI. REV. 658 (1984).

2. *Id.* at 670.

3. REICH, *supra* note 9 (ch. 1), at 264. This ideology, of course, seems hauntingly similar to modern-day terrorist statements and justifications.

4. Rapoport, *supra* note 1, at 666.

5. REICH, *supra* note 9 (ch. 1), at 265.

6. *Id.* at 266.

7. The report designates seven countries as state sponsors of terrorism: Cuba, Iran, Iraq, Libya, North Korea, Syria, and Sudan. Inclusion on this terrorist list imposes four main sets of U.S. sanctions: a ban on arms-related exports and sales, controls over exports of other items that could enhance military capability, prohibitions on economic assistance, and miscellaneous financial aid restrictions.

8. Likely targets for recruitment also include disaffected Americans, particularly those with extensive criminal histories, who may have a motive to seek revenge against America and its justice system. American law enforcement identifies this as the most pernicious form of recruitment because American terrorists could ostensibly "blend in" to American society and go undetected until they unleash a deadly attack. This reality pinpoints precisely why a counterterrorism program focusing on ethnicity as a basis for suspicion will be short-sighted and ineffectual.

9. Yonah Alexander, *Terrorism in the Twenty-first Century: Threats and Responses*, 12 DEPAUL BUS. L.J. 59, 79 (fall 1999).

10. The report, "Significant Terrorist Incidents, 1961–2001: A Brief Chronology," can be found at www.state.gov/r/pa/ho/pubs/fs/5902.htm.

11. The Department of State had confirmed that between 10 and 14

American citizens were onboard the ship. Fortunately, at the time of the hijacking, the majority of the 680 passengers had already disembarked at a previous port and were expected to reboard the ship at a later port of call.

12. There were conflicting reports concerning whether the Italian government had information about the killing during conversations with the captain prior to the release of the ship. The U.S. government's suspicion that Italy agreed to allow the hijackers safe passage with full knowledge that a vicious crime had been committed aboard led to increased tension and distrust between the two governments.

13. The *Achille Lauro* Hijacking (B), Kennedy School of Government Case Program, Case #864.0 (1988).

14. Abul Abbas was eventually convicted in absentia in an Italian court and remained a fugitive from justice for 18 years until his capture in April 2003 by U.S. Special Forces in Iraq after the toppling of Saddam Hussein's regime.

15. ALLAN GERSON AND JERRY ADLER, THE PRICE OF TERROR: ONE BOMB, ONE PLANE, 270 LIVES: THE HISTORY-MAKING STRUGGLE FOR JUSTICE AFTER PAN AM 103 3 (2001).

16. *Report of the President's Commission on Aviation Security and Terrorism* (May 1990).

17. Later, at the end of the trial, prosecutors dropped the lesser charges of conspiracy and contravention of the act. Dropping the conspiracy charge was significant because it, at minimum, suggested that there was insufficient evidence to demonstrate that others were involved in the bombing. The families of the American victims had hoped that the trial would produce evidence of the Libyan government's involvement.

18. Although Yousef was a fugitive at the time of the trial, he was subsequently apprehended, tried, convicted, and sentenced to life in prison in 1997.

19. Harry S. Truman, NEW YORK TIMES, Nov. 17, 1953.

20. Majid Tehranian's article may be found in draft format at www.toda.org/grad/mt1/global_terrorism.html (2001).

21. *Id.*

Chapter 3

1. *Past Terrorist Targets*, USA TODAY, Oct. 18, 2001, at 10A.

2. Bill Keller, *Nuclear Nightmares*, NEW YORK TIMES MAGAZINE, May 26, 2001, at 22; BBC News, *US Terror Experts Set for UK Ports*, July 10, 2002 <http://news.bbc.co.uk/1/hi/uk/2119071.stm>.

3. Joel Brinkley, *Coast Guard Encounters Big Hurdles in New Effort to Screen Arriving Ships*, NEW YORK TIMES, Mar. 16, 2002, at A9.

4. Jay Kral, *A New Bureaucracy Takes Flight, Air-Safety Agency's First Steps Look Plodding, Inefficient*, WALL STREET JOURNAL, July 16, 2002, at A4.

5. Sara Kehaulani Goo, *Fledgling TSA Offers Clues*, WASHINGTON POST, July 22, 2002, at A13.

6. Office of the Coordinator for Counterterrorism, U.S. State Dept., *Patterns of Global Terrorism* (2002), App. A: Chronology of Significant Terrorist Incidents. Available at www.state.gov/s/ct/rls/pgtrpt/2002/html/19990.htm.

7. Peter L. Bergen, *Picking up the Pieces*, 81 FOREIGN AFFAIRS 169 (March/April 2002).

8. James Risen and David Johnston, *Agency Is under Scrutiny for Overlooked Messages*, NEW YORK TIMES, June 20, 2002, at A20; James Bramford, *Too Much, Not Enough*, WASHINGTON POST, June 2, 2002, at B1.

9. Subcommittee on Terrorism and Homeland Security, *Counterterrorism Intelligence Capabilities and Performance Prior to 9–11*, Report to the Speaker of the House of Representatives and Minority Leader (July 2002); Kathy Kiely, *House Panel Flags Intelligence Flops*, USA TODAY, July 17, 2002, at 5A.

10. John Diamond, *Shackles Loosened on U.S. Intelligence*, USA TODAY, July 9, 2002, at 8A.

11. Statement of Robert S. Mueller III, director of FBI, on *New FBI Focus*, Subcommittee for the Departments of Commerce, Justice, State, the Judiciary, and Related Agencies of the House Committee on Appropriations (June 21, 2002). Available at <http://www.fbi.gov/congress/congress02/mueller062102.htm>.

12. William Safire, *J. Edgar Mueller*, NEW YORK TIMES, June 3, 2002, at A15.

13. Kathy Kiely and Jim Drinkard, *Ridge Lacks Clout, Critics Say*, USA TODAY, June 6, 2002, at 4A.

14. Thomas S. Foley and Newt Gingrich, *If Congress Were Attacked*, WASHINGTON POST, Mar. 17, 2002, at B9.

15. Thom Shanker and James Risen, *Rumsfeld Weighs New Covert Acts by Military Units*, NEW YORK TIMES, Aug. 12, 2002, at A1.

16. Bergen, *supra* note 7.

17. Joe Hallett and Catherine Candisky, *Why Do People Hate America Enough to Kill?* COLUMBUS DISPATCH, Sep. 13, 2001, at 1A; Joseph S. Nye, *Why Do They Hate Us? The Reasons Are Many, The History Long 'America Represents Global Capitalism,'* BOSTON GLOBE, Sep. 16, 2001, at D1; Editorial, *Why Do They Hate Us So Much?* ST. LOUIS POST-DISPATCH, Sep. 16, 2001, at B6.

18. Fouad Ajami, *The Sentry's Solitude*, 80 FOREIGN AFFAIRS 2, 7 (Nov./Dec. 2001).

19. *Id.* at 5–12.

20. The minority view is actually a radicalized version of the already conservative form of Wahabbi Islamic clericism that controls religious life in Saudi Arabia. Examples of how wildly out of touch Wahabbi clerics are include the continued declaration only twenty years ago by the head of the sect that the earth was flat because the Koran told him that was so and the recent *fatwah* against the Japanese children's toy Pokémon trading cards. *Fresh Air: Interview with Newsweek Correspondent Christopher Dickey* (NPR radio broadcast, Nov. 13, 2001).

21. Douglas Jehl, *Newspapers and T.V. Paint U.S. Action as a Kind of Terrorism*, NEW YORK TIMES, Nov. 11, 2001, at B5: This attitude "permeate[s] a region that sees itself as having been cheated, maligned, outsmarted and outmuscled by Westerners for much of its modern history."

22. Milton Bearden, *Afghanistan, Graveyard of Empires*, 80 FOREIGN AFFAIRS 17, 23–26 (Nov./Dec. 2001).

23. *The Propaganda War—It Is Needed to Sustain the Immediate Battle, But Also to Win the Peace*, ECONOMIST, Oct. 6, 2001, at 11. After some initial stumbles in the communication strategy—such as President Bush's early reference to the coming conflict as a "crusade" and Italian prime minister Berlusconi's remarks about Christian superiority and the need to "occidentalise" the Middle East (*A Battle on Many Fronts*, ECONOMIST, Oct. 6, 2001, at 16)—the concerted effort to signal increased sensitivity appears to be coming together.

24. Peter Tomsen, *Untying the Afghan Knot*, 25 FLETCHER F. WORLD AFF. 17, 19 (winter 2001).

25. Mohammad Bazzi, *Power Struggle: Tribal Divisions Threaten a New Afghan Government*, NEWSDAY (New York), Nov. 18, 2001, at A5; Reuters, *Five Years After Ouster, a Professor Returns to Uneasy Alliance*, NEW YORK TIMES, Nov. 18, 2001, at B3; *After the Taliban*, ECONOMIST, Oct. 6, 2001, at 17.

26. Stephen Kinzer, *Why They Don't Know Us*, NEW YORK TIMES, Nov. 11, 2001, at WK5.

27. *Id.*

28. Fouad Ajami, *What the Muslim World Is Watching*, NEW YORK TIMES MAGAZINE, Nov. 18, 2001, at 48.

29. *Islam and the West, Never the Twain Shall Peacefully Meet?* ECONOMIST, Nov. 17, 2001, at 17, 19.

30. *America and the Arabs, Why Not Democracy?* ECONOMIST, Mar. 23, 2002, at 11.

31. Bergen, *supra* note 7.

32. *Id.*

33. *Id.*

34. *America and the Arabs*, *supra* note 30.

35. *Islam and the West, They Can Live Together*, ECONOMIST, Nov. 17, 2001, at 10.

36. *U.S. to Track Visitors Deemed a Security Risk*, WASHINGTON POST, June 6, 2002, at A1.

37. *Id.*

38. John Kifner, *The New Power of Arab Public Opinion*, NEW YORK TIMES, Nov. 11, 2001, at WK1:

It is on just this Arab—or, better, Islamic—street that President Bush must fight in his war against Osama bin Laden and his terrorists, a battleground for the public's mood that may ultimately be more important than the mountains and deserts of Afghanistan. . . . And in this conflict, Mr. bin Laden has an edge in weaponry—the vocabulary with which to define the conflict. For what he seeks to do is cast this the cataclysmic clash of civilizations: Islam against the West, believer against infidel.

39. *The Battle for Hearts and Minds, Relaunching the Propaganda War*, ECONOMIST, Nov. 10, 2001.

40. J. William Fulbright, NEW YORKER, May 10, 1958.

41. *Judges* 16:29, 30 (emphasis added).

42. Ariel Merari, *The Readiness to Kill and Die: Suicidal Terrorism in the Middle East, in* ORIGINS OF TERRORISM: PSYCHOLOGIES, IDEOLOGIES, THEOLOGIES, STATES OF MIND 193–207 (Walter Reich ed., 2000).

43. *Id.*

44. *Id.* at 197.

45. Gregg Zoroya, *Her Decision to Be a Suicide Bomber,* USA TODAY, Apr. 22, 2002, at A1.

46. Merari, *supra* note 42, at 199.

47. *Id.* at 200.

48. Zoroya, *supra* note 45.

49. Jan Lodal, The Price of Dominance: The New Weapons of Mass Destruction and Their Challenge to American Leadership 95 (Council on Foreign Relations 2001).

50. Guy Gugliotta, *Report: U.S. Vulnerable to Attack,* WASHINGTON POST, June 25, 2002, at A2.

51. Jessica Stern, *Terrorist Motivations and Unconventional Weapons, in* PLANNING THE UNTHINKABLE 203 (Peter R. Lavoy et al. eds. 2000).

52. *Word for Word Early Warnings; The Surprise Was More When Than Whether or How,* NEW YORK TIMES, May 19, 2002, at D7.

53. Stern, *supra* note 51, at 223.

54. GARY K. BERTSCH AND WILLIAM C. POTTER, DANGEROUS WEAPONS, DESPERATE STATES (1999).

55. Stern, *supra* note 51.

56. William J. Broad et al., *Assessing Risks, Chemical, Biological, Even Nuclear,* NEW YORK TIMES, Nov. 1, 2001, at A1.

57. Christopher F. Chyba, *Toward Biological Security,* 81 FOREIGN AFFAIRS 122–23 (May/June 2002).

58. Stern, *supra* note 51, at 221.

59. TOM MANGOLD AND JEFF GOLDBERG, PLAGUE WARS: THE TERRIFYING REALITY OF BIOLOGICAL WARFARE 379, 381–83 (1999).

60. *Id.* at 380, 383–86.

61. *Id.* at 380, 387–88.

62. Rick Weiss, *Clarifying the Facts and Risks of Anthrax,* WASHINGTON POST, Oct. 18, 2001, at A12.

63. Guy Gugliotta, *Study: Anthrax Tainted up to 5,000 Letters,* WASHINGTON POST, May 14, 2002, at A2.

64. *Id.*

65. Ellen Nakashima, *USPS Sees New Way to Spot Biohazards,* WASHINGTON POST, March 9, 2002, at A13.

66. MADELINE DREXLER, SECRET AGENTS: THE MENACE OF EMERGING INFECTIONS 234 (2002).

67. JEANNE GUILLEMIN, ANTHRAX: THE INVESTIGATION OF A DEADLY OUTBREAK (1999).

68. William J. Broad, *Sowing Death: How Japan Germ Terror Alerted the World,* NEW YORK TIMES, May 26, 1998, at A1.

69. *Id.*

70. *Id.*

71. Shannon Brownlee, *Clear and Present Danger: We Thought We'd*

Wiped Out Smallpox, a Highly Contagious Disease That Has Killed Countless Millions. Could an Ancient Scourge, in Enemy Hands, Come Back to Haunt Us? WASHINGTON POST MAGAZINE, Oct. 28, 2001, at W08.

72. *Id.*

73. *Id.*

74. *Id.* See also Ceci Connolly, *Smallpox Vaccine Program Readied: Inoculations May Surpass 500,000 under U.S. Plan,* WASHINGTON POST, July 8, 2002, at A1; Elizabeth Olson, *Panel Urges Shift of Focus in Preparing for Small Pox,* NEW YORK TIMES, Aug. 13, 2003, at A22.

75. RICHARD PRESTON, THE HOT ZONE (1994).

76. MANGOLD AND GOLDBERG, *supra* note 59, at 384.

77. PLANNING THE UNTHINKABLE: HOW NEW POWERS WILL USE NUCLEAR, BIOLOGICAL AND CHEMICAL WEAPONS 202–29 (Peter R. Lavoy et al. eds., 2000).

78. Chyba, *supra* note 57, at 128.

79. *Id.* at 126–28.

80. *Id.*

81. New York Times Service, *Scientists Create Virus from Scratch Using Information on Web,* OMAHA WORLD-HERALD, July 12, 2002, at 3A.

82. KEN ALIBEK, BIOHAZARD 275–76 (1999).

83. Bill Miller, *Bioterror Defense Bill Signed,* WASHINGTON POST, June 13, 2002, at A16.

84. Guy Gugliotta, *A First Step on U.S. Biodefense,* WASHINGTON POST, July 14, 2002, at A10.

85. Lodal, *supra* note 49, at 95–96.

86. ABC News, *Types of Chemical Weapons: A Horrific Battlefield Legacy* <http://ABCNews.com> (Oct. 4, 2001); National Library of Medicine, Specialized Information Services, *Chemical Warfare Agents.*

87. Timothy V. McCarthy and Jonathan B. Tucker, *Saddam's Toxic Arsenal: Chemical and Biological Weapons in the Gulf Wars, in* PLANNING THE UNTHINKABLE 47–78 (Peter R. Lavoy et al. eds. 2000).

88. Teresa Watanabe, *Cult Leader's Day in Court Arrives,* LOS ANGELES TIMES, April 24, 1996, at A8.

89. Stern, *supra* note 51, at 202–29.

90. Marlise Simons, *Money Short for Battle on Chemicals Used in War,* NEW YORK TIMES, Oct. 5, 2001, at A9.

91. James Risen and Judith Miller, *Al Qaeda Sites Point to Tests of Chemicals,* NEW YORK TIMES, Nov. 11, 2001, at B1.

92. Simons, *supra* note 90; Patrick E. Tyler, *In a Changed World, Qadaffi Is Changing, Too,* NEW YORK TIMES, Dec. 20, 2001, at B1; Chyba, *supra* note 57, at 126.

93. Patrick E. Tyler, *Russia Vows to Start Destroying Chemical Arms,* NEW YORK TIMES, Feb. 9, 2001, at A10; Judith Miller, *U.S. Warns Russia of Need to Verify Treaty Compliance,* NEW YORK TIMES, April 8, at A1; David E. Sanger, *$10 Billion Pledge to Ex-Soviets to Dispose of Unconventional Arms,* NEW YORK TIMES, June 28, 2002, at A8.

94. Broad et al., *supra* note 56.

95. Stern, *supra* note 51, at 224.

96. Tim Weiner, *Bin Laden Asserts He Has Nuclear Arms*, NEW YORK TIMES, Nov. 10, 2001, at B4.

97. Associated Press, *Europe Tightens Security at Nuclear and Other Sensitive Areas*, NEW YORK TIMES, Oct. 25, 2001; John Tagliabue, *Threat of Nuclear Terror Has Increased, Official Says*, NEW YORK TIMES, Nov. 2, 2001, at B4.

98. Keller, *supra* note 2.

99. *Id.*; Stephen Erlanger, *Lax Nuclear Security in Russia Is Cited as Way for bin Laden to Get Arms*, NEW YORK TIMES, Nov. 12, 2001, at B1; David E. Sanger and Michael Wines, *Bush and Putin Sign Pact for Steep Nuclear Arms Cuts*, NEW YORK TIMES, May 25, 2002, at A1.

100. Douglas Frantz, *Nuclear Booty: More Smugglers Use Asia Route*, NEW YORK TIMES, Sept. 11, 2001, at A1.

101. Keller, *supra* note 2.

102. Mansoor Ijaz and R. James Woolsey, *How Secure Is Pakistan's Plutonium?* NEW YORK TIMES, Nov. 28, 2001, at A25; David E. Sanger, *Nuclear Experts in Pakistan May Have Links to al Qaeda*, NEW YORK TIMES, Dec. 9, 2001, at A1.

103. Keller, *supra* note 2.

104. *Id.*

105. Joby Warrick, *NRC Warns of Missing Radioactive Materials*, WASHINGTON POST, May 4, 2002, at A13.

106. Susan S. Hsu, *Plan Urged for 'Dirty' Explosive*, WASHINGTON POST, May 4, 2002, at B1.

107. *Id.*

108. Howard W. French, *Japanese Shipment of Nuclear Fuel Raises Security Fears*, NEW YORK TIMES, July 5, 2002, at A3.

109. Keller, *supra* note 2; Editorial, *Nuclear Reactors as Terrorist Targets*, NEW YORK TIMES, Jan. 21, 2002, at A14; Matthew L. Wald: *Suicidal Nuclear Threat Is Seen at Weapons Plants*, NEW YORK TIMES, Jan. 23, 2002, at A9; *A-Plant Drill for Guards Is Inadequate, Group Says*, NEW YORK TIMES, Dec. 17, 2001, at B6; *Security at U.S. Reactors Criticized by Congressman*, NEW YORK TIMES, Mar. 25, 2002, at A13.

110. *Pills for Nuclear Plant Radiation*, NEW YORK TIMES, June 13, 2002, at A38.

111. Matthew L. Wald, *White House Cut 93% of Funds Sought to Guard Atomic Arms*, NEW YORK TIMES, Apr. 23, 2002, at A8.

112. Jayson Blair, *Post-9/11, Questions About Security at Electric Plants*, NEW YORK TIMES, May 17, 2002, at B3; Matthew L. Wald, *Private Flights Are Halted Near Nuclear Installations*, NEW YORK TIMES, Oct. 31, 2001, at B11; John Ritter et al., *Report Card on Homeland Security*, USA TODAY, June 9, 2002 (online ed.).

113. Barton Gellman, *Cyber-Attacks by Al Qaeda Feared; Terrorists at Threshold of Using Internet as Tool of Bloodshed, Experts Say*, WASHINGTON POST, June 27, 2002, at A01.

114. *Id.*

115. Cyberterrorism, Testimony before the Special Oversight Panel on Terrorism, Committee on Armed Services, U.S. House of Representatives, May 23, 2000.

116. *Cybercrime, Cyberterrorism, Cyberwarfare: Averting an Electronic Waterloo* xii (Center for Strategic and International Studies 1998) [hereinafter *Cyberterrorism*].

117. *Cyberterrorism, supra* note 116.

118. *Id.* .

119. *Id.* at xiii.

120. Report of the Defense Science Board Task Force on Information Warfare—Defense (November 1996).

121. *Id.*

122. *Id.*

123. *Cyberterrorism, supra* note 116, at 16–17.

124. *Cyberterrorism, supra* note 116, at 29.

125. *Cyberterrorism, supra* note 116, at 36. The report offers as an example the possibility that, prior to launching an attack against Saudi Arabia, Iran could trigger viruses and time bombs previously planted in the electronic inventory systems in the United States. Because the United States would be hampered by the technological confusion and operational delays, it would be unable to immediately deploy reinforcements to the region, thereby giving Iran a tactical, and possibly decisive, advantage.

126. Report of the Defense Science Board, *supra* note 120.

127. *Cyberterrorism, supra* note 116, at xix.

128. Available at www.fas.org/irp/congress/2002_cr/51900.html.

129. Information Warfare and International Security, Draft Report, NATO Parliamentary Assembly, Science and Technology Committee (1999).

130. Barton Gellman, *Struggles Inside the Government Defined Campaign*, WASHINGTON POST, Dec. 20, 2001, at A01.

131. *Id.* at A7

132. David Johnston et al., *Qaeda's New Links Increase Threats from Far-Flung Sites*, NEW YORK TIMES, June 16, 2002, at A1; David Johnston, *The Warning du Jour Comes via Rumsfeld, But Worriers Abound*, HOUSTON CHRONICLE, May 22, 2002, at A23; Dana Priest and Douglass Farah, *Terror Alliance Has U.S. Worried; Hezbollah, Al Qaeda Seen Joining Forces*, WASHINGTON POST, June 30, 2002, at A1.

133. James Risen, *Qaeda Still Able to Strike the U.S., Head of CIA Says*, NEW YORK TIMES, Feb. 7, 2002, at A1.

134. *Bin Laden's Foreign Fighters: Follow the Leader*, ECONOMIST, Dec. 21, 2001, at 23.

135. Los Angeles Times, *Ashcroft: Al-Qaeda Alive in U.S.*, OMAHA WORLD-HERALD, July 12, 2002, at 8A.

Chapter 4

1. SELECT COMMITTEE TO STUDY GOVERNMENTAL OPERATIONS, 94TH CONG., 2D SESS., *Intelligence Activities and the Rights of Americans*, BK. II, FINAL RPT., NO. 94–755, at 165.

2. *Id.* at 171.

3. *Id.* at 174.

4. *Id.* at 169 (emphasis added).

5. *Anti-Terrorism Act of 2001, Section by Section Analysis* (proposal of Att'y Gen. John Ashcroft, draft Sept. 19, 2001).

6. CONG. REC. S10990–S11060 (Oct. 25, 2001).

7. The Combating Terrorism Act authorized, among other things, more wiretap and surveillance authority to law enforcement officials. According to one of the bill's sponsors, Senator Orrin Hatch, "It is essential that we give our law enforcement authorities every possible tool to search out and bring to justice those individuals who have brought such indiscriminate death into our backyard." Statement of Senator Orrin Hatch during floor debate of the Combating Terrorism Act, CONG. REC. S9362–87 (Sept. 13, 2001).

8. CONG. REC. S9362–87 (Sept. 13, 2001).

9. *Id.*

10. Edmund Burke, Speech on Conciliation with the Colonies (March 22, 1775).

11. Levy, *supra* note 18 (ch. 1), at 143.

12. *Id.* at 146.

13. Frisbie v. Butler, 1 Kirby 213 (1787).

14. *Id.* (emphasis added).

15. *Id.*

16. Griswold v. Connecticut, 381 U.S. 479, 484 (1965).

17. *Id.*

18. Katz v. U.S. 389 U.S. 347, 357 (1967).

19. *Id.* at 358–59 (quoting Beck v. Ohio, 379 U.S. 89, 97).

20. 18 U.S.C. 2515.

21. The list of felonies is quite lengthy and includes espionage, bribery, presidential assassination, mail and wire fraud, murder, kidnapping, extortion, and robbery. Essentially, Congress sought to limit authorization for intrusive surveillance practices to serious crimes.

22. 18 U.S.C.S. 2518 (4).

23. United States v. United States Dist. Court, 407 U.S. 297, 322–3 (1972).

24. A "U.S. person" is defined as a "citizen of the United States, an alien lawfully admitted for permanent residence, and unincorporated association a substantial number of which are citizens of the United States or aliens lawfully admitted for permanent residence, or a corporation which is incorporated in the United States, but does not include a corporation or an association which is a foreign power."

25. This section amends 18 U.S.C. 3121 et seq., which establishes standards for the use of pen registers and trap and trace devices on telephonic communications.

26. *Supra* note 5.

27. Karen Branch-Brioso, *Fight Over Rights Rages On*, ST. LOUIS POST-DISPATCH, September 8, 2002, at B1.

28. Wilson v. Arkansas, 514 U.S. 927, 934 (1995).

29. Dalia v. United States, 441 U.S. 238, 247–48 (1979).

30. *Id.* at 253.

31. United States v. Freitas, 800 F.2d 1451, 1456 (9th Cir. 1986). The

Freitas court further concluded that notice should be provided "within a reasonable, but short, time subsequent to the surreptitious entry. Such time should not exceed seven days except upon a strong showing of necessity." Cf. United States v. Villegas, 899 F.2d 1324 (2nd. Cir. 1990). In *Villegas*, the court reasoned that

> two limitations on the issuance of warrants for covert-entry searches for intangibles are appropriate. First, the court should not allow the officers to dispense with advance or contemporaneous notice of the search unless they have made a showing of reasonable necessity for the delay. Second, if a delay in notice is to be allowed, the court should nonetheless require the officers to give the appropriate person notice of the search within a reasonable time after the covert entry. What constitutes a reasonable time will depend on the circumstances of each individual case. We would, however, agree with the Freitas court that as an initial matter, the issuing court should not authorize a notice delay of longer than seven days. (United States v. Villegas, at 1337; citations omitted)

32. *See* Zadvydas v. Davis, 533 U.S. 678 (2001); see also United States v. Verdugo-Urquidez, 494 U.S. 259, 269, 108 L. Ed. 2d 222, 110 S. Ct. 1056 (1990) (the Fifth Amendment's protections do not extend to aliens outside the territorial boundaries); Johnson v. Eisentrager, 339 U.S. 763, 784, 94 L. Ed. 1255, 70 S. Ct. 936 (1950) (same).

33. *See* Yick Wo v. Hopkins, *supra* note 25 (ch. 1), at 369. *See also* Plyler v. Doe, 457 U.S. 202 (1982); Mathews v. Diaz, 426 U.S. 67 (1976); Kwong Hai Chew v. Colding, 344 U.S. 590 (1953).

34. Indeed, many criminal forfeiture provisions contain what is known as a "relation back" provision, which converts unlawfully acquired proceeds to the government's possession at the time the unlawful act is committed. For example, the RICO forfeiture statute reads, in pertinent part:

> All right, title, and interest in property described in subsection (a) vests in the United States upon the commission of the act giving rise to forfeiture under this section. Any such property that is subsequently transferred to a person other than the defendant may be the subject of a special verdict of forfeiture and thereafter shall be ordered forfeited to the United States, unless the transferee establishes in a hearing pursuant to subsection (l) that he is a bona fide purchaser for value of such property who at the time of purchase was reasonably without cause to believe that the property was subject to forfeiture under this section.

18 U.S.C. §1963(c).

35. *See* Nancy Chang, *The USA Patriot Act: What's So Patriotic About Trampling on the Bill of Rights?* <http://www.ccr-ny.org/whatsnew/usa_patriot_act_2.asp>

36. Senator Edward Livingston, U.S. Senate Debate on the Alien and Sedition Acts of 1798.

37. Katharine Q. Seelye, *Guantánamo Bay Faces Sentence of Life as Permanent U.S. Prison* NEW YORK TIMES, Sept. 16, 2002.

38. It is noteworthy that several of the Patriot Act provisions authorizing expansive government surveillance powers contain sunset clauses, which means that the provisions will expire on December 31, 2005, unless renewed by Congress. Ironically, many of the provisions lack reporting or other legislative oversight requirements, arguably leaving Congress with no reasonable basis to measure the implementation and impact of these provisions.

39. *In re* All Matters Submitted to the Foreign Intelligence Surveillance Court, 218 F. Supp. 2d 611, 615 (U.S. Dist., 2002).

40. *Id.* at 616.

41. *Id.* at 620.

42. Notwithstanding the "wall" requirement, in September 2000, the government confessed that, in at least seventy-five instances, there had been inappropriate dissemination of foreign intelligence information to criminal investigators.

43. *Supra* note 39, at 623 (emphasis added).

44. *Id.*

45. *Id.* at 625. This FISA court ruling and the first ever FISA appellate court opinion are more fully explored in chapter 6, under the section "Non-Article III Courts."

46. Statement of Senator Patrick Leahy hailing the release of the FISA court opinion (Aug. 23, 2002).

47. Eric Lichtblau with Adam Liptak, *On Terror and Spying, Ashcroft Expands Reach,* NEW YORK TIMES, Mar. 15, 2003.

48. Fact Sheet on Murkowski Legislation.

49. Inspector General, Department of Justice, Report to Congress on Implementation of Section 1001 of the USA PATRIOT Act, at 6 (July 17, 2003).

Chapter 5

1. David Abramowitz, *The President, the Congress, and Use of Force: Legal and Political Considerations in Authorizing Use of Force Against International Terrorism,* 43 HARV. INT'L L.J. 71, 73 (winter 2002).

2. *Id.*

3. Authorization for Use of Military Force, S.J. Res. 23, 107th Congress, 115 Stat. 224 (2001). This joint resolution was passed by the Senate 98–0 and the House 420–1 on September 14 and signed by the president on September 18.

4. *A United Response,* Statement of Senator Joseph Biden, 147 CONG. REC., S9422 (September 14, 2001).

5. Abramowitz, *supra* note 1, at 77.

6. Lori Fisler Damrosch, *The Constitution under Clinton: A Critical Assessment: The Clinton Administration and War Powers,* 63 LAW & CONTEMP. PROBS. 125 (winter/spring 2000).

7. *Id.* at 131.

8. Louis Fisher, *War Powers and Foreign Affairs: Sidestepping Congress: Presidents Acting under the U.N. and N.A.T.O.* 47 CASE W. RES. L. REV. 1237 (summer 1997).

9. War Powers Resolution, Public Law 93–148, 93rd Congress, H. J. Res. 542 (November 7, 1973).

10. *Id.* at Section 5.

11. Derived from BBC News, *War on Terror, Where Next?* <http://news.bbc.co.uk/hi/english/static/in_depth/world/2001/war _on_terror/what_next> (visited July 11, 2002); Peter Charles Choharis, *The Case for a Wider War Against Terrorism,* WASHINGTON POST NATIONAL WEEKLY EDITION, Jan. 14–20, 2002, at 22; Leslie Lopez, *Portrait of a Radical Network in Asia,* WALL STREET JOURNAL, Aug. 13, 2002, at A14.

12. Madeleine K. Albright, *Where Iraq Fits in the War on Terror,* NEW YORK TIMES, Sept. 13, 2002.

13. Robert J. Delahunty and John C. Yoo, *The President's Constitutional Authority to Conduct Military Operations Against Terrorist Organizations and the Nations that Harbor or Support Them,* 25 HARV. J.L. & PUB. POL'Y 487 (spring 2002).

14. For more information on this point, see Michael J. Kelly, *Time Warp to 1945—Resurrection of the Reprisal and Anticipatory Self-Defense Doctrines in International Law,* 13 FLA. ST. UNIV. J. TRANSNAT'L. L. & POL'Y. 1 (fall 2003).

15. The White House, *Executive Order Establishing Office of Homeland Security* <http://www.whitehouse.gov/news/releases/2001/10/ 20011008–2 .html> (Oct. 8, 2001).

16. *Id.*

17. Dan Eggen, *Ashcroft Plans to Reorganize Justice, Curtail Programs,* WASHINGTON POST, Nov. 9, 2001, at A17.

18. Cheryl W. Thompson, *Reorganization, Anti-Terrorism Effort Keeping INS Chief Busy,* WASHINGTON POST, Jan. 21, 2002, at A15.

19. Dan Eggen, *FBI Director to Propose 'Super Squad' for Terror; Special D.C. Unit Would Lead Investigations Worldwide,* WASHINGTON POST, May 15, 2002, at A01; Bill Miller and Dan Eggen, *FBI Memo Author Did Not Envision Sept. 11; Phoenix Agent Who Marked Warning 'Routine' Finishes Congressional Testimony,* WASHINGTON POST, May 23, 2002, at A08; Cheryl W. Thompson, *New Security Checks Swamp INS Offices; Applications Pile Up Because Workers Lack Database Access, Training,* WASHINGTON POST, May 16, 2002, at A01.

20. Susan Schmidt, *Terrorism Focus Set for FBI; Mueller's Reorganization Would Shift 480 Agents,* WASHINGTON POST, May 29, 2002, at A1.

21. *'Overriding and Urgent Mission' for New Agency,* WASHINGTON POST, June 7, 2002, at A19.

22. Dan Eggen and Dana Priest, *Intelligence Powers Set for New Agency; Department Would Shape Response to Threats,* WASHINGTON POST, June 8, 2002, at A01.

23. *Testimony of Director of Central Intelligence before the Government Affairs Subcommittee* <http://www.cia.gov/cia/public_affairs/speeches/2002/dci_speech_06272002.html> (June 27, 2002); Robert S. Mueller, III, *Statement for the Record on Homeland Security*, Congressional Statement <http://www.fbi.gov/congress/congress02/mueller062702.htm> (June 27, 2002); Bill Miller and Christine Haughney, *President to Detail Security Strategy; Plan Seeks Public, Private Teamwork on Array of Threats*, WASHINGTON POST, July 16, 2002, at A01.

24. Office of Homeland Security, *The National Strategy for Homeland Security* (July 2002) <http://www.whitehouse.gov/homeland/book/index.html>.

25. Helen Thomas, *Bush Acting as Imperial President*, SEATTLE POST-INTELLIGENCER, July 3, 2002, at B6.

26. Ex Parte Milligan, 71 U.S. 2 (1866).

27. President's Military Order, 66 Fed. Reg. 57833 (Nov. 15, 2001).

28. George Lardner, Jr., *Legal Scholars Criticize Wording of Bush Order; Accused Can Be Detained Indefinitely*, WASHINGTON POST, Dec. 3, 2001, at A10.

29. President's Military Order, *supra* note 27.

30. Geneva Convention Relative to the Treatment of Prisoners of War, Aug. 12, 1949, 75 U.N.T.S. 287.

31. Youngstown Sheet & Tube Co. v. Sawyer, 343 U.S. 579, 72 S.Ct. 863 (1952).

32. President's Address to Joint Session of Congress (Sept. 20, 2001) <http://www.whitehouse.gov/news/releases/2001/09/20010920-8.html>; President's State of the Union Message (Jan. 29, 2002) <http://www.whitehouse.gov/news/releases/2002/01/20020129 11.html>; President's Remarks at the Pentagon Marking the One Year Anniversary of September 11th (Sept. 11, 2002) <http://www.white house.gov/news/releases/2002/09/20020911.html>; President's Remarks to the Nation Marking the One Year Anniversary of September 11th—Ellis Island (Sept. 11, 2002) <http://www.whitehouse.gov/news/releases/2002/09/20020911-3.html>.

33. *Supra* note 4, at S9422–23.

34. INGRID DETTER, THE LAW OF WAR 327–28 (2d ed. 2000).

35. Joan Biskupic and Richard Willing, *Military Tribunals: Swift Judgments in Dire Times*, USA TODAY, Nov. 15, 2001, at 1A.

36. *Id.*

37. *Excerpts from the President's Remarks on the War on Terrorism*, NEW YORK TIMES, Oct. 12, 2001, at B4; *Excerpts From Attorney General's Testimony Before Senate Judiciary Committee*, NEW YORK TIMES, Dec. 7, 2001, at B6; Katharine Q. Seelye, *Justice Department Decision to Forgo Tribunal Bypasses Pentagon*, NEW YORK TIMES, Dec. 13, 2001, at B6; William Glaberson, *U.S. Asks to Use Secret Evidence in Many Cases of Deportation*, NEW YORK TIMES, Dec. 9, 2001, at B1; Elisabeth Bumiller and Katharine Q. Seelye, *Bush Defends Wartime Call for Tribunals*, NEW YORK TIMES, Dec. 5, 2001, at A1.

38. William Glaberson, *Arguing Tribunals v. Courts-Martial, False Comparison Creates Confusion, Military Lawyers Say*, NEW YORK TIMES, Dec. 2, 2001, at B6.

39. Ruth Wedgwood, *The Law's Response to September 11ᵗʰ* <http://www.carnegiecouncil.org/lib_pov_rules.html#wedgewood>.

40. SENATE COMMITTEE ON FOREIGN RELATIONS, 82ND CONG., REPORT ON THE GENEVA CONVENTIONS FOR THE PROTECTION OF WAR VICTIMS (Comm. Print 1955).

41. Glaberson, *supra* note 38.

42. Sean D. Murphy, ed., *Contemporary Practice of the United States Relating to International Law—U.S. Department of Defense Rules on Military Commissions*, 96 AM. J. INT'L L. 706, 733 (July 2002).

43. Jordan J. Paust, *Antiterrorism Military Commissions: The Ad Hoc DOD Rules of Procedure*, 23 MICH. J. INT'L L. 677–79 (spring 2002).

44. *Id.*

45. Murphy, *supra* note 41.

46. Jordan J. Paust, *Antiterrorism Military Commissions: Courting Illegality*, 23 MICH. J. INT'L L. 1, 11 (fall 2001).

47. Robin Toner, *Civil Liberty vs. Security: Finding a Wartime Balance*, NEW YORK TIMES, Nov. 18, 2001, at A1.

48. Carola Hoyos, *U.N. Charter and Resolutions Offer U.S. Action Legal Backing*, FINANCIAL TIMES, Oct. 8, 2001.

49. S/Res/1368 (Sept. 12, 2001); S/Res/1373 (Sept. 28, 2001).

50. Statement by NATO Secretary General, October 2, 2001, 40 I.L.M. 1268 (2001).

51. North Atlantic Treaty, April 4, 1949, Art. 5, 63 Stat. 2241, 2244, 34 U.N.T.S. 243, 246.

52. Alan Sipress and Colum Lynch, *Turkey, Britain, France to Head Peacekeeping Forces*, WASHINGTON POST, Nov. 16, 2001, at A29.

53. President's Message to Joint Session of Congress Responding to the Terrorist Attacks of September 11th, PUB. PAPERS (Sept. 24, 2001).

54. Stephen Erlanger, *So Far, Europe Breathes Easier over Free Hand Given to U.S.*, NEW YORK TIMES, Sept. 29, 2001 at B1.

55. Gregory M. Travalio, *Terrorism, International Law, and the Use of Military Force*, 18 WIS. INT'L L.J. 145, 166 (winter 2000).

56. *Id.*

57. CHRISTINE GRAY, INTERNATIONAL LAW AND THE USE OF FORCE 108–18 (2000).

58. Andrew D. Mitchell, *Does One Illegality Merit Another? The Law of Belligerent Reprisals in International Law*, 170 MIL. L. REV. 155 (Dec. 2001). Mitchell ultimately concludes that the potential for abuse outweighs such deterrent value.

59. *Id.* at 156–57.

60. Michael F. Noone, Jr., *Applying Just War Jus in Bello Doctrine to Reprisals: An Afghan Hypothetical*, 51 CATH. U. L. REV. 27, 28 (fall 2001).

61. *Id.*

62. *Id.* at 30.

63. The incentive package to Pakistan in exchange for rekindling an old alliance was expensive but necessary in the grand scheme:

Since [September 11], Washington has rescheduled $396 million of Islamabad's debt; approved a $300 million line of credit for prospective investors in Pakistan; and offered $73 million to patrol Pakistani borders and $34 million to fight drug trafficking. On November 15th, Washington gave Pakistan $600 million in foreign aid to address the impact of a terror-induced global recession.

Michael Wines, *Leasing, If Not Building, an Anti-Taliban Coalition*, NEW YORK TIMES, Nov. 18, 2001, at WK3.

64. Elaine Sciolino and Neil A. Lewis, *Iran Dances a 'Ballet' with U.S.*, NEW YORK TIMES, Oct. 16, 2001, at B1. Usually, when an administration intervenes in such a case, compensation is granted to those litigants negatively affected by the government's action for foreign policy reasons.

65. Erlanger, *supra* note 54; Marc Lacey, *U.S. Envoy Looks for Change in Sudan*, NEW YORK TIMES, Nov. 18, 2001, at A8.

66. Serge Schmemann, *Syria Is Likely to Join U.N. Security Council*, NEW YORK TIMES, Oct. 7, 2001, at A28; Christopher S. Wren, *U.S. Advises U.N. Council More Strikes Could Come*, NEW YORK TIMES, Oct. 9, 2001, at B5.

67. Hugh Dellios, *Sharon Firm on Calm Before Talks; Powell to Outline U.S. Peace Vision*, CHICAGO TRIBUNE, Nov. 19, 2001, at 3; Alan Sipress, *Powell Vows U.S. Role in Mideast*, WASHINGTON POST, Nov. 20, 2001, at A1.

68. Associated Press Poll conducted Aug. 2–6, 2002. N = 1,001 adults nationwide. MoE ± 3 <www.pollingreport.com>; Associated Press, *Terrorist Attacks Prompt Changes in Americans' Legal Rights After Sept. 11*, DAILY RECORD (Omaha), Aug. 29, 2002, at 4.

Chapter 6

1. Jess Braven, *White House Seeks to Expand Indefinite Detentions in Brigs*, WALL STREET JOURNAL, Aug. 8, 2002:

Stung by the courtroom circus that yet another accused terrorist, Zacarias Moussaoui, has created, and the aggressive defense marshaled by John Walker Lindh before he plea-bargained his way out of a possible life sentence, the Bush administration is preparing to expand its policy of indefinitely detaining in U.S. military jails people it designates as "enemy combatants." Such prisoners— whether Americans or foreigners captured in the U.S.—aren't afforded the same constitutional rights as criminal defendants, or even the limited rights allowed in military tribunals. . . . Officials said they selected brigs in South Carolina and Virginia [for Hamdi and Padilla] partly because they fall under the jurisdiction of courts that are more conservative and presumably more sympathetic to the administration.

2. Ex Parte Milligan, 71 U.S. 2, 121; 18 L. Ed. 281, 295 (1866).

3. Anne English French, *Trials in Times of War: Do the Bush Military Commissions Sacrifice Our Freedoms?* 63 OHIO ST. L.J. 1225 (2002/2003).

4. Ex Parte Milligan, 71 U.S. 2, 109; 18 L. Ed. 281, 292.

5. *Id.* at 115–16; 18 L. Ed. 281, 294.

6. *Id.*

7. *Id.* at 131; 18 L. Ed. 281, 299.

8. *Id.* at 125; 18 L. Ed. 281, 297.

9. Watts v. Indiana, 338 U.S. 49, 54 (1949).

10. The case of the alleged "shoe bomber" Richard Reid is not discussed here as it raises no new significant issues not already raised in the Lindh and Moussaoui cases. The divergent areas of the Reid indictment relate to his actions on board an aircraft—namely attempting to detonate an explosive contained in the sole of his shoe. His case was heard before the federal district court in Boston and was resolved with an agreement giving him sixty years to life in exchange for a plea of guilty. Reid admitted he attended terrorist training camps in Afghanistan and was a follower of Osama bin Laden. *See* Reid indictment and legal documents at <http://news.findlaw.com/legalnews/us/terrorism/cases/index2.html>; Associated Press, *Venting Hate; Voicing Regret, Staying Loyal to bin Laden,* NEWSDAY (New York), Oct. 5, 2002, at A4.

11. Rene Sanchez, *John Walker's Restless Quest Is Strange Odyssey,* WASHINGTON POST, Jan. 14, 2002, at A1.

12. Brooke A. Masters, *American Taliban Suspect Appears in Alexandria Court,* WASHINGTON POST, Jan. 25, 2002, at A1; Brooke A. Masters and Patricia Davis, *Walker's Long Trip Ends in Alexandria Jail,* WASHINGTON POST, Jan. 24, 2002, at A24; 18 U.S.C. §§ 2332(b), 2339; 31 C.F.R. §§ 545.201, 545.204; Exec. Ord. 13129; 50 U.S.C. §§ 1702, 1705; 18 U.S.C. § 2.

13. Brooke A. Masters and Dan Eggen, *Lindh Indicted on Conspiracy, Gun Charges,* WASHINGTON POST, Feb. 6, 2002, at A1.

14. Brooke A. Masters and Edward Walsh, *U.S. Taliban Fighter to Have His Rights, Rumsfeld Says,* WASHINGTON POST, Dec. 5, 2001, at A13.

15. Defendants Motion for a Bill of Particulars, United States v. Lindh, Crim. No. 02–37-A (E.D. Va. 2002); Defendant's Motion of March 15, 2002, available at <http://news.findlaw.com/hdocs/docs/lindh/uslindh31502mot4bop.pdf>.

16. Naftali Bendavid, *U.S.: No Evidence Lindh Killed Agent; Prison Riot Victim Cited in Indictment,* WASHINGTON POST, Apr. 2, 2002, at A7.

17. Brooke A. Masters and Dan Eggen, *Walker Statements a Trial Issue; Defense Will Contest Interviews with FBI,* WASHINGTON POST, Jan. 17, 2002, at A14.

18. Neil A. Lewis, *Admitting He Fought in Taliban, American Agrees to 20-year Term,* NEW YORK TIMES, July 16, 2002, at A1.

19. Suzanne Daley, *Mysterious Life of a Suspect from France,* NEW YORK TIMES, Sept. 21, 2001, at B1; David Johnston and Philip Shenon, *F.B.I. Curbed Scrutiny of Man Now a Suspect in the Attacks,* NEW YORK TIMES, Oct. 6, 2001, at A1; Philip Shenon, *Flight School Warned F.B.I. of Suspicions,* NEW YORK TIMES, Dec. 22, 2001, at B1.

20. David Johnston, *Not-Guilty Plea Is Set for Man in Terror Case,* NEW YORK TIMES, Jan. 3, 2002, at A1.

21. Neil A. Lewis, *Moussaoui's Defense Plan Complicates Terror Trial,* NEW YORK TIMES, Apr. 26, 2002, at A12; Philip Shenon, *Sept. 11 Defendant Who Wants to Represent Himself Is Busy Doing So,* NEW YORK TIMES, Apr. 30, 2002, at A22.

22. Philip Shenon, *Judge Agrees to New Delay in Trial in Conspiracy Case,* NEW YORK TIMES, Oct. 1, 2002, at A20.

23. United States v. Moussaoui, 333 F.3d 509 (4th Cir. 2003).

24. Philip Shenon, *Terror Suspect Says He Wants U.S. Destroyed,* NEW YORK TIMES, Apr. 23, 2002, at A1; Neil A. Lewis, *Defense Seeks Extensive Tests on Mental Health of Suspect,* NEW YORK TIMES, Apr. 29, 2002, at A16.

25. Philip Shenon and Benjamin Weiser, *Prosecutors Seek a Death Sentence in Terrorism Case,* NEW YORK TIMES, Mar. 19, 2002, at A1; Philip Shenon and Neil A. Lewis, *U.S. to Seek Death Penalty for Moussaoui in Terror Case,* NEW YORK TIMES, Mar. 29, 2002, at A20.

26. Adam Liptak, *A Host of Legal Questions on U.S. Action in Bomb Case,* NEW YORK TIMES, June 11, 2002.

27. Anthony Lewis, *The Silencing of Gideon's Trumpet,* NEW YORK TIMES, Apr. 20, 2003.

28. Adam Liptak et al., *After Sept. 11, a Legal Battle on the Limits of Civil Liberty,* NEW YORK TIMES, Aug. 4, 2002, at A1.

29. President's Military Order, 66 Fed. Reg. 57833 (Nov. 15, 2001).

30. Geneva Convention Relative to the Treatment of Prisoners of War, Aug. 12, 1949, 75 U.N.T.S. 287.

31. Michael J. Kelly, *Understanding September 11th —An International Legal Perspective on the War in Afghanistan,* 35 CREIGHTON L.REV. 283, 289–92 (2002).

32. Karen Branch-Brioso, *Fight over Rights Rages On,* ST. LOUIS POST-DISPATCH, Sept. 8, 2002, at B1.

33. *Id.*

34. Neil A. Lewis, *Detention Upheld in Enemy Combatant Case,* NEW YORK TIMES, Jan. 9, 2003.

35. Tom Jackson, *Judges Uphold U.S. Detention of Hamdi,* WASHINGTON POST, Jan. 9, 2003, at A1.

36. Hamdi v. Rumsfeld, 316 F.3d 450 (4th Cir. 2003).

37. *Id.*

38. *Id.*

39. Jess Braven, *Judge Declares Padilla Has Right to Counsel,* WALL STREET JOURNAL, Dec. 4, 2002.

40. Padilla v. Rumsfeld, 243 F. Supp.2d 42 (S.D.N.Y. 2003).

41. Braven, *supra* note 1.

42. Charles Lane, *In Terror War, 2nd Track for Suspects; Those Designated 'Combatants' Lose Legal Protections,* WASHINGTON POST, Dec. 1, 2002, at A1.

43. Ex Parte Quirin, 317 U.S. 1 (1942).

44. Diane F. Orentlicher and Robert Kogod Goldman, *The Military Tribunal Order: When Justice Goes to War: Prosecuting Terrorists Before Military Commissions,* 25 HARV. J.L. & PUB. POL'Y 653, 657 (spring 2002):

Much like the Supreme Court's validation of President Roosevelt's decision to intern American citizens of Japanese descent during World War II, *Quirin* has long been criticized as an abdication of independent judicial judgment during war time and an unwarranted surrender of constitutional rights. Even the author of the Court's opinion, Chief Justice Stone, reportedly had grave misgivings about the judgment he penned.

45. Adam Liptak, *Accord Suggests U.S. Prefers to Avoid Courts*, New York Times, July 16, 2002, at A14:

> Legal scholars found it hard to identify a rationale that would call for an ordinary criminal prosecution of Mr. Lindh but military detention of Mr. Padilla and Mr. Hamdi. The search for a unifying principle becomes even more difficult if Zacarias Moussaoui and Richard C. Reid are added to the mix. . . . Efforts to distinguish the treatment of these prisoners on consistent grounds tend to fail. The distinguishing factor is not citizenship: Mr. Moussaoui is French, and Mr. Reid is British; the others claim American citizenship. Nor is it the place of arrest: Mr. Lindh and Mr. Hamdi were captured in Afghanistan, the others in the United States. Nor is it the nature of the central criminal charge: Mr. Moussaoui, Mr. Reid and Mr. Padilla are accused of attempting or conspiring to commit terrorist acts, the others of fighting on the wrong side abroad.
>
> "You do worry about equal treatment and having a consistent theory about who ends up where," said Ruth Wedgwood, a law professor at Yale. The only factor that seems to explain the disparity in how the men were treated is time. The later detentions were military, suggesting that the government may now view ordinary trials as more trouble than they are worth.

46. Presidential Order Transferring Custody of Ali Saleh Kahlah al-Marri from the Department of Justice to the Department of Defense (June 23, 2003), Al-Marri v. Bush, No. 03 CV 1220 (C.D. Ill. 2003) <http://news.findlaw.com/cnn/docs/almarri/almarri62303exord.pdf>.

47. Respondent's Motion to Dismiss or Transfer Petition for Writ of Habeas Corpus, Al-Marri v. Bush, No. 03 CV 1220 (C.D. Ill. 2003) <http://news.findlaw.com/cnn/docs/almarri/almarribush71603gmot.pdf>.

48. For the sake of brevity and to reduce repetitiveness of issues, the federal indictments of James Ujaama in Seattle in August 2002 for allegedly planning to create a training camp in Oregon, and the four foreign nationals arrested in Detroit for alleged conspiracy to obtain weaponry and intelligence and create safe houses and fake IDs, are not discussed. However, for further reading on these cases, *see* Timothy Egan, *Riddle in Seattle: Is Man Held by U.S. a Terrorist or Just a Hustler?* New York Times, Oct. 6, 2002, at A24; United States v. Ujaama (W.D. Wash. 2002); grand jury indictment available at <http://news.findlaw.com/hdocs/docs/terrorism/usujaama82802ind.pdf>; Danny Hakim, *4 Are Charged with Belonging to a Terror Cell*, New York Times, Aug. 29, 2002, at A1.

49. United States v. Goba, Mosed, Taher, Galeb, Al-Bakri and Alwan

(W.D. NY 2002); grand jury indictment of May 2002 available at <http://news.findlaw.com/hdocs/docs/terrorism/ussattar040902ind.pdf>.

50. One of the defendants, Faysal Galab, entered a plea agreement on January 10, 2003, with prosecutors. In exchange for dropping his indictment to a lesser charge, he supplied information on the other five cell members and agreed to testify against them, admitting attending the al Farooq terrorist training camp in Afghanistan with them, and was told afterward to deny it. Robert F. Worth, *Accused Member of Terror Cell Near Buffalo Agrees to Guilty Plea*, NEW YORK TIMES, Jan. 11, 2003, at A9.

51. United States v. Battle, Ford, Bilal, Al Saoub and Lewis, No. CR 02–399 HA (D. Or 2002); grand jury indictment of Oct. 31, 2002, available at <http://news.findlaw.com/hdocs/docs/terrorism/usbattle100302 ind.pdf>; Associated Press, *Malaysia to Deport 5th Oregon Suspect*, NEW YORK TIMES, Oct. 8, 2002, at A15.

52. Eric Lichtblau, *4 in U.S. Charged in Post-9/11 Plan to Join al Qaeda*, NEW YORK TIMES, Oct. 5, 2002, at A1.

53. *Id.*

54. The president's order designating al-Marri an enemy combatant, *supra* note 46, only states that he is associated with al Qaeda, is "engaged in conduct that constituted hostile and war-like acts . . . that had the aim to cause injury to . . . the United States," possesses intelligence that would aid the United States in its war on terror, and represents a continuing grave danger to American national security.

55. Lane, *supra* note 42.

56. 18 U.S.C. §2339A.

57. *Id.* at (b).

58. David Cole, Opinion, *Fight Terrorism Fairly*, NEW YORK TIMES, Oct. 19, 2002, at A17.

59. *Id.:*

America has had these kinds of laws before. In the McCarthy era, Congress and the states passed numerous statutes that made it a crime to have an association with the Communist Party. But the Supreme Court repeatedly ruled that only those individuals who specifically intended to further the party's unlawful ends could be punished. Guilt by association, the court proclaimed, is "alien to the traditions of a free society and to the First Amendment itself."

60. Humanitarian Law Project v. Reno, 9 F. Supp. 2d 1176 (C.D. Cal. 1998).

61. *Id.* at 1180–81.

62. *Id.* at 1204.

63. Greg Winter, *Judge Drops Case Against 7 Tied to Group Called Terrorist*, LOS ANGELES TIMES, June 24, 2002, at A13.

64. Greg Winter, *Fund-Raising; Aiding Friend or Iranian Foe is Issue in Case*, LOS ANGELES TIMES, Mar. 22, 2002, at A13.

65. Winter, *supra* note 63.

66. Attorney General's Press Conference, Department of Justice (Nov. 14, 2003) <http://www.usdoj.gov/ag/speeches/2001/agcrisisremarks11_14.htm>.

67. Susan Sachs, *Judge Rejects U.S. Policy of Secret Hearings*, NEW YORK TIMES, May 30, 2002, at A21.

68. American Civil Liberties Union, *ACLU Joins in FOIA Request for Information on Detainees, Says Government Has Refused to Answer Previous Inquiries* <http://www.aclu.org/news/2001/n102901a.html> (Oct. 29, 2001); Amy Goldstein, *A Deliberate Strategy of Disruption; Massive, Secretive Detention Effort Aimed Mainly at Preventing More Terror*, WASHINGTON POST, Nov. 4, 2001, at A01; *In First Lawsuit Filed Regarding Mass Detentions, Civil Liberties Groups Demand Release of Essential Information Under FOIA*. American Civil Liberties Union <http://www.aclu.org/news/2001/n120501b.html> (Dec. 5, 2001).

69. Liptak et al., *supra* note 28.

70. Neil A. Lewis, *Judge Orders U.S. to Release Names of 9/11 Detainees*, NEW YORK TIMES, Aug. 3, 2002, at A1; Linda Greenhouse, *Judicial Restraint; The Imperial Presidency vs. The Imperial Judiciary*, NEW YORK TIMES, Sept. 8, 2002, at D3.

71. Steve Fainaru and Dan Eggen, *Judge Rules U.S. Must Release Detainees' Names*, WASHINGTON POST, Aug. 3, 2002, at A1.

72. Steve Fainaru, *U.S. Deported 131 Pakistanis In Secret Airlift; Diplomatic Issues Cited; No Terror Ties Found*, WASHINGTON POST, July 10, 2002, at A1.

73. Josh Meyer, *Bar Assn. Assails U.S. on Detainees*, LOS ANGELES TIMES, Aug. 14, 2002, at 1.

74. Detroit Free Press v. Ashcroft, 195 F. Supp. 2nd 937 (E.D. Mich 2002).

75. Detroit Free Press v. Ashcroft, 2002 U.S. App. LEXIS 17646 (6th Cir. 2002).

76. *Id.*

77. Sachs, *supra* note 67.

78. *Id.*

79. *Appeals Panel Upholds Ruling for Open Court*, NEW YORK TIMES, June 19, 2002, at A19.

80. Susan Sachs, *Ashcroft Petitions Justices for Secrecy in Deportations*, NEW YORK TIMES, June 22, 2002, at A9.

81. *Supreme Court Allows Secrecy to Stand in Deportation Cases*, NEW YORK TIMES, June 29, 2002, at A10.

82. North Jersey Media Group, Inc, et al. v. Ashcroft, No. 02–2524 (3rd Cir. 2002) <http://news.findlaw.com/hdocs/docs/terrorism/ashnjmg108020pn.pdf>.

83. Adam Liptak and Robert Hanley, *Court Upholds Secret Hearings on Deportation*, NEW YORK TIMES, Oct. 9, 2002, at A1.

84. *Id.*

85. *Id.*

86. Inspector General, Department of Justice, Report on the September 11th Detainees: A Review of the Treatment of Aliens Held on Immigration Charges in Connection with the Investigation of the September 11th Attacks (April 2003).

87. Eric Lichtblau, *Ashcroft Seeks More Power to Pursue Terror Suspects,* NEW YORK TIMES, June 6, 2003, at A1.

88. Benjamin Weiser, *Judge Rules Against U.S. on Material Witness Law,* NEW YORK TIMES, May 1, 2002, at A10 (emphasis added); Steve Fainaru and Amy Goldstein, *Judge Rejects Jailing of Material Witnesses; Ruling Imperils Tool in Sept. 11 Probe,* WASHINGTON POST, May 1, 2002, at A1.

89. Steve Fainaru, *Judge: U.S. May Jail Material Witnesses; N.Y. Ruling Conflicts with Decision in Prior Case in Same Federal Court,* WASHINGTON POST, July 12, 2002, at A12.

90. Margaret Graham Tebo, *Courts Wrestle with Keeping Secret Detainees,* ABA JOURNAL, Sept. 2002, at 46.

91. Editorial, *At What Cost?* ST. LOUIS POST-DISPATCH, May 6, 2002, at B6.

92. Washington Post, *Nearly Half of 'Material Witnesses' Haven't Testified,* OMAHA WORLD-HERALD, Nov. 24, 2002, at 16A.

93. *Newshour with Jim Lehrer: The Detainees,* by Jeffrey Kaye (PBS television broadcast, Jan. 22, 2003) <http://www.pbs.org/newshour/bb/military/jan-june03/detainees_1–22.html>.

94. Geneva Convention, *supra* note 30.

95. Thom Shanker and Katharine Q. Seelye, *Behind-the-Scenes Class Led Bush to Reverse Himself on Applying Geneva Conventions,* NEW YORK TIMES, Feb. 22, 2002, at A12: "By denying captives full Geneva protections, the administration said, it could more thoroughly interrogate them to uncover future terrorist plots, bring a wide array of charges against them, try them before military tribunals and administer the death penalty."

96. William Glaberson, *Critics' Attack on Tribunals Turns to Law Among Nations,* NEW YORK TIMES, Dec. 26, 2001, at B1.

97. Military Order, *supra* note 29.

98. Thom Shanker and Katharine Q. Seelye, *The Geneva Conventions, Who Is a Prisoner of War? You Could Look It Up. Maybe,* NEW YORK TIMES, March 10, 2002, at D9.

99. Geneva Convention Relative to the Protection of Civilian Persons in Time of War, Aug. 12, 1949, 75 U.N.T.S. 287.

100. Chambers v. Florida, 309 U.S. 227, 241 (1940).

101. Mapp v. Ohio, 367 U.S. 643, 648 (1961) (quoting Weeks v. United States, 232 U.S. 383, 393 (1914)).

102. Miranda v. Arizona, 384 U.S. 436, 457–58 (1966).

103. Although there are variations among jurisdictions, the *Miranda* warning is generally expressed as follows:

You have the right to remain silent. Anything you say can and will be used against you in a court of law. You have the right to speak

Notes to Pages
215–23

283

to an attorney and to have an attorney present during any questioning. If you cannot afford a lawyer, one will be provided for you at government expense.

104. Rosen v. United States, 161 U.S. 29, 40 (1896).

105. Gideon v. Wainwright, 372 U.S. 335, 344–5 (1963) (quoting Powell v. Alabama, 287 U.S. 45, 68–69) (1932).

106. New York Times, *New Power in Terror Inquiries Put to Use*, OMAHA WORLD-HERALD, Nov. 24, 2002, at 16A.

107. *Feds Get Wide Wiretap Authority* (CBS News) <http://www.cbsnews.com/stories/2002/08/23/attack/printable519606.shtml> (Nov. 18, 2002).

108. In re Sealed Case No. 02–001, 310 F.3d 717, 731 (U.S. App., 2002).

109. *Id.* at 734.

110. *Id.* at 746.

111. In re All Matters Submitted to the Foreign Intelligence Surveillance Court, 218 F.Supp. 2d 611, 614 (U.S. Dist., 2002).

112. *Supra* note 108, at 734.

113. *Id.*

114. *Id.* at 730.

115. *Supra* note 111, at 625.

116. *Id.* at 621.

117. Statement of Senator Patrick Leahy during Senate floor debate on Patriot Act, CONG. REC. S10990–S11060 (Oct. 25, 2001).

118. *Supra* note 108, at 744.

119. Joint Investigation into September 11: Third Public Hearing, statement of Eleanor Hill, Sept. 20, 2002.

120. *Id.*

121. *Supra* note 111, at 614.

122. *Id.* at 617.

123. Military Order, *supra* note 29.

124. Katharine Q. Seelye, *Government Sets Rules for Military on War Tribunals*, NEW YORK TIMES, Mar. 21, 2002, at A1; see Military Commission Order No. 1 (Dept. of Defense, Mar. 21, 2002) <http://defenselink.mil/news/mar2002/d20020321ord.pdf>.

125. Coalition of Clergy v. Bush, 189 F. Supp. 2nd 1036 (D. Ca. 2002).

126. Neil A. Lewis, *Judge Rebuffs Detainees at Guantanamo*, NEW YORK TIMES, Aug. 1, 2002, at A20.

127. Lauritzen v. Larsen, 345 U.S. 571 (1952) ("a ship is constructively a floating part of the flag-state"); U.N. Convention on the Law of the Sea, Art. 91 & 92, 21 I.L.M. 1261 (1982).

128. Sarah Lyall, *Death Penalty Ruled Out for Two British Detainees*, NEW YORK TIMES, July 23, 2003, at A4.

129. Harvey Rishikof, *A New Court for Terrorism*, NEW YORK TIMES, June 8, 2002, at A15.

130. *Id.*

131. *Id.*

132. WILLIAM H. REHNQUIST, ALL THE LAWS BUT ONE: CIVIL LIBERTIES IN WARTIME (1998).

133. Olmstead v. United States, 277 U.S. 438, 478 (1928).

134. William H. Rehnquist, Remarks of the Chief Justice of the United States, 47 DRAKE L.R. 201–208 (1999) (delivering the Dwight D. Opperman Lecture at Drake University School of Law, Sept. 18, 1998).

135. Adam Cohen, *Justice Rehnquist's Ominous History of Wartime Freedom*, NEW YORK TIMES, Sept. 22, 2002.

136. United States v. Verdugo-Urquidez, 494 U.S. 259 (1990).

137. Rehnquist, *supra* note 132.

Chapter 7

1. Ex Parte Merryman 17 F. Cas. 144 (D. Md. 1861).

2. Abraham Lincoln, Letter to Matthew Birchard (June 29, 1863), in COLLECTED WORKS OF ABRAHAM LINCOLN 6:302 (Roy P. Basler ed., 1953).

3. Woodrow Wilson, Speech, Chicago (Jan. 31, 1916), in PRESIDENT WILSON'S STATE PAPERS AND ADDRESSES 181–82 (Albert Shaw ed., 1917).

4. Editorial, *Justice Deformed: War and the Constitution*, NEW YORK TIMES, Dec. 2, 2001, at 14.

5. Laura Parker, Kevin Johnson, and Toni Locy, *Secure Often Means Secret*, USA TODAY, May 16, 2002, at 1A.

Bibliography

18 U.S.C. §1963(c).

18 U.S.C. §2515.

18 U.S.C. §2518 (4).

Abramowitz, David. *The President, the Congress, and Use of Force: Legal and Political Considerations in Authorizing Use of Force Against International Terrorism.* 43 HARV. INT'L L.J. 71 (winter 2002).

The *Achille Lauro* Hijacking (B). Kennedy School of Government Case Program, Case #864.0 (1988).

Alexander, Yonah. *Terrorism in the Twenty-first Century: Threats and Responses.* 12 DEPAUL BUS. L.J. 59 (fall 1999).

ALIBEK, KEN. BIOHAZARD (1999).

Authorization for Use of Military Force. S.J. Res. 23, 107th Congress, 115 Stat. 224 (2001).

Bassiouni, M. Cherif. *Legal Control of International Terrorism: A Policy-Oriented Assessment.* 43 HARV. INT'L L.J. 83 (winter 2002).

BERTSCH, GARY K., AND WILLIAM C. POTTER. DANGEROUS WEAPONS, DESPERATE STATES (1999).

Caldwell v. Texas, 137 U.S. 692 (1891).

CARR, CALEB. THE LESSONS OF TERROR (2002).

Chambers v. Florida, 309 U.S. 227 (1940).

Chyba, Christopher F. *Toward Biological Security.* 81 FOREIGN AFFAIRS 122 (May/June 2002).

Coalition of Clergy v. Bush, 189 F. Supp. 2nd 1036 (D. Ca. 2002).

Cooper v. Aaron, 358 U.S. 1 (1958).

Cybercrime, Cyberterrorism, Cyberwarfare: Averting an Electronic Waterloo. Center for Strategic and International Studies (1998).

Damrosch, Lori Fisler. *The Constitution under Clinton: A Critical Assessment: The Clinton Administration and War Powers.* 63 LAW & CONTEMP. PROBS. 125 (winter/spring 2000).

Delahunty, Robert J., and John C. Yoo. *The President's Constitutional Authority to Conduct Military Operations Against Terrorist Organizations and the Nations That Harbor or Support Them.* 25 HARV. J.L. & PUB. POL'Y 487 (spring 2002).

287

Detroit Free Press v. Ashcroft, 195 F. Supp. 2nd 937 (E.D. Mich 2002).

Detroit Free Press v. Ashcroft, 2002 U.S. App. LEXIS 17646 (6th Cir. 2002).

DETTER, INGRID. THE LAW OF WAR (2d ed., 2000).

DREXLER, MADELINE. SECRET AGENTS: THE MENACE OF EMERGING INFECTIONS (2002).

The Economic Consequences of 11 September and the Economic Dimension of Anti-Terrorism. Draft General Report, NATO Parliamentary Assembly, Economics and Security Committee (2002).

Ex Parte Milligan, 71 U.S. 2 (1866).

Ex Parte Quirin, 317 U.S. 1 (1942).

Fisher, Louis. *War Powers and Foreign Affairs: Sidestepping Congress: Presidents Acting under the U.N. and N.A.T.O.* 47 CASE W. RES. L. REV.1237 (summer 1997).

Frisbie v. Butler, 1 Kirby 213 (1787).

GALSTON, WILLIAM. JUSTICE AND THE HUMAN GOOD (1980).

Gellman, Barton. *Cyber-Attacks by Al Qaeda Feared; Terrorists at Threshold of Using Internet as Tool of Bloodshed, Experts Say.* WASHINGTON POST, June 27, 2002, A01.

Gellman, Barton. *Struggles Inside the Government Defined Campaign.* WASHINGTON POST, Dec. 20, 2001, A01.

Geneva Convention Relative to the Treatment of Prisoners of War, Aug. 12, 1949, 75 U.N.T.S. 287.

GERSON, ALLAN, AND JERRY ADLER. THE PRICE OF TERROR: ONE BOMB, ONE PLANE, 270 LIVES: THE HISTORY-MAKING STRUGGLE FOR JUSTICE AFTER PAN AM 103 (2001).

Gideon v. Wainwright, 372 U.S. 335 (1963).

GRAY, CHRISTINE. INTERNATIONAL LAW AND THE USE OF FORCE (2000).

GUILLEMIN, JEANNE. ANTHRAX: THE INVESTIGATION OF A DEADLY OUTBREAK (1999).

Howard v. Fleming, 191 U.S. 126 (1903).

Information Warfare and International Security. Draft Report, NATO Parliamentary Assembly, Science and Technology Committee (1999).

Johnson v. Eisentrager, 339 U.S. 763 (1950).

Katz v. United States 389 U.S. 347 (1967).

Korematsu v. United States, 323 U.S. 214 (1944).

Korematsu v. United States, 584 F.Supp. 1406 (N. D. Cal. 1984).

Kwong Hai Chew v. Colding, 344 U.S. 590 (1953).

LAVOY, PETER R., SCOTT D. SAGAN, AND JAMES J. WIRTZ, EDS. PLANNING THE UNTHINKABLE: HOW NEW POWERS WILL USE NUCLEAR, BIOLOGICAL AND CHEMICAL WEAPONS (2000).

LEVY, LEONARD W. ORIGINAL INTENT AND THE FRAMERS' CONSTITUTION (1988).

LINCOLN, ABRAHAM. COLLECTED WORKS OF ABRAHAM LINCOLN (Roy P. Basler ed., 1953).

Lodal, Jan. The Price of Dominance: The New Weapons of Mass Destruction and Their Challenge to American Leadership. Council on Foreign Relations (2001).

Mangold, Tom, and Jeff Goldberg. Plague Wars: The Terrifying Reality of Biological Warfare (1999).

Mapp v. Ohio, 367 U.S. 643 (1961).

Mathews v. Diaz, 426 U.S. 67 (1976).

Merari, Ariel. *The Readiness to Kill and Die: Suicidal Terrorism in the Middle East. In* Origins of Terrorism: Psychologies, Ideologies, Theologies, States of Mind (Walter Reich ed., 2000).

Miranda v. Arizona, 384 U.S. 436 (1966).

Mitchell, Andrew D. *Does One Illegality Merit Another? The Law of Belligerent Reprisals in International Law.* 170 Mil. L. Rev. 155 (Dec. 2001).

Nobles v. Georgia, 168 U.S. 398 (1897).

Noone, Michael F., Jr. *Applying Just War Jus in Bello Doctrine to Reprisals: An Afghan Hypothetical.* 51 Cath. U. L. Rev. 27 (fall 2001).

North Atlantic Treaty, April 4, 1949, Art. 5, 63 Stat. 2241, 2244, 34 U.N.T.S. 243, 246.

Office of Homeland Security. *The National Strategy for Homeland Security* (July 2002).

Olmstead v. United States, 277 U.S. 438 (1928).

Orentlicher, Diane F., and Robert Kogod Goldman. *The Military Tribunal Order: When Justice Goes to War: Prosecuting Terrorists before Military Commissions.* 25 Harv. J.L. & Pub. Pol'y 653 (spring 2002).

Paust, Jordan J. *Antiterrorism Military Commissions: Courting Illegality.* 23 Mich. J. Int'l L. 1 (fall 2001).

Paust, Jordan J. *Antiterrorism Military Commissions: The Ad Hoc DOD Rules of Procedure.* 23 Mich. J. Int'l L. 677 (spring 2002).

Plyler v. Doe, 457 U.S. 202 (1982).

Pollock, Joycelyn M. Ethics in Crime and Justice: Dilemmas and Decisions (1998).

President's Message to Joint Session of Congress Responding to the Terrorist Attacks of September 11th. Pub. Papers, Sept. 24, 2001.

President's Military Order, 66 Fed. Reg. 57833 (Nov. 15, 2001).

Preston, Richard. The Hot Zone (1994).

Rapoport, David C. *Fear and Trembling: Terrorism in Three Religious Traditions.* 78 Am. Pol. Sci. Rev. 658 (1984).

Reich, Walter. Understanding Terrorist Behavior: The Limits and Opportunities of Psychological Inquiry in Origins of Terrorism: Psychologies, Ideologies, Theologies, States of Mind (1998).

Report of the Defense Science Board Task Force on Information Warfare—Defense (November 1996).

Richardson, James D., ed. Messages and Papers of the Presidents (1898).

Rosen v. United States, 161 U.S. 29 (1896).

Schmid, Alex P. *The Response Problem as a Definition Problem. In* Western Responses to Terrorism (Alex P. Schmid and Ronald P. Crelinsten eds., 1993).

Shaughnessy v. Mezei, 345 U.S. 206 (1953).

Stern, Jessica. *Terrorist Motivations and Unconventional Weapons. In* Planning the Unthinkable (Peter R. Lavoy et al. eds., 2000).

Subcommittee on Terrorism and Homeland Security. *Counterterrorism Intelligence Capabilities and Performance Prior to 9–11*. Report to the Speaker of the House of Representatives and Minority Leader (July 2002).

Tehranian, Majid. *Global Terrorism: Searching for Appropriate Responses.* <http://www.toda.org/grad/mt1/global_terrorism.html> (2001).

Travalio, Gregory M. *Terrorism, International Law, and the Use of Military Force.* 18 WIS. INT'L L.J. 145 (winter 2000).

United Nations Charter.

A United Response. Statement of Senator Joseph Biden. Congressional Record, S9422 (September 14, 2001).

United States v. Armstrong, 208 U.S. 481 (1908).

United States v. Freitas, 800 F.2d 1451 (9th Cir. 1986).

United States v. United States Dist. Court, 407 U.S. 297 (1972).

United States v. Verdugo-Urquidez, 494 U.S. 259 (1990).

War Powers Resolution, Public Law 93–148, 93rd Congress, H. J. Res. 542 (Nov. 7, 1973).

Watts v. Indiana, 338 U.S. 49 (1949).

Wilson v. Arkansas, 514 U.S. 927 (1995).

WILSON, WOODROW. PRESIDENT WILSON'S STATE PAPERS AND ADDRESSES (Albert Shaw ed., 1917).

Wong Wing v. United States, 163 U.S. 228 (1896).

Yick Wo v. Hopkins, 118 U.S. 356 (1886).

Youngstown Sheet & Tube Co. v. Sawyer, 343 U.S. 579 (1952).

Index

Achille Lauro hijacking, 31, 32–36
Afghanistan, 3, 10, 42–45, 59, 65, 67–68, 92, 109, 157, 160, 201, 206, 217–21, 231, 238; John Walker Lindh and, 195–200; terrorist connections to, 161–80; U.S. invasion of, 183–89
Alien and Sedition Acts, 144
Alien Registration Act, 46–47
al Qaeda, 3, 12–13, 28, 77, 80, 86, 104, 109, 146, 147, 154, 156, 171, 173, 175, 180, 187–89, 190–91, 197–98, 200–201, 205–7, 239; captured detainees with connections to, 218–20; continuing threat from, 110–13; defense against, 55–67; network and connections of, 160–65; tactics of, 50–54; weapons of mass destruction and, 92–95
anthrax, 57, 81–89
Ashcroft, John D., 3, 13, 73, 86, 168–69, 171, 188, 201, 238–40; disdain for dissenters, 23; enemy combatants and, 204; misuse of material witness statute by, 215–18; Patriot Act and, 150–52; on political opposi-

tion, ix; Safire's criticism of, 61–62; on sleeper cells, 111; Thomas's criticism of, 173; treatment of immigrants by, 210–15
"axis of evil," 28, 45, 163–65

Biden, Joseph, 157
Bill of Rights, 120, 123, 213
bin Laden, Osama, 10, 104, 160–62, 206; al Qaeda connection, 110–12; claim of nuclear capability by, 93; goals of, 65–70; terrorist acts by, 56–57; use of suicide bombers by, 77–80
Black, Justice Hugo, 220, 235
Bush, George W., 1–2, 38, 41, 46, 67, 74, 87, 110, 177, 194, 202, 205, 219, 230, 233; on "axis of evil," 28, 163–65; and invasion of Afghanistan, 155–58; joint resolution and, 154; military action under international law by, 183–85; military order and, 145, 178–83; and Office of Homeland Security, 62–63; order to shoot down passenger jets, 53; Patriot Act and, 116–17; response to September 11 attacks, 166–71;

291